MW00813202

Taylor Swift
FAVORITES

Cover photo by Sarah Barlow

ISBN 978-1-4803-2441-1

Visit Hal Leonard Online at
www.halleonard.com

BACK TO DECEMBER

Words and Music by
TAYLOR SWIFT

Moderately, in 2
F
5
Dm
2
Bb
mf
1
3
F
Dm
Bb
F
Dm
1. I'm so glad you made time to see me. How's life?
2. (See additional lyrics)
1
Bb
Tell me, how's your fam - 'ly? I have - n't seen them in a

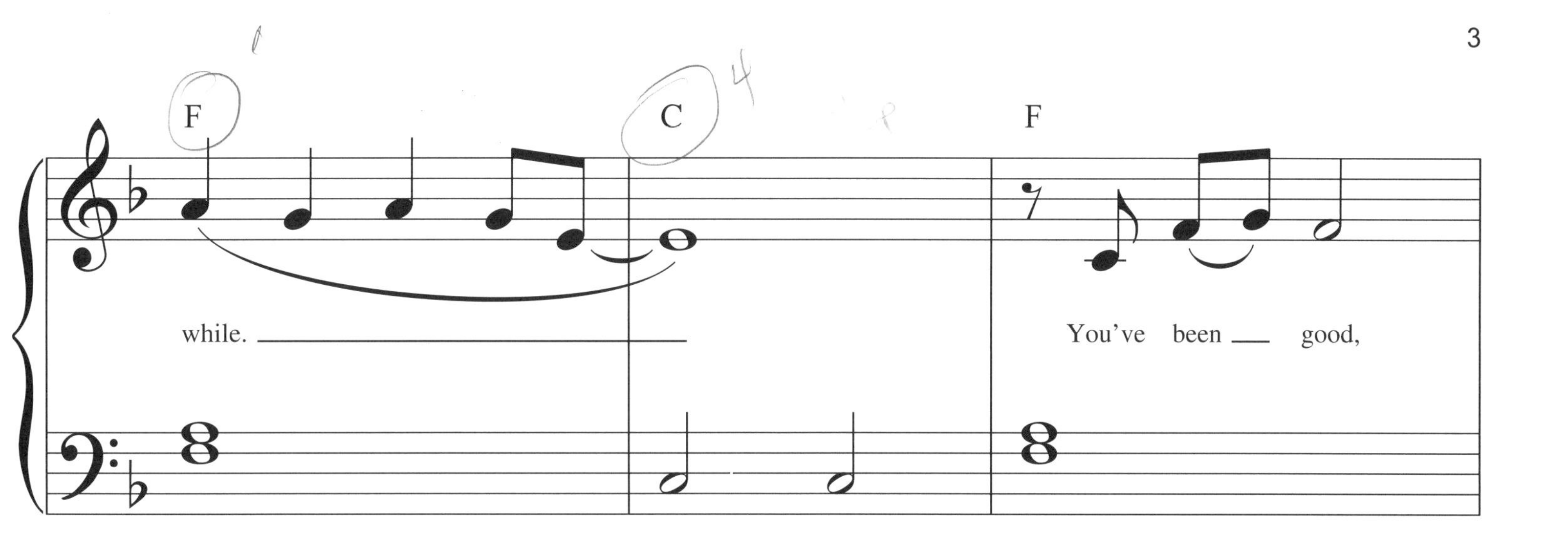
F
C
F
while.
You've been good,

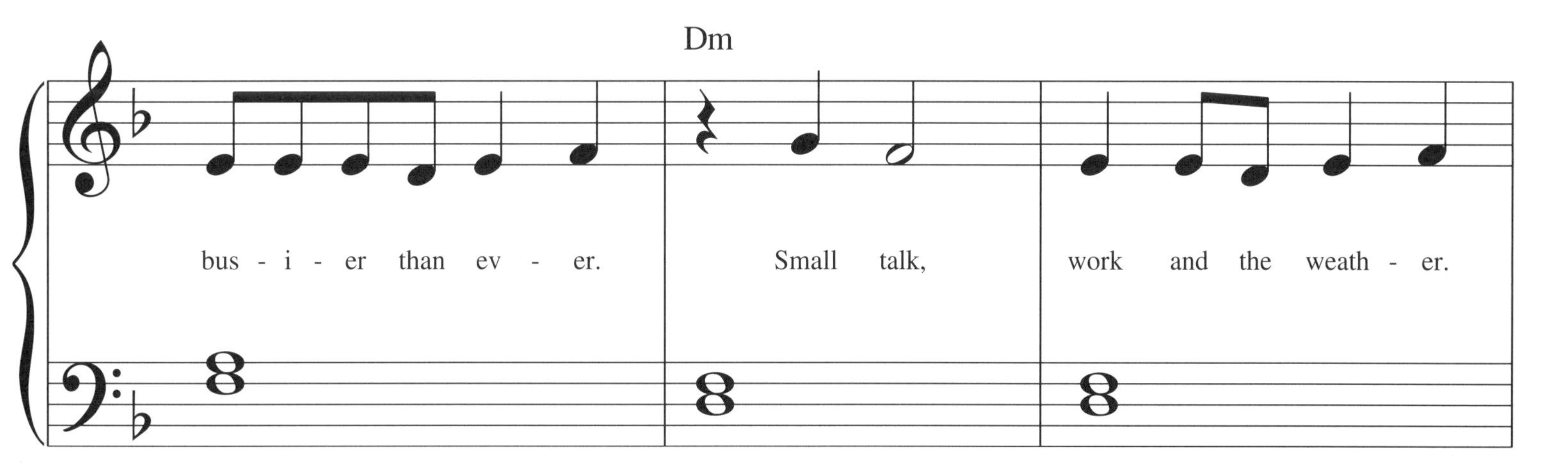
Dm
bus - i - er than ev - er.
Small talk,
work and the weath - er.

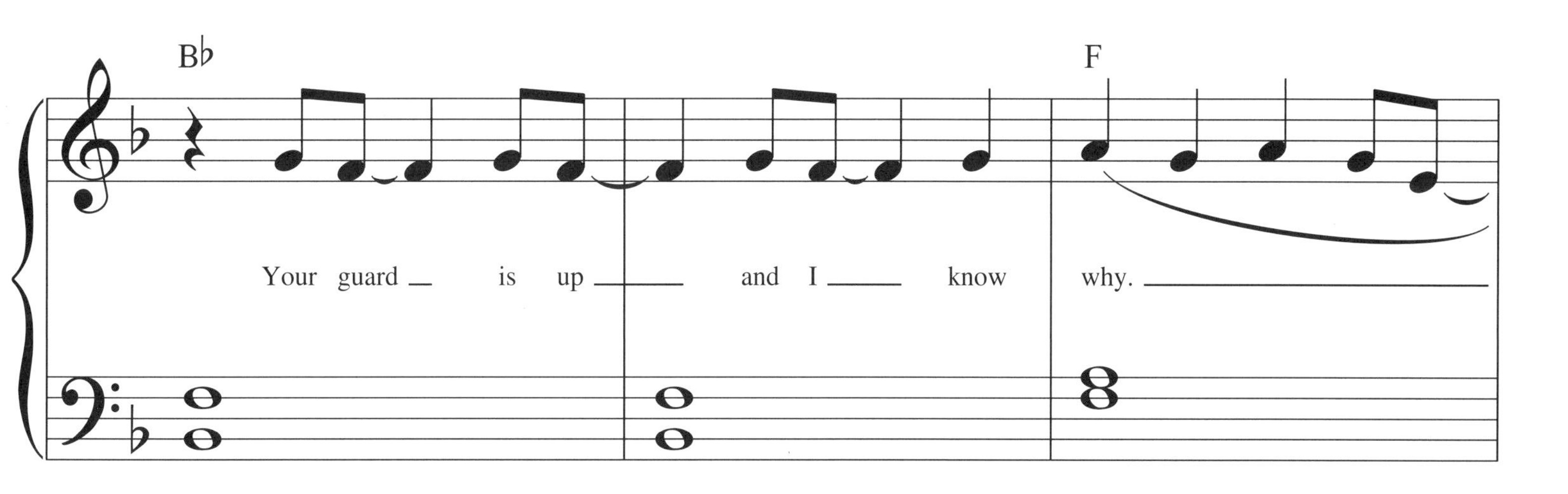
B♭
F
Your guard is up and I know
why.

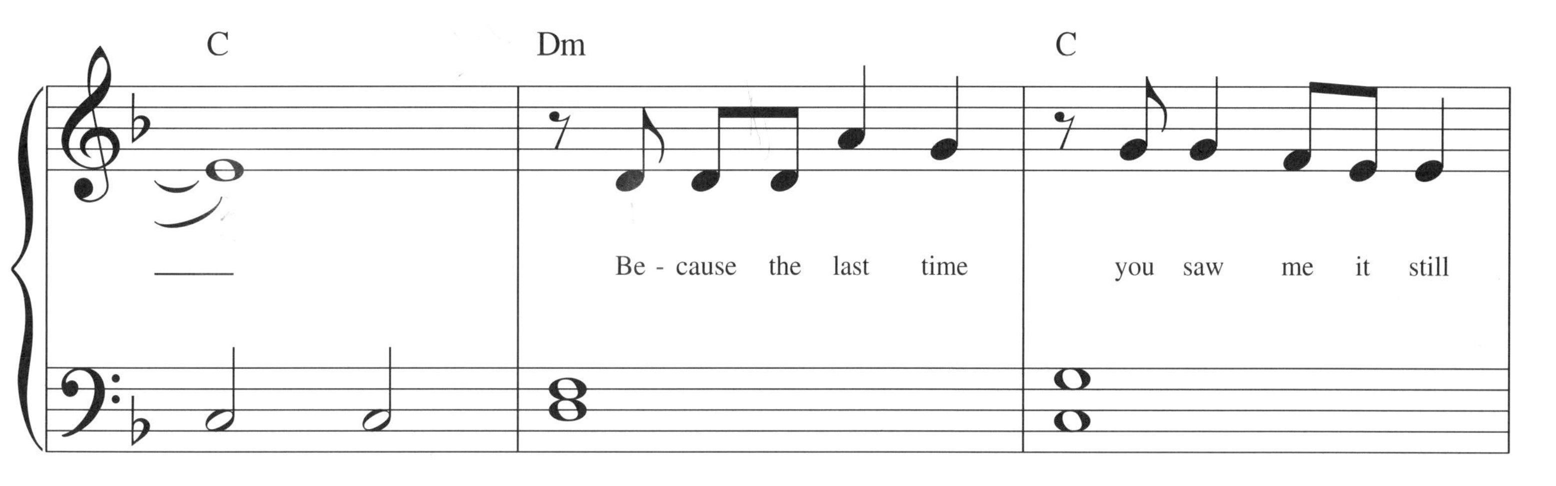
C
Dm
C
Be - cause the last time
you saw me it still

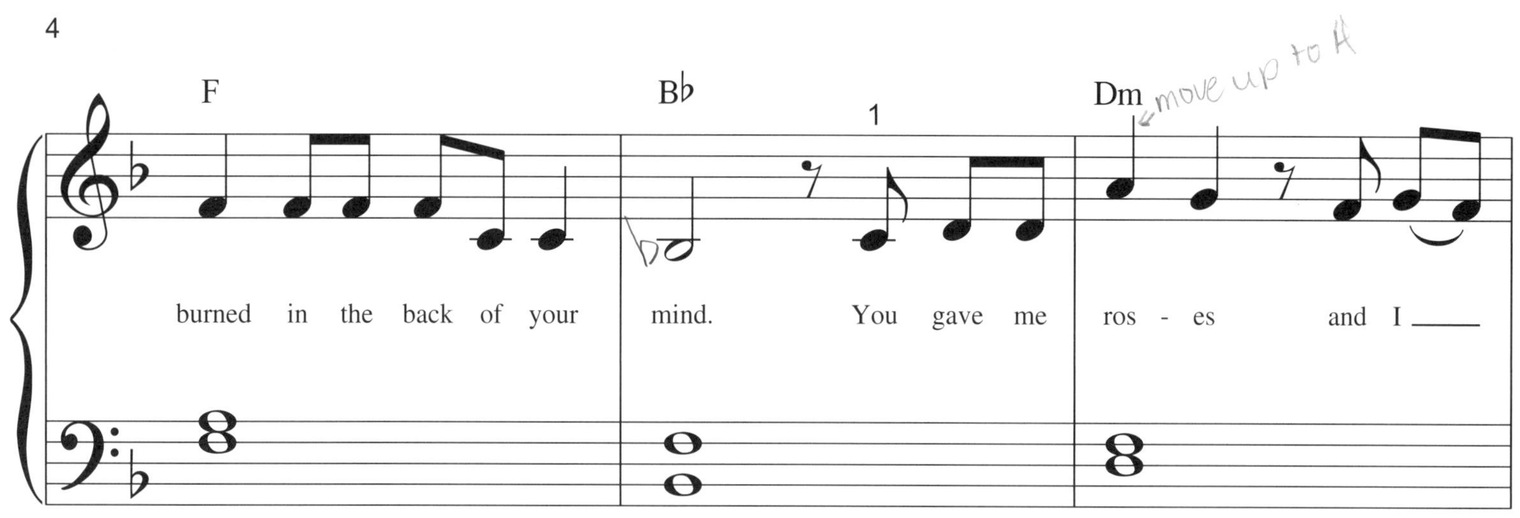
F
B♭
1
Dm
move up to A
burned in the back of your
mind. You gave me
ros - es and I

C
B♭
go farther
left them there to die.
So,
F
Am
this is me swal - low - in'
my pride stand - in' in
front of you, say - in' I'm

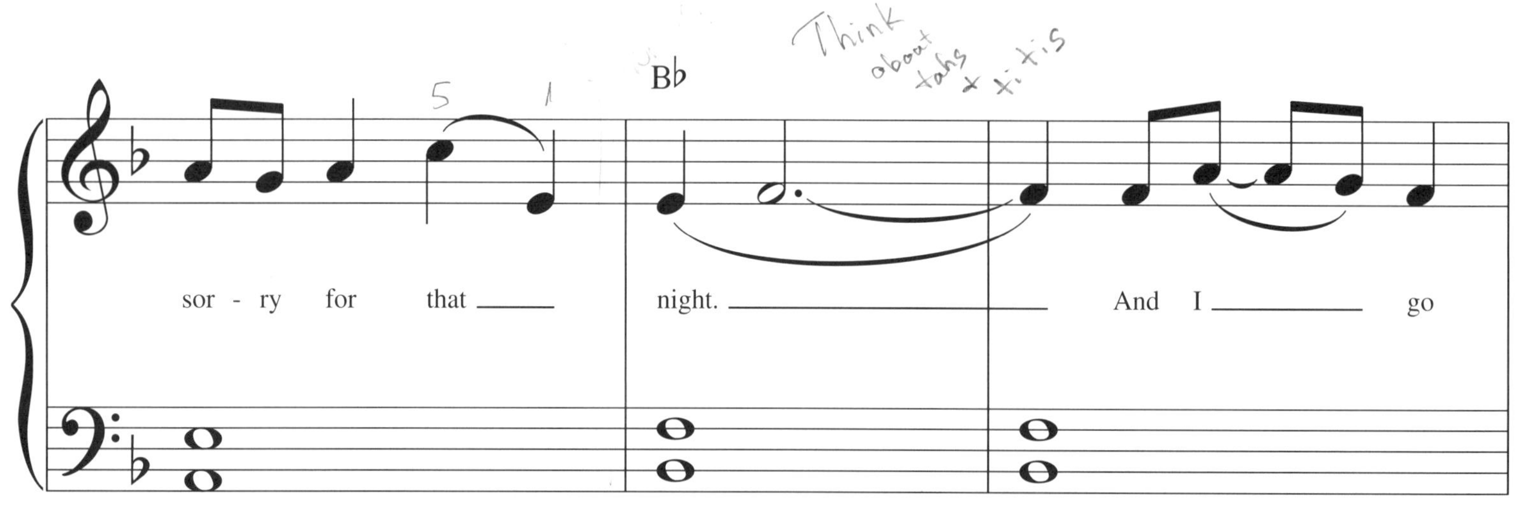
5
1
B♭
Think about tahs + ti-tis
sor - ry for that
night.
And I
go

F
C
3
F
back to De - cem - ber all the time. It turns out free - dom ain't

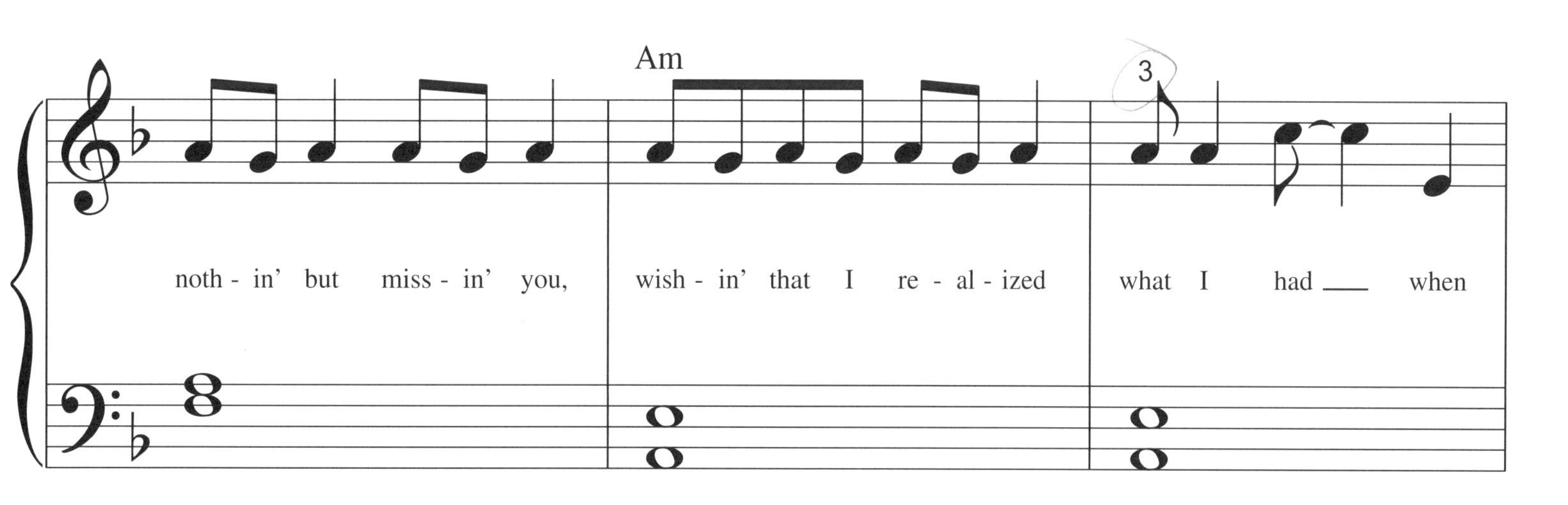
Am
3
noth - in' but miss - in' you, wish - in' that I re - al - ized what I had when

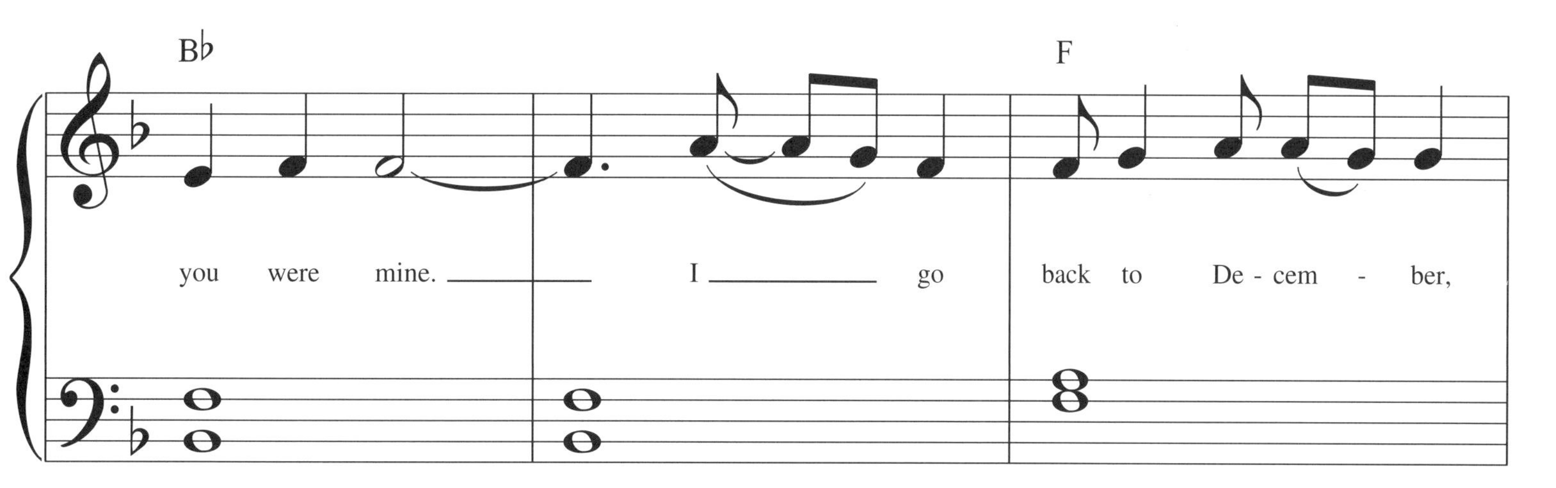
B♭
F
you were mine. I go back to De - cem - ber,

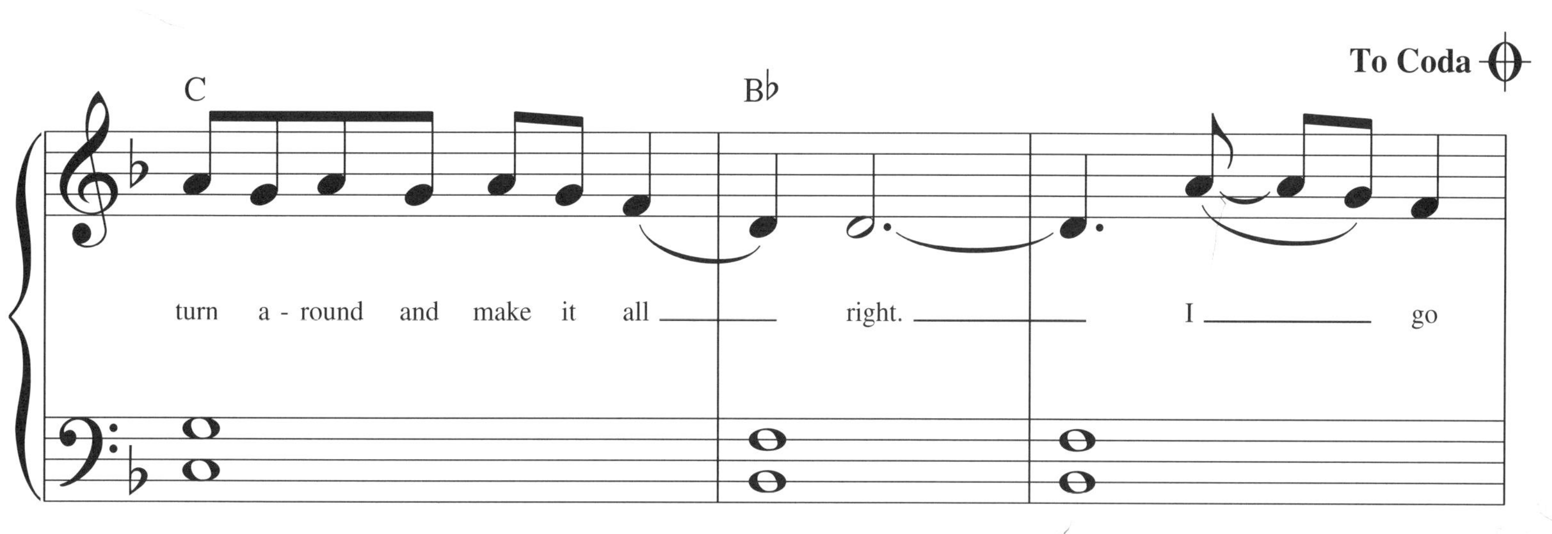
To Coda
C
B♭
turn a - round and make it all right. I go

1.
Dm
C
F
back to De - cem - ber all the time.
Dm
B♭
F
Dm
B♭
2.
F
Dm
B♭
F

Dm
Bb
Dm
I miss your tan skin, your
Bb
F
C
sweet smile, so good to me, so right; and how you
Dm
Bb
F
held me in your arms that Sep - tem - ber night, the first time you
C
Dm
N.C.
ev - er saw me cry. May - be this is wish - ful think - in',

B♭
N.C.
F
3
2
2
prob - a - bly
mind - less dream - in'.
If we loved a - gain,

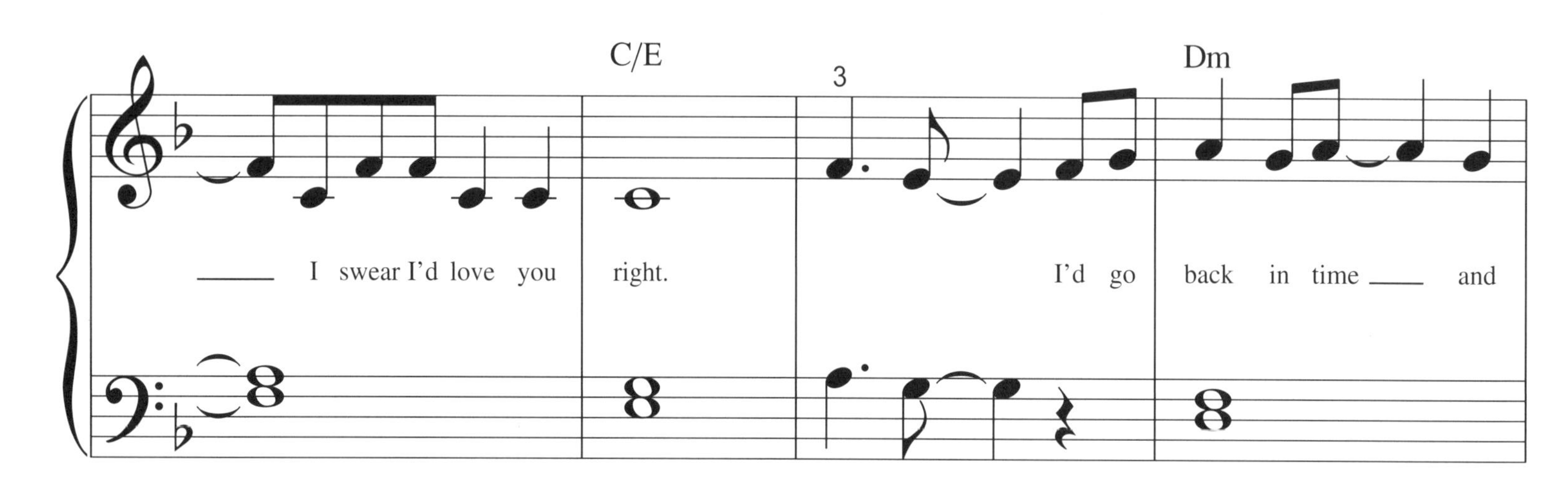
C/E
Dm
3
I swear I'd love you
right.
I'd go
back in time and

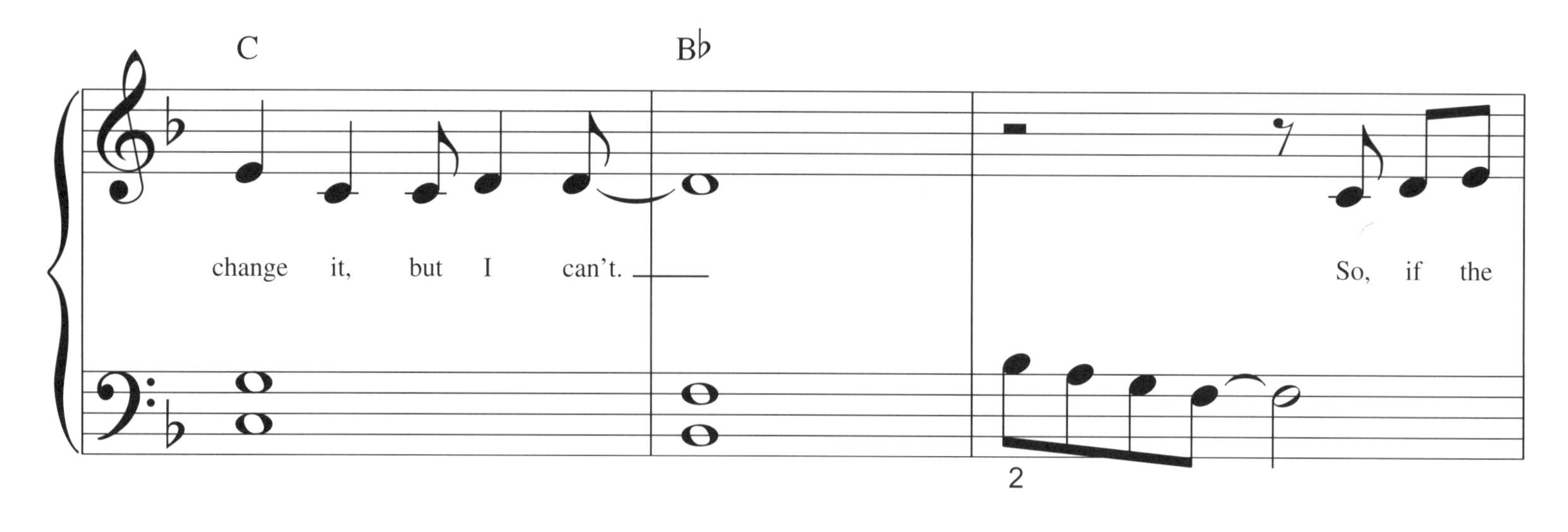
C
B♭
change it, but I can't.
So, if the
2

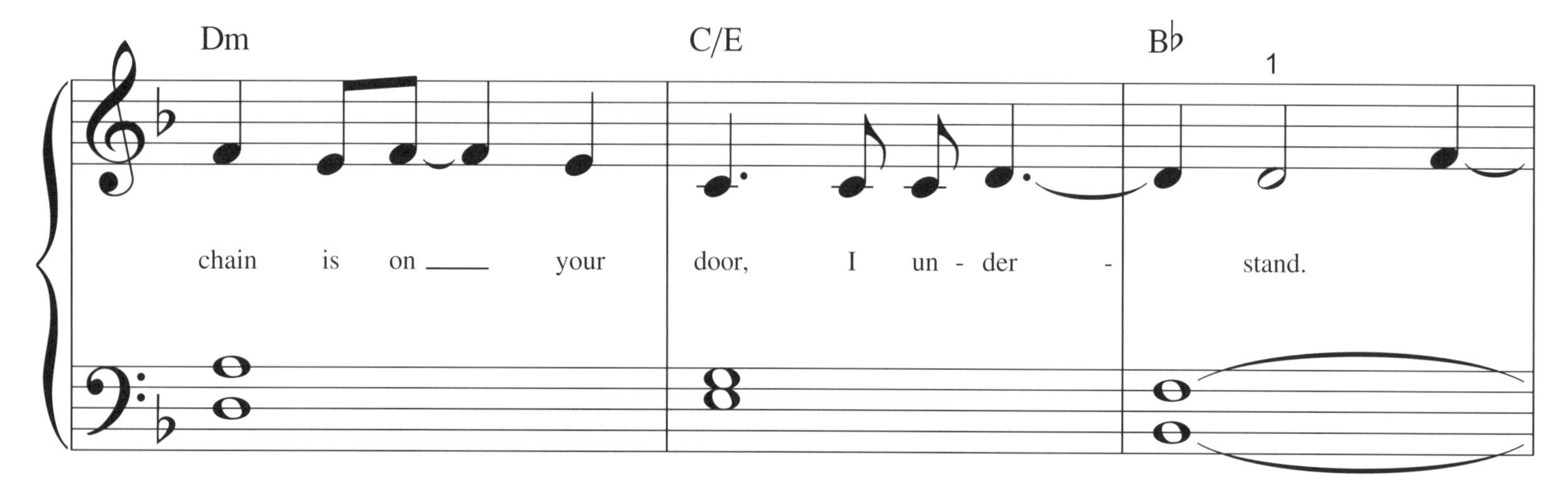
Dm
C/E
B♭
1
chain is on your
door, I un - der -
stand.

Additional Lyrics

2. These days I haven't been sleepin';
Stayin' up, playin' back myself leavin',
When your birthday passed and I didn't call.
Then I think about summer, all the beautiful times
I watched you laughin' from the passenger side
And realized I loved you in the fall.
And then the cold came, the dark days
When fear crept into my mind.
You gave me all your love and
All I gave you was goodbye.

So, this is me swallowin' my pride...

BEGIN AGAIN

Words and Music by
TAYLOR SWIFT
Moving gently, in 2
C
mf
Took a deep breath in the mir - ror.
Turn the lock and put my head - phones on.
He did - n't like it when I wore high heels, but
He al - ways said he did - n't get this song, but
1.
F
I do.
2.
F
I do.
I do.

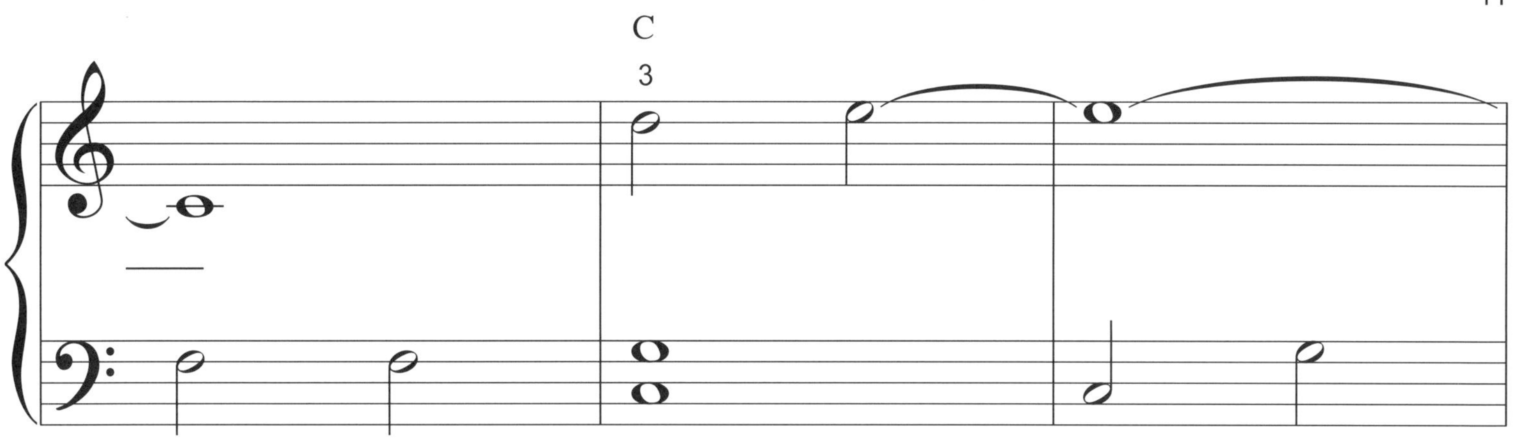
C
3

4
Walked in ex - pect - ing
You say you nev - er met

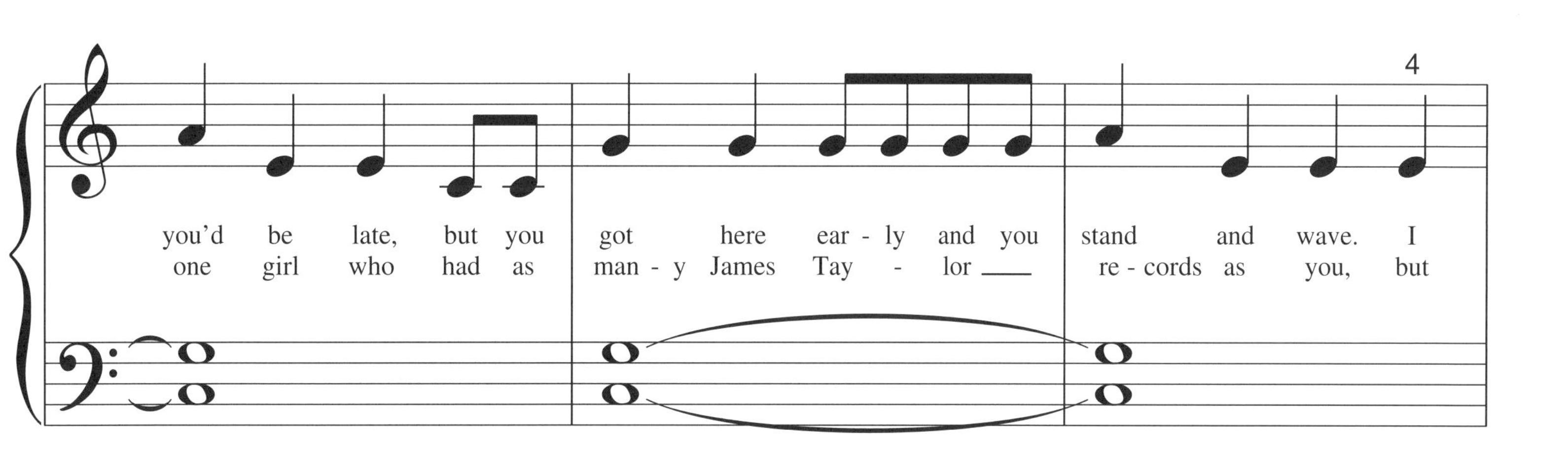
4
you'd be late, but you got here ear - ly and you stand and wave. I
one girl who had as man - y James Tay - lor re - cords as you, but

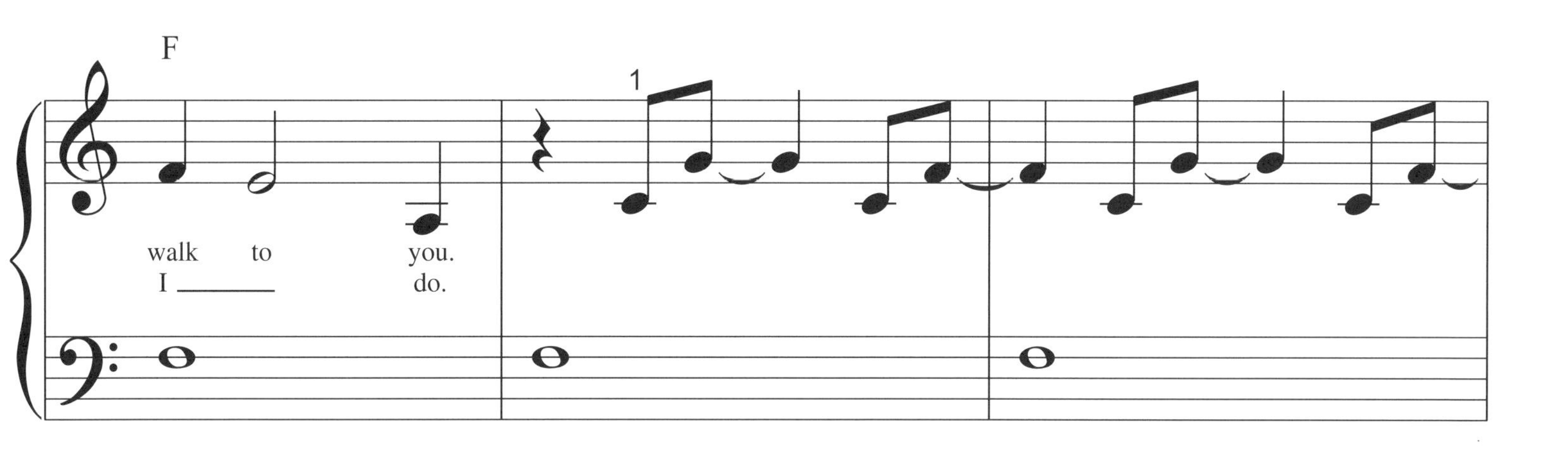
F
1
walk to you.
I do.

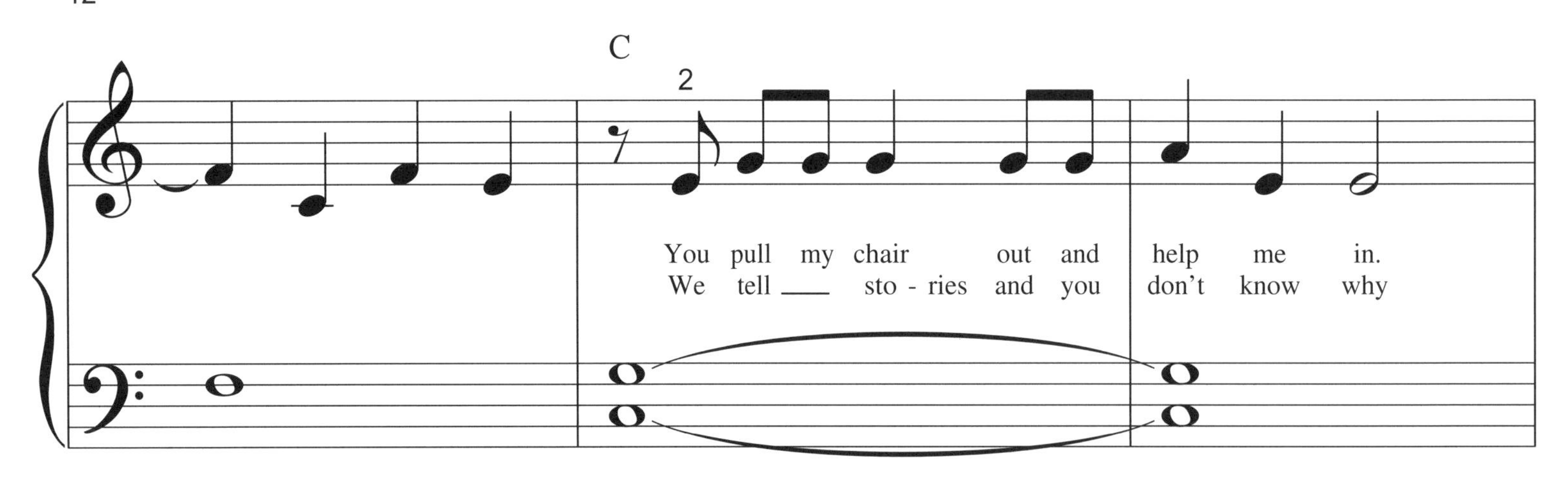
C
2
You pull my chair out and help me in.
We tell ___ sto - ries and you don't know why

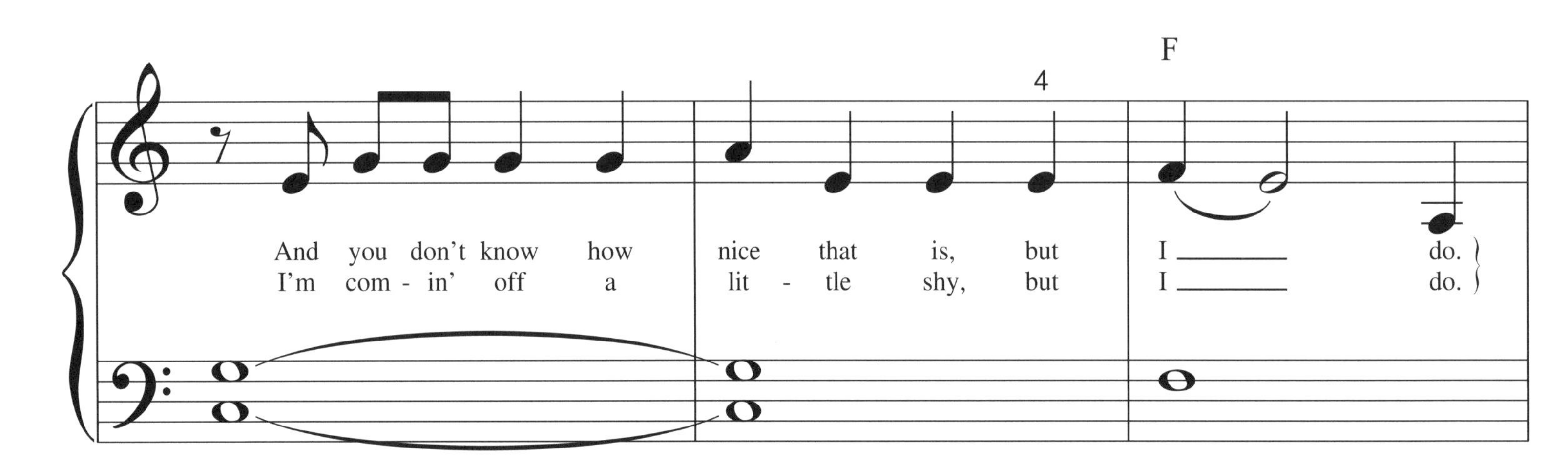
F
4
And you don't know how nice that is, but I ___ do.
I'm com - in' off a lit - tle shy, but I ___ do.

1
3

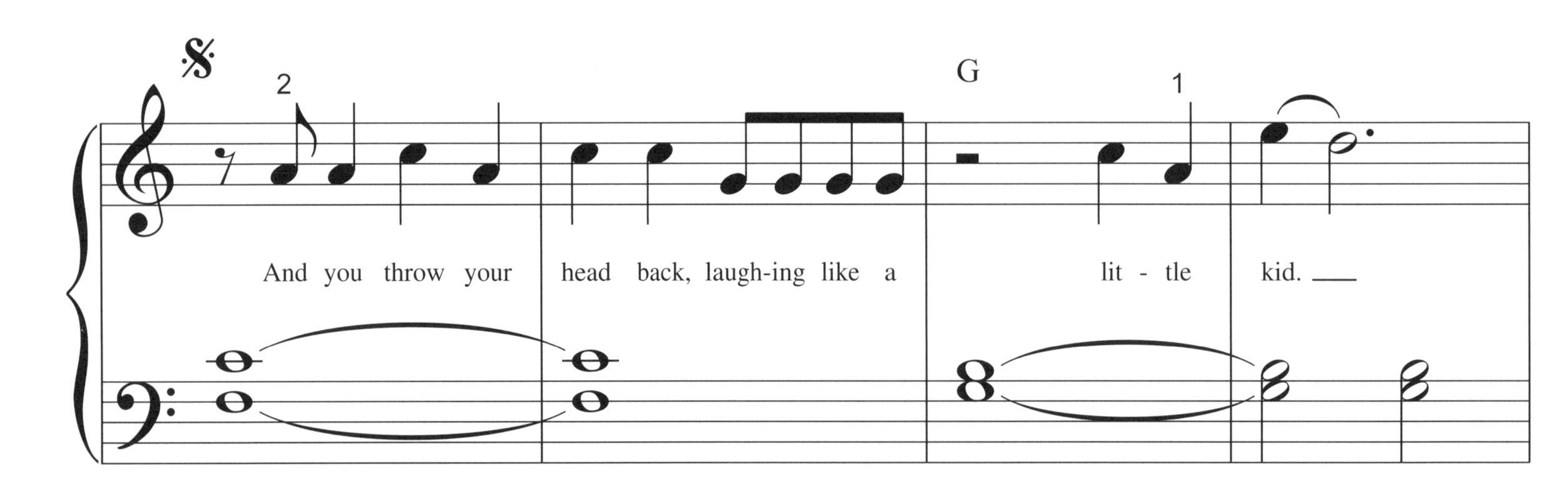
G
2
1
And you throw your head back, laugh-ing like a lit - tle kid. ___

Am
2
I think it's strange that you think I'm fun - ny 'cause he nev - er
C
3

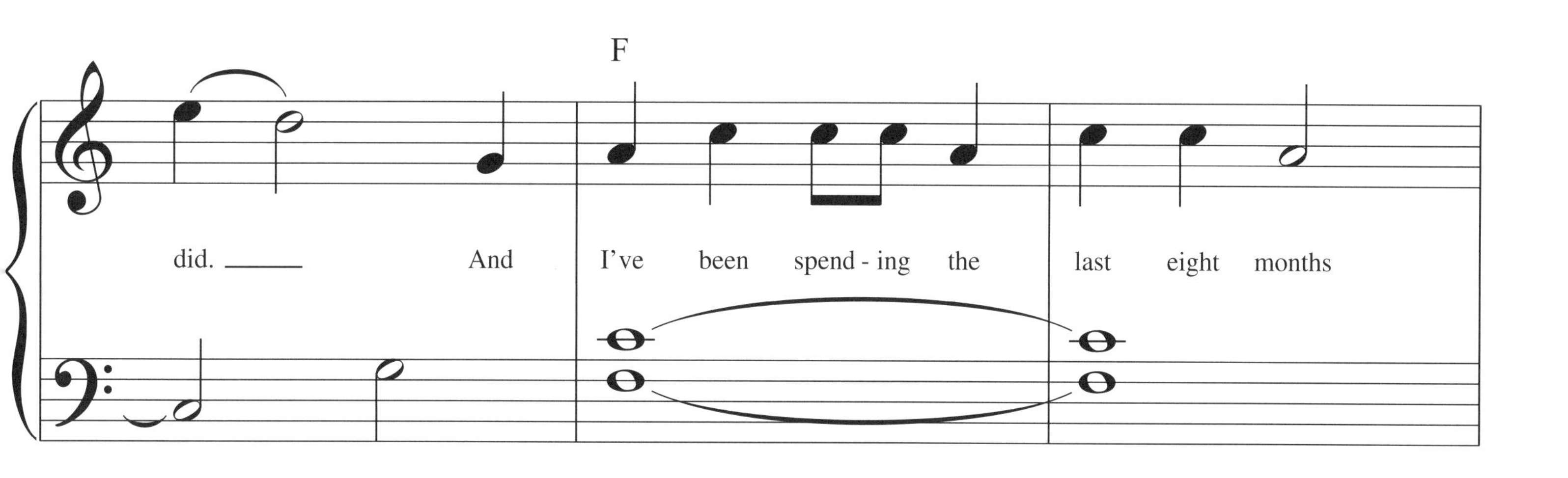
F
did. And I've been spend - ing the last eight months

G
4
C
think - ing all love ev - er does is break and

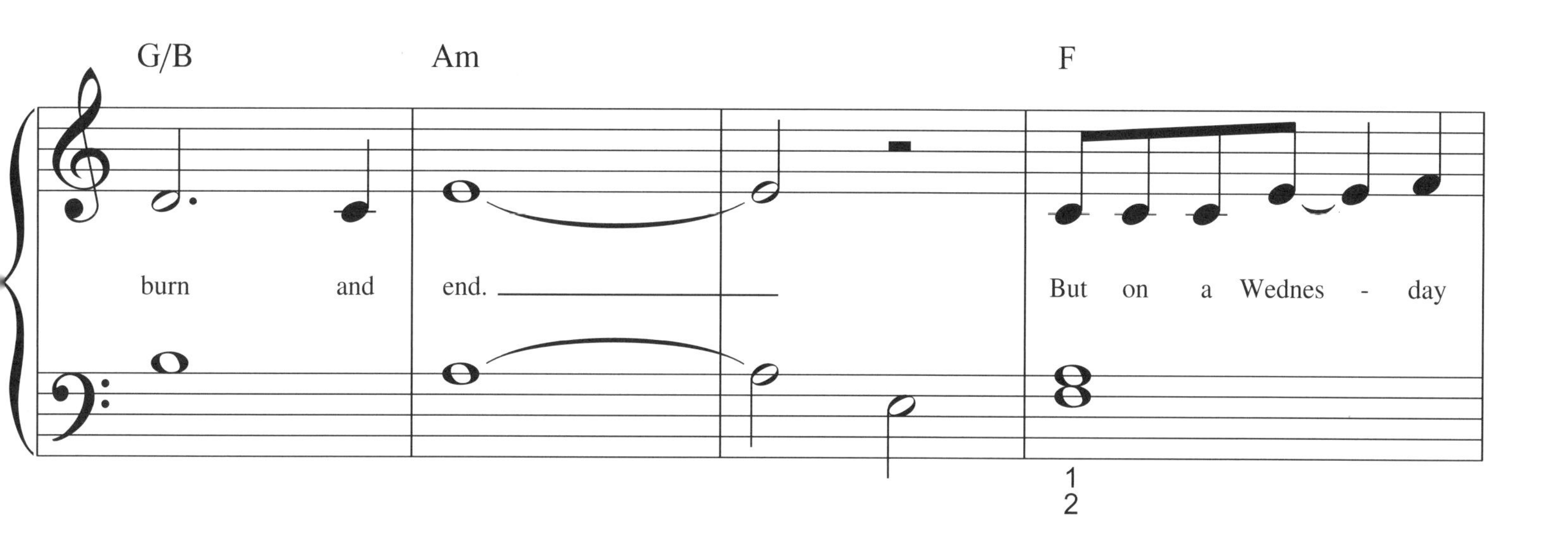
G/B
Am
F
burn and end. But on a Wednes - day
1
2

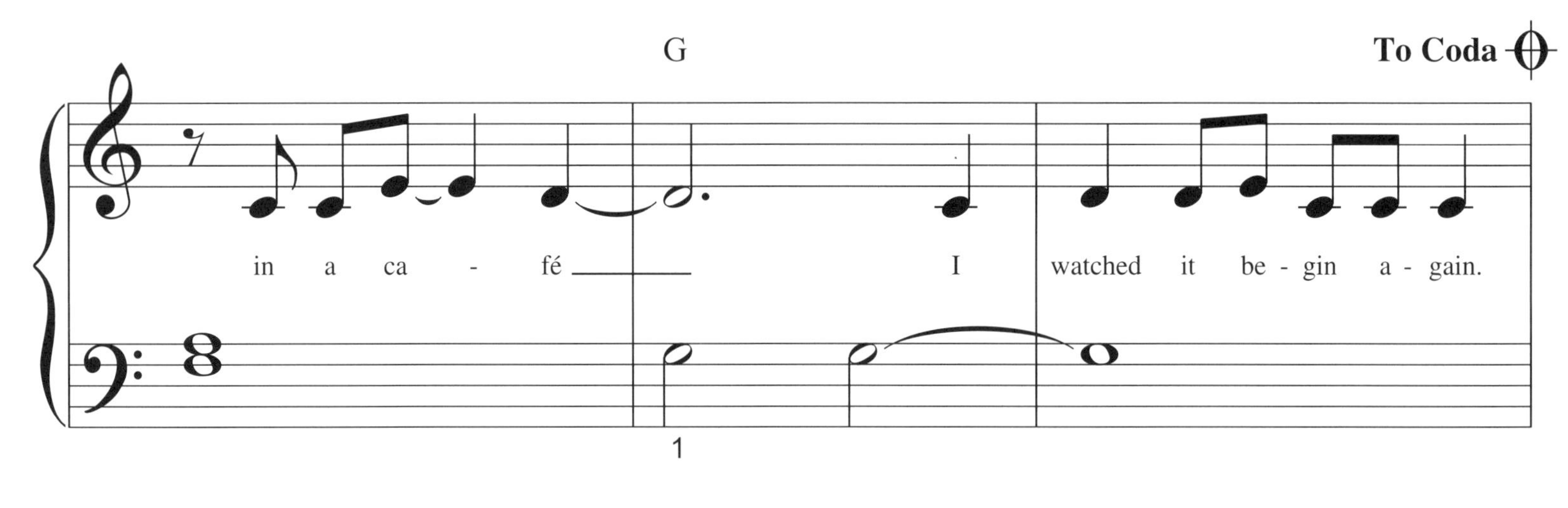
G
To Coda
in a ca - fé
I
watched it be - gin a - gain.
1

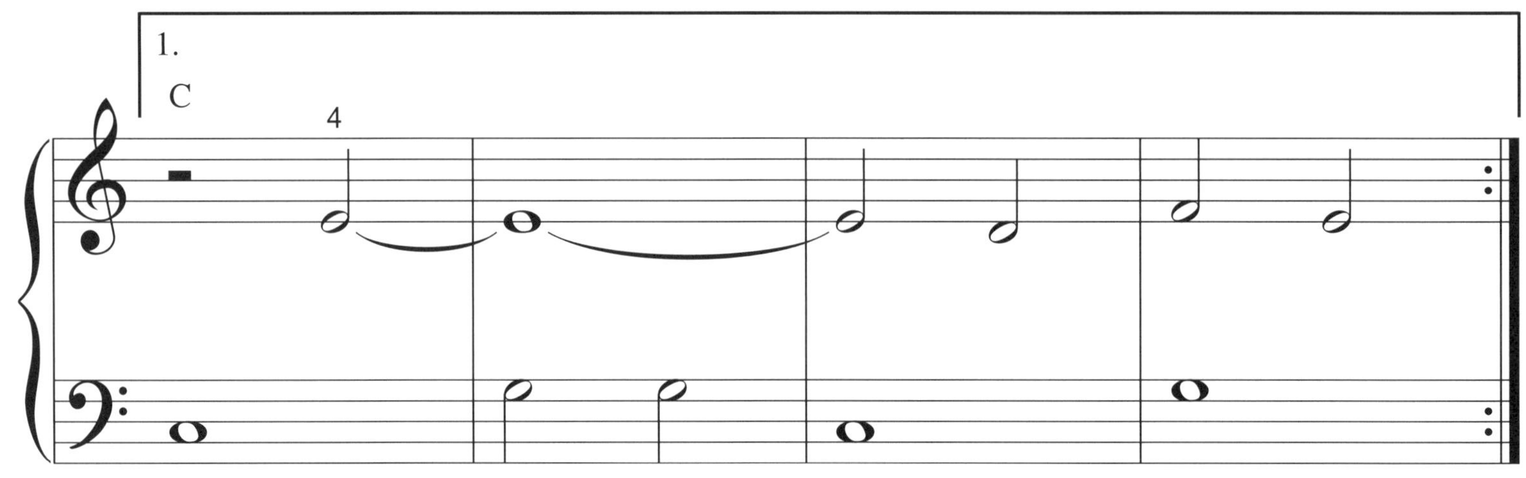
1.
C
4

2.
C
4

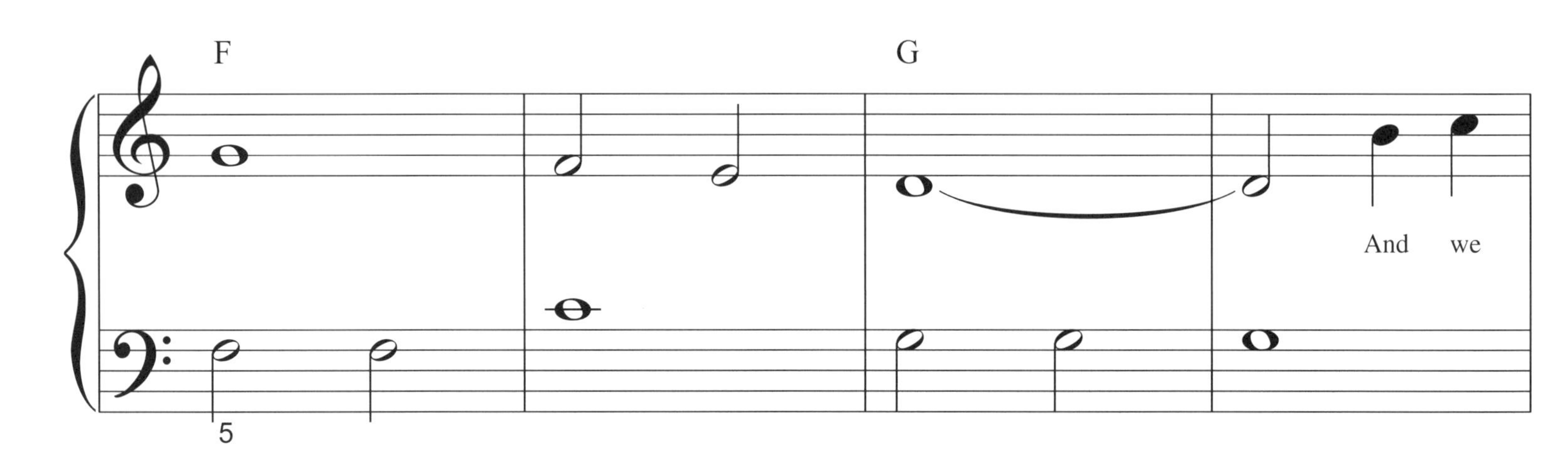
F
G
And we
5

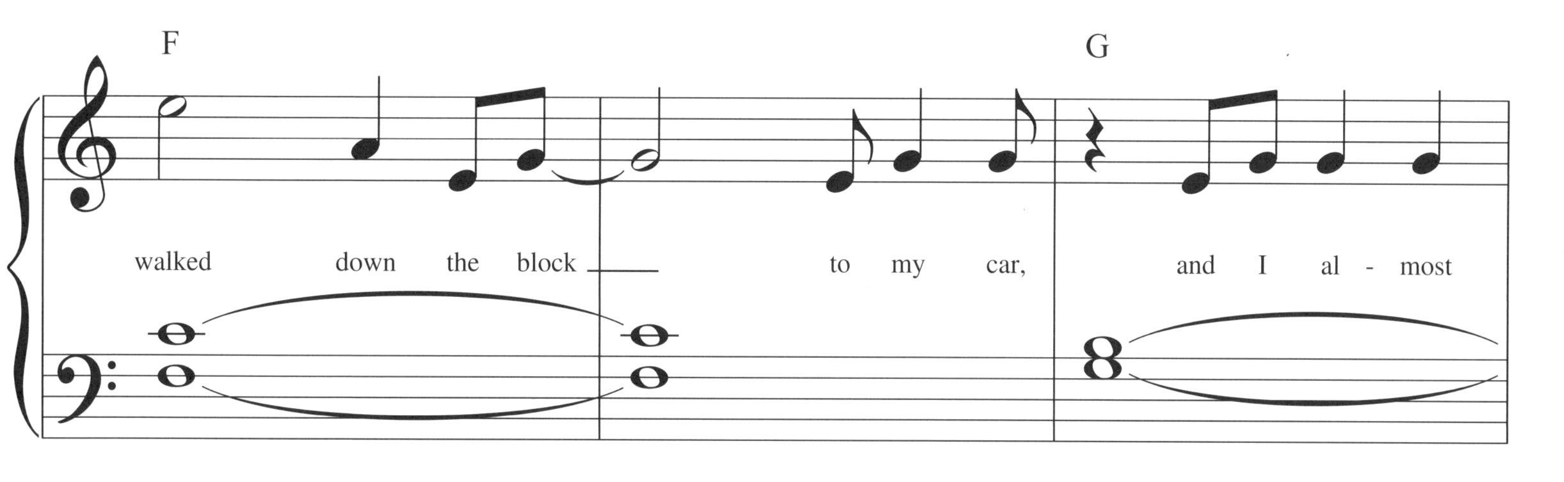
F
G
walked down the block to my car, and I al - most

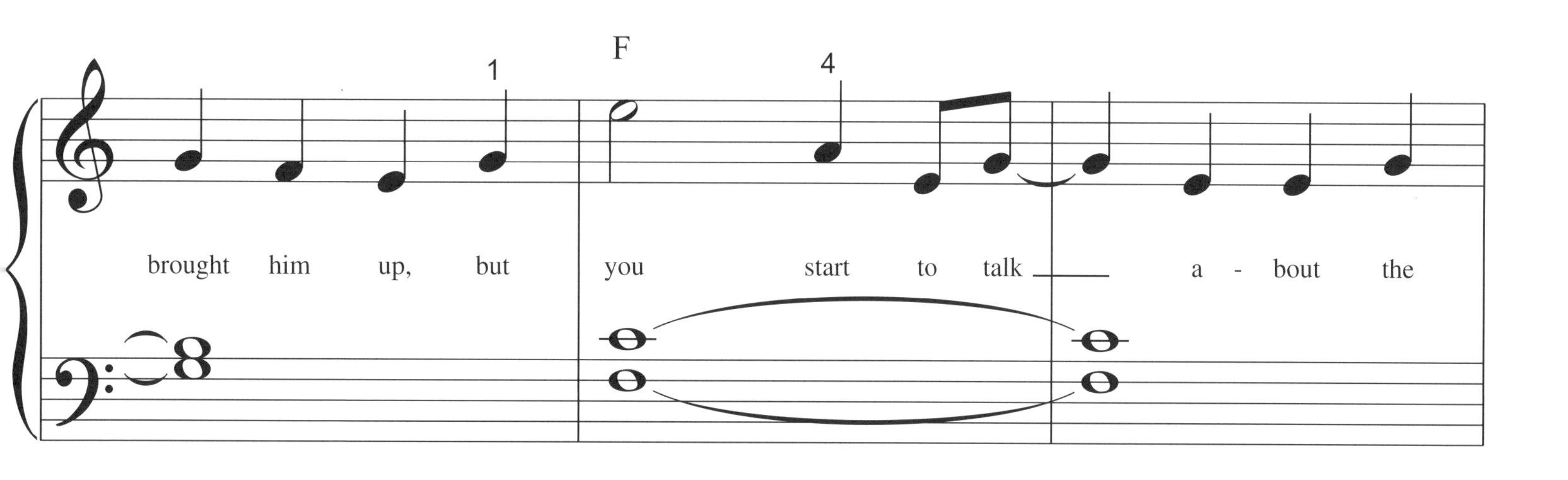
1
F
4
brought him up, but you start to talk a - bout the

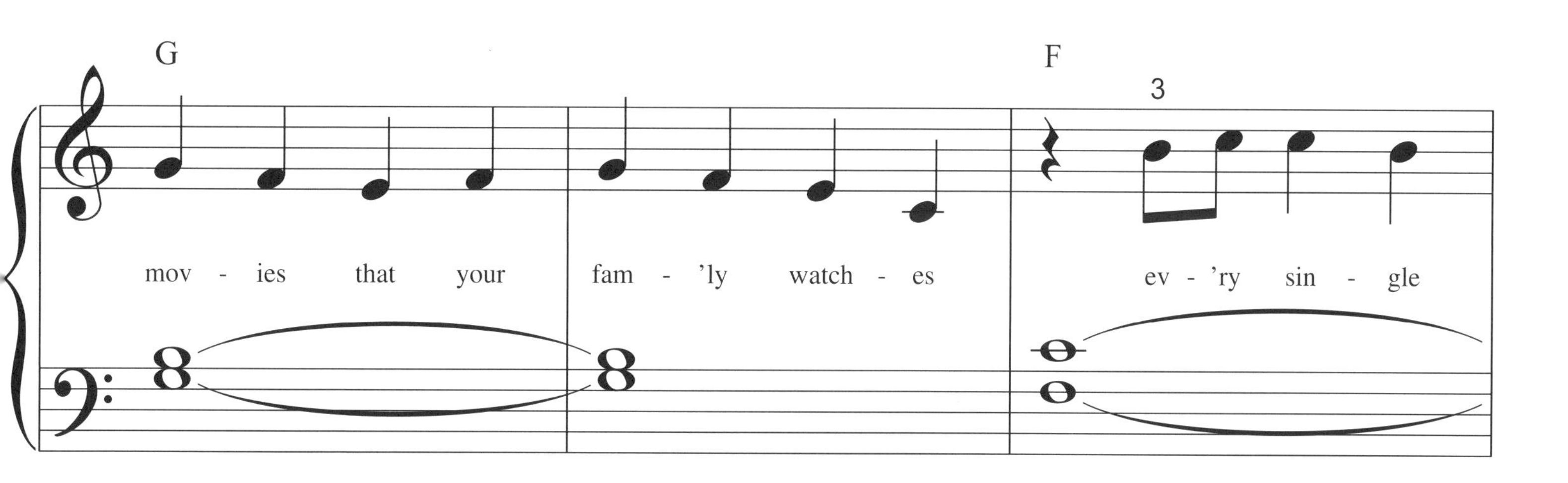
G
F
3
mov - ies that your fam - 'ly watch - es ev - 'ry sin - gle

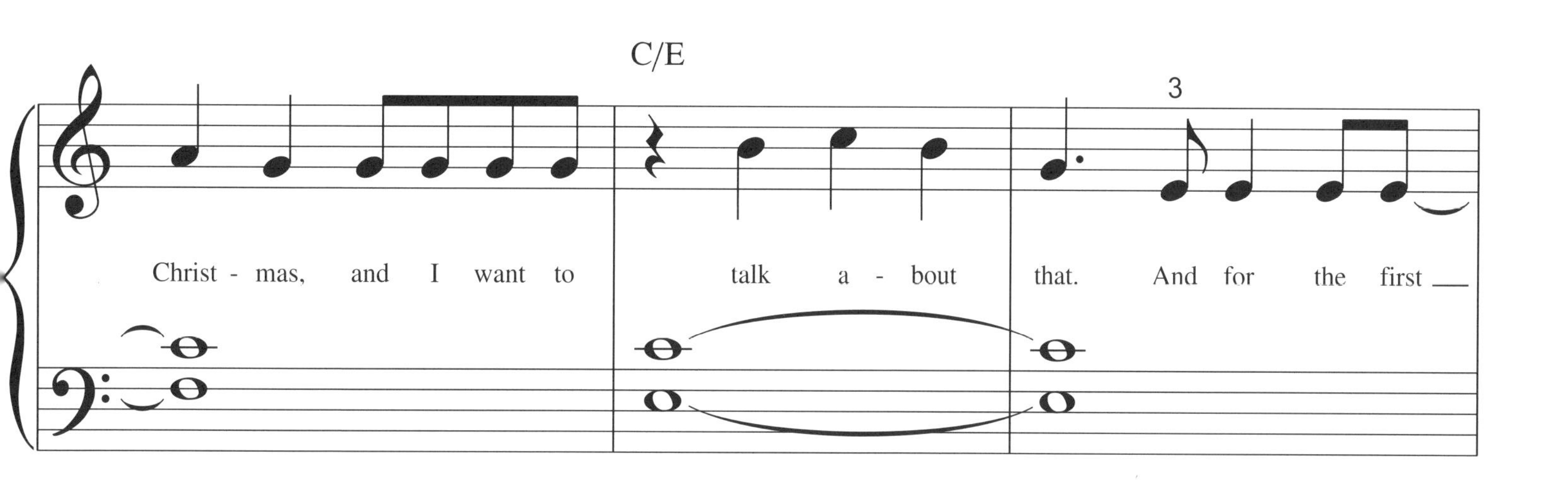
C/E
3
Christ - mas, and I want to talk a - bout that. And for the first

F
time,
what's past
is
past.
3
5
D.S. al Coda
CODA
C
G
5
Am
F
1
But on a Wednes - day
1
3
G
N.C.
in a ca - fé
I
watched it be - gin a - gain.

ENCHANTED

Words and Music by
TAYLOR SWIFT

Moderately

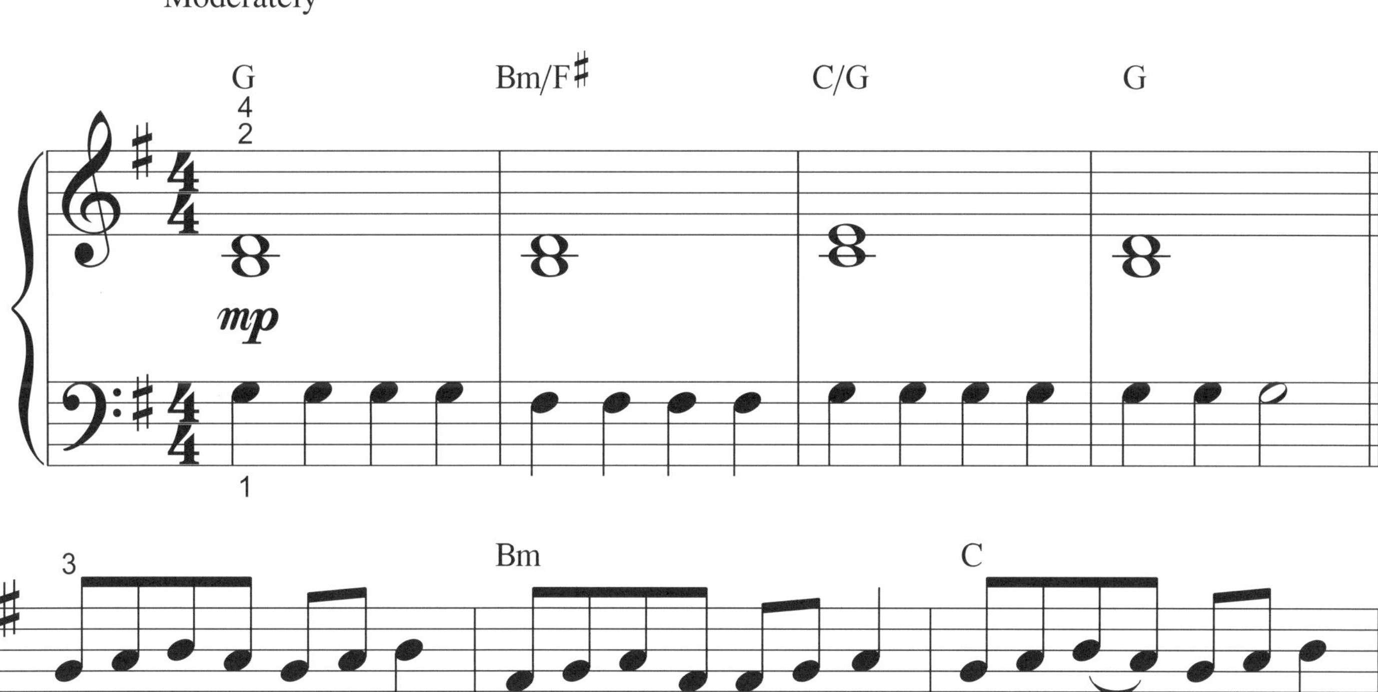
G
Bm/F♯
C/G
G
mp

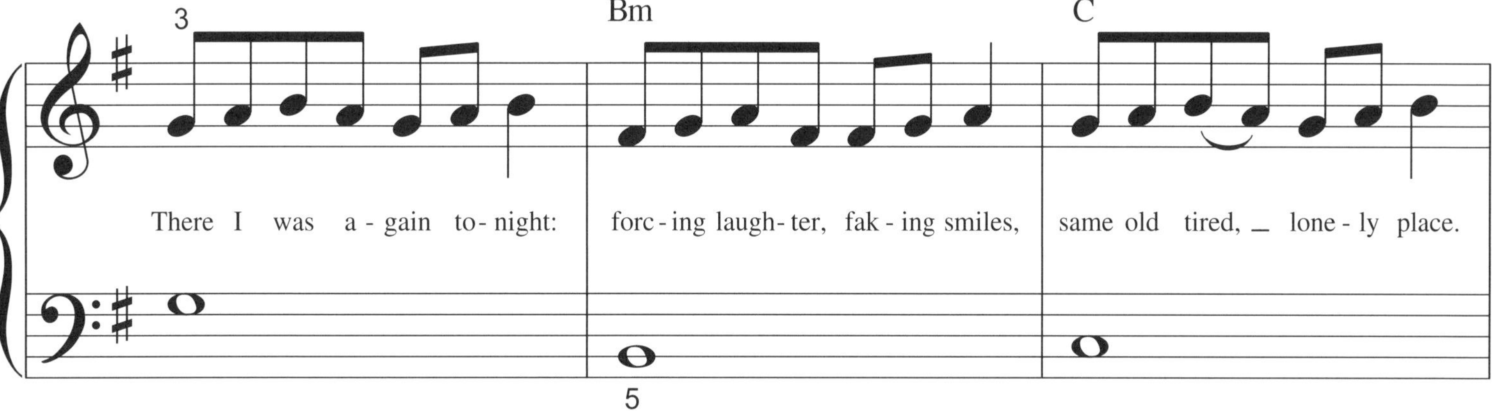
Bm
C
There I was a-gain to-night:
forc-ing laugh-ter, fak-ing smiles,
same old tired, lone-ly place.

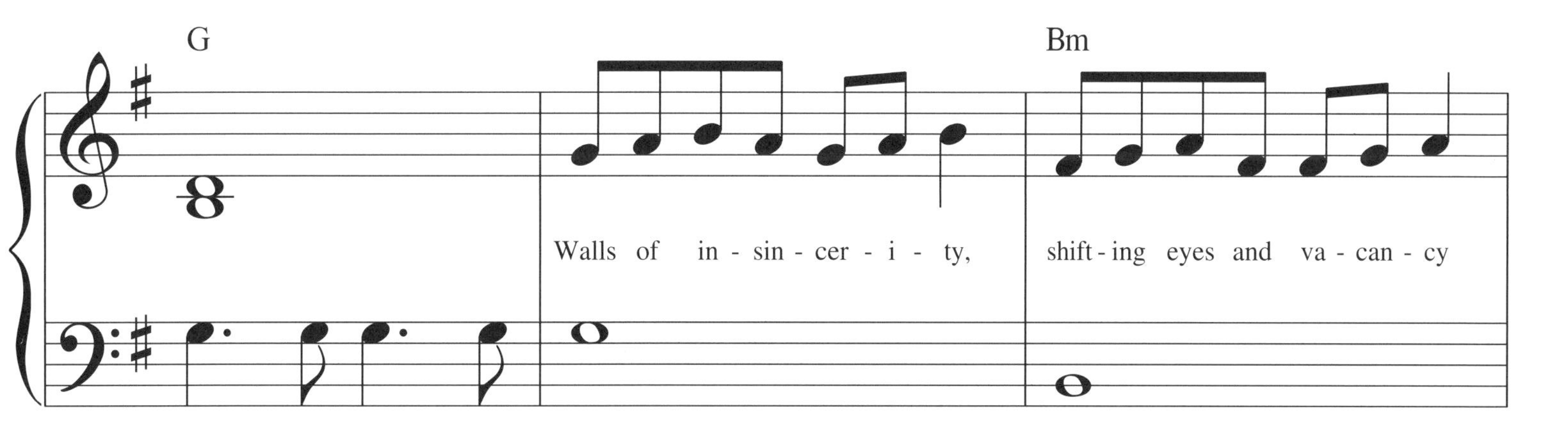
G
Bm
Walls of in-sin-cer-i-ty,
shift-ing eyes and va-can-cy

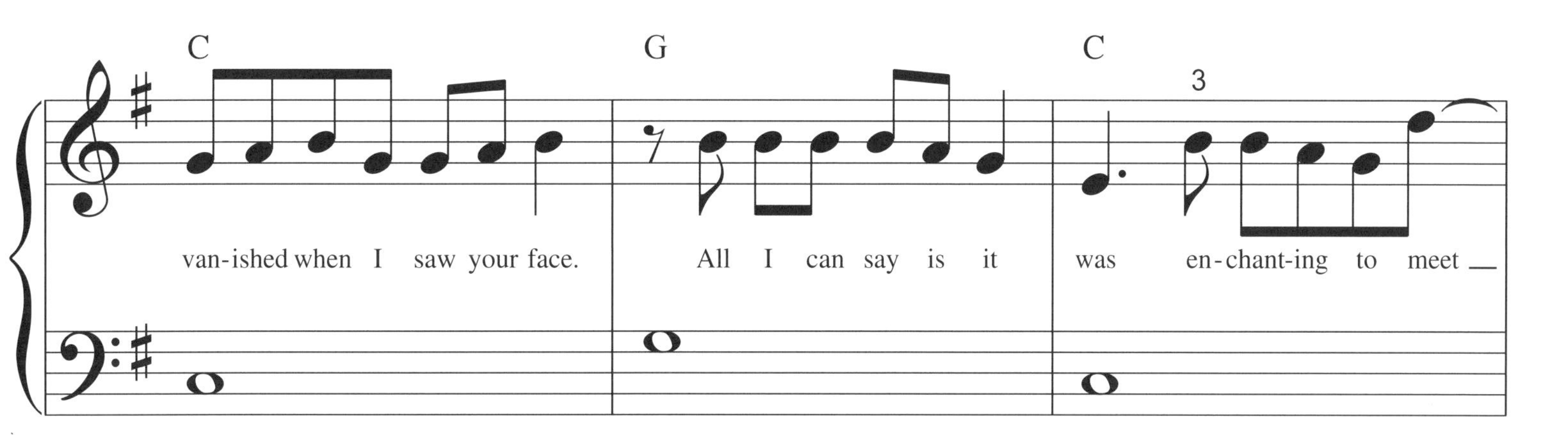
C
G
C
van-ished when I saw your face.
All I can say is it
was en-chant-ing to meet

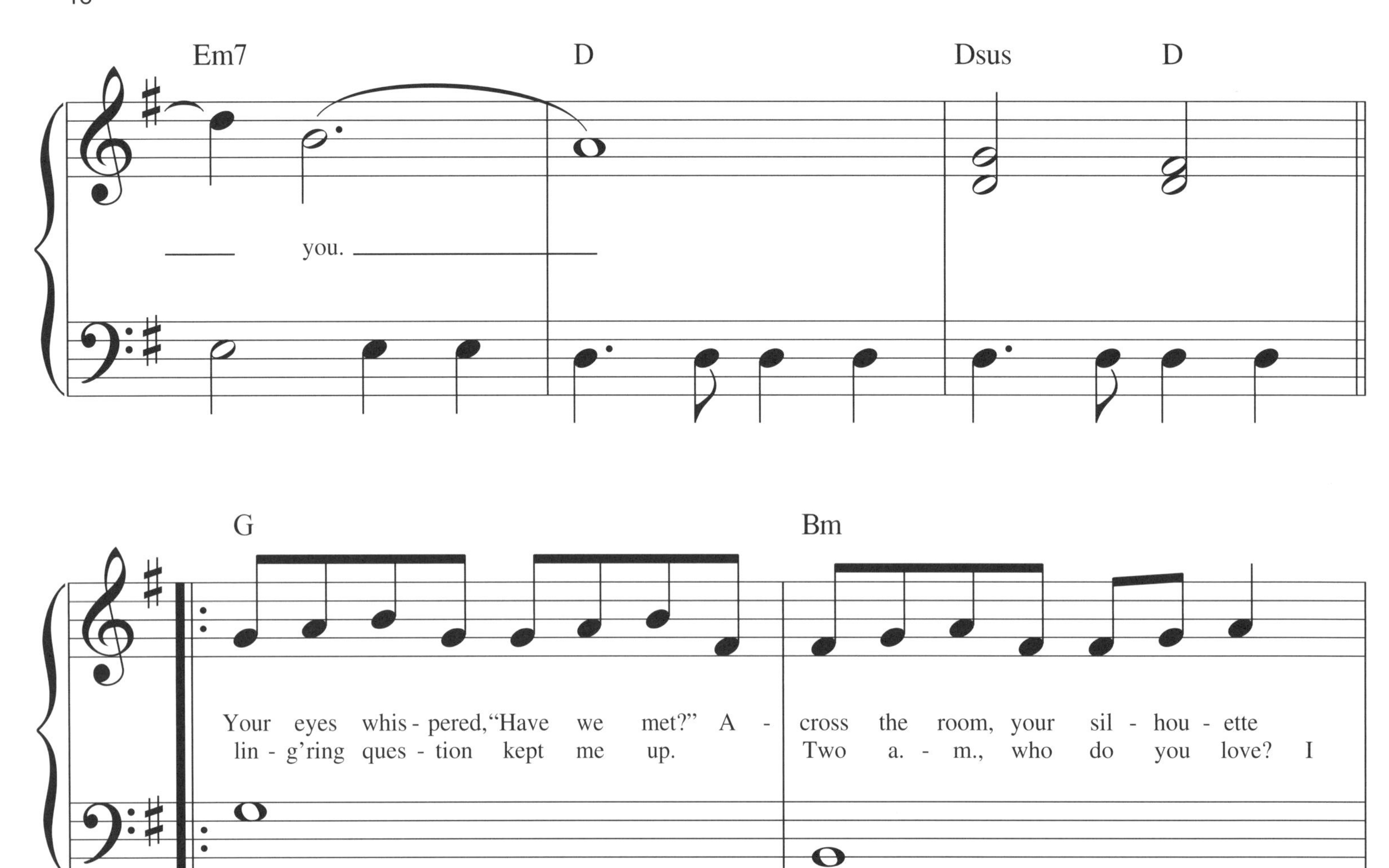
Em7
D
Dsus
D
you.
G
Bm
Your eyes whis - pered, "Have we met?" A - cross the room, your sil - hou - ette
lin - g'ring ques - tion kept me up. Two a. - m., who do you love? I

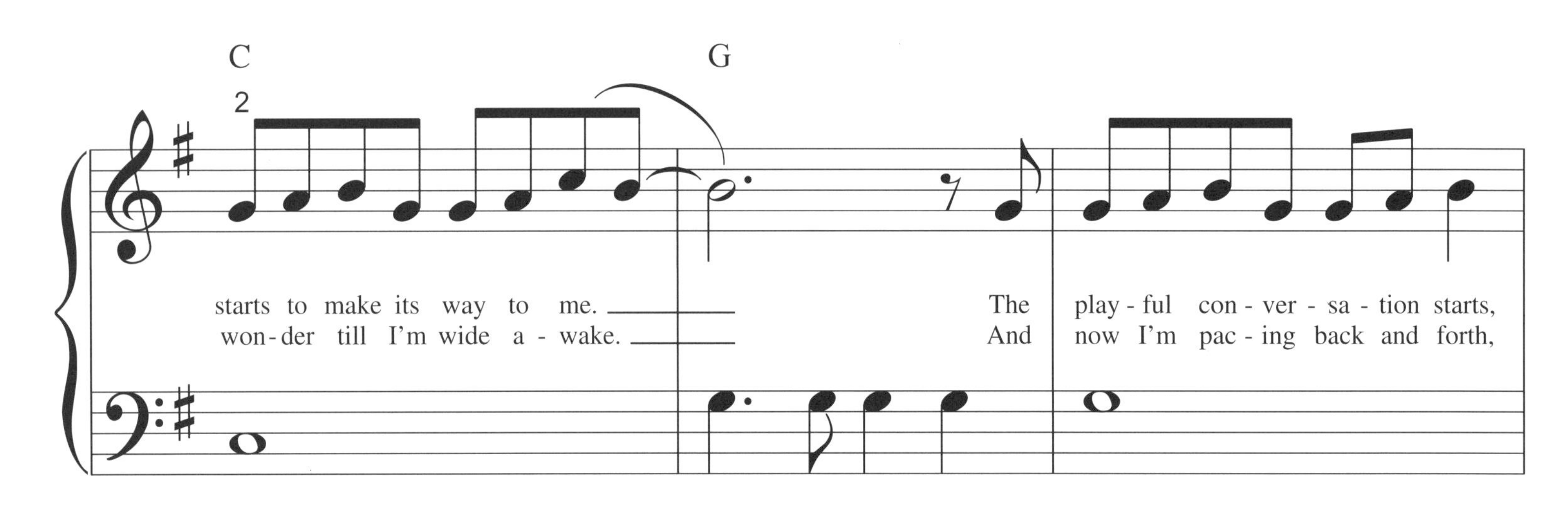
C
G
2
starts to make its way to me. The play - ful con - ver - sa - tion starts,
won - der till I'm wide a - wake. And now I'm pac - ing back and forth,

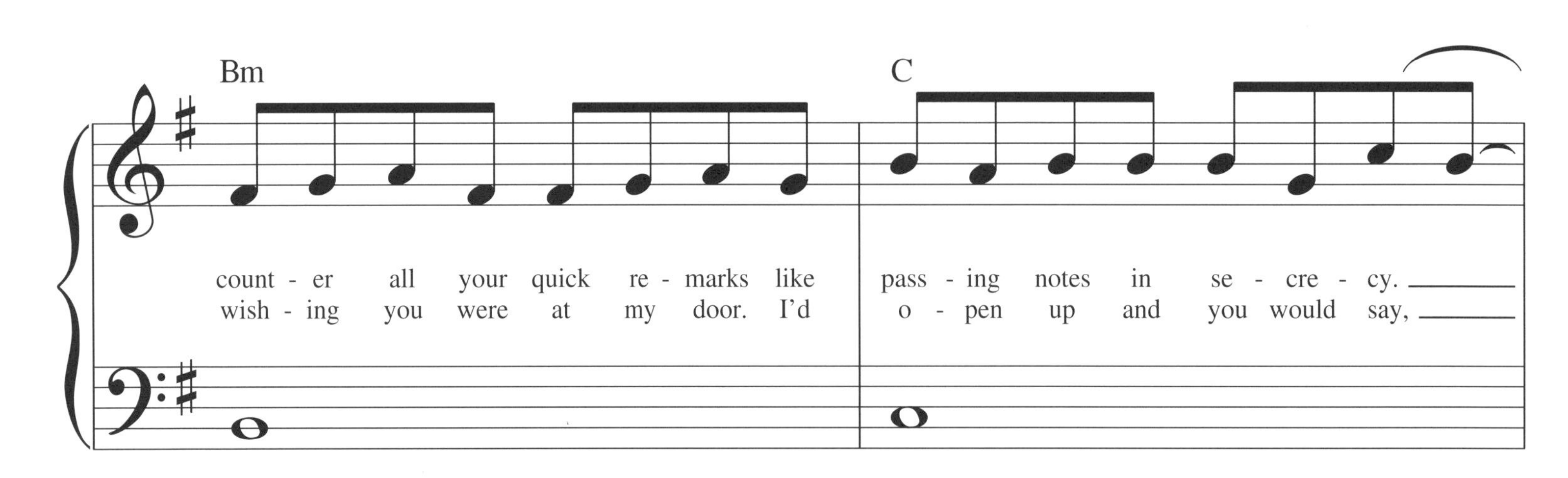
Bm
C
count - er all your quick re - marks like pass - ing notes in se - cre - cy.
wish - ing you were at my door. I'd o - pen up and you would say,

G
C
Em7
3
And it
was en - chant - ing to meet you.
"Hey, it
was en - chant - ing to meet you."
D
Dsus
C
3
All I can say is I
was en - chant - ed to meet
All I know is it
was en - chant - ing to meet
Em7
D
Dsus
D
you.
you.
C
G
D
C
This night is
spar - kling. Don't you let it
go. I'm won - der -

To Coda
G D C G D
struck, blush-ing all the way home. I'll spend for - ev - er won-d'ring if you
1.
C Em D G
3
knew I was en-chant-ed to meet you.
The
2.
C Em D
knew.
C G D C
This night is flaw - less. Don't you let it go. I'm won - der -

G D C G D
struck, danc - ing 'round all a - lone. I'll spend for - ev - er won - d'ring if you
C Em D G
2 1
knew I was en - chant - ed to meet you.
Bm C
D C Em D
This is me pray - ing that this was the ver - y first page, not where the sto - ry - line ends.

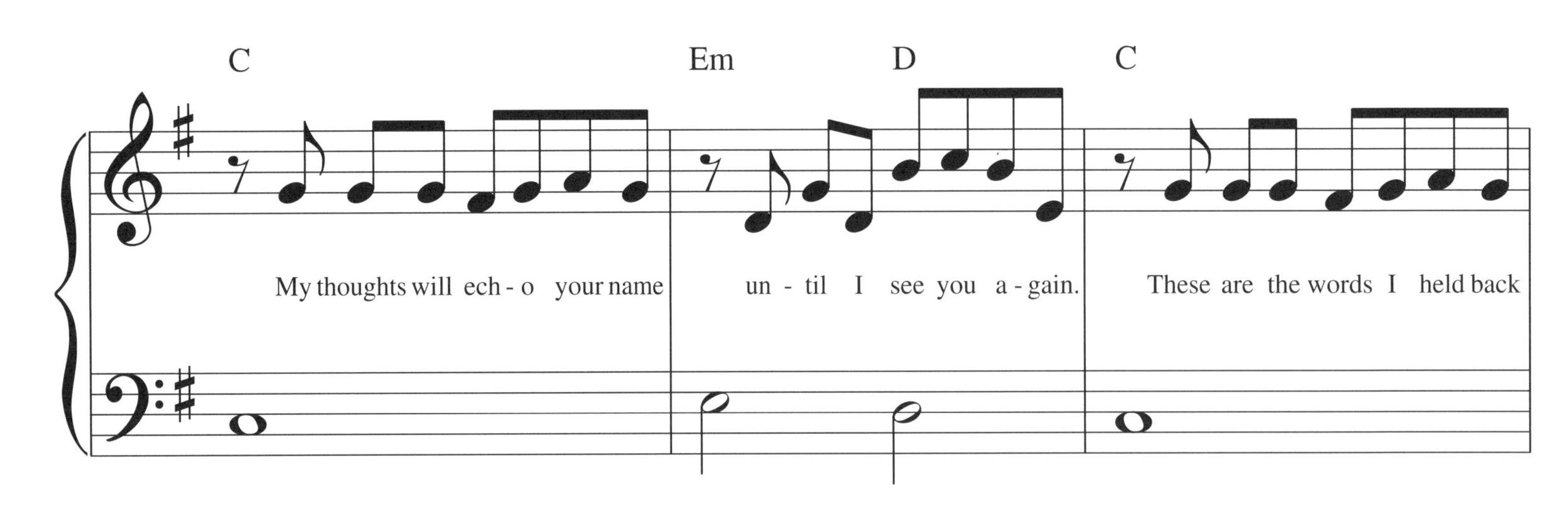
C
Em
D
C
My thoughts will ech - o your name
un - til I see you a - gain.
These are the words I held back

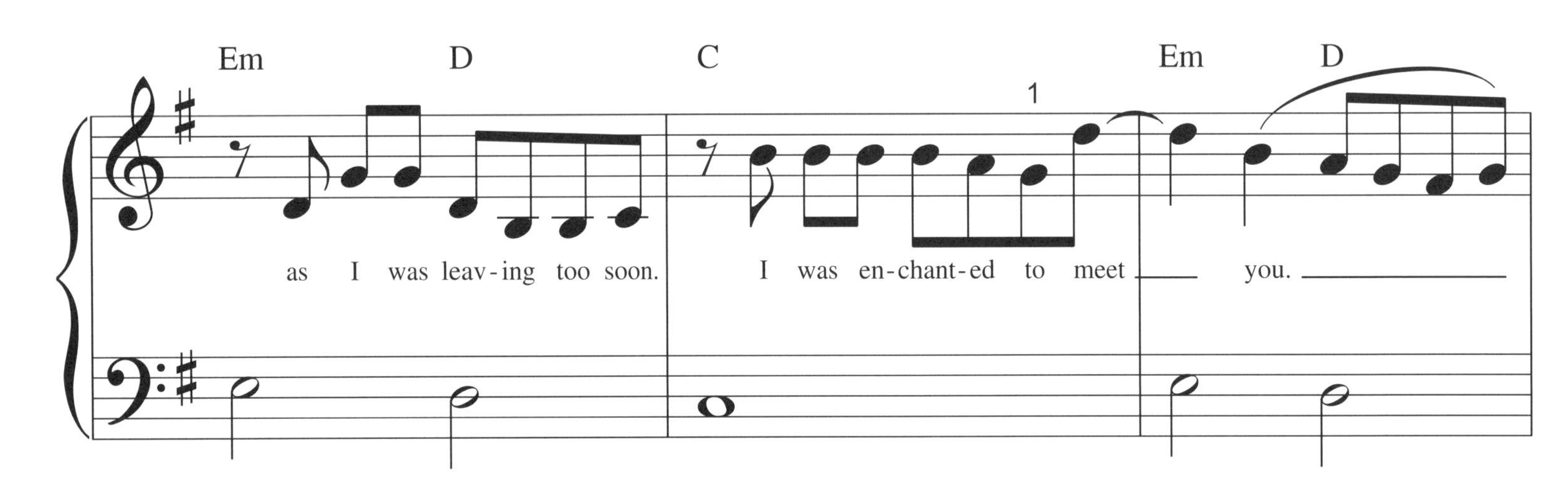
Em
D
C
Em
D
1
as I was leav - ing too soon.
I was en - chant - ed to meet
you.

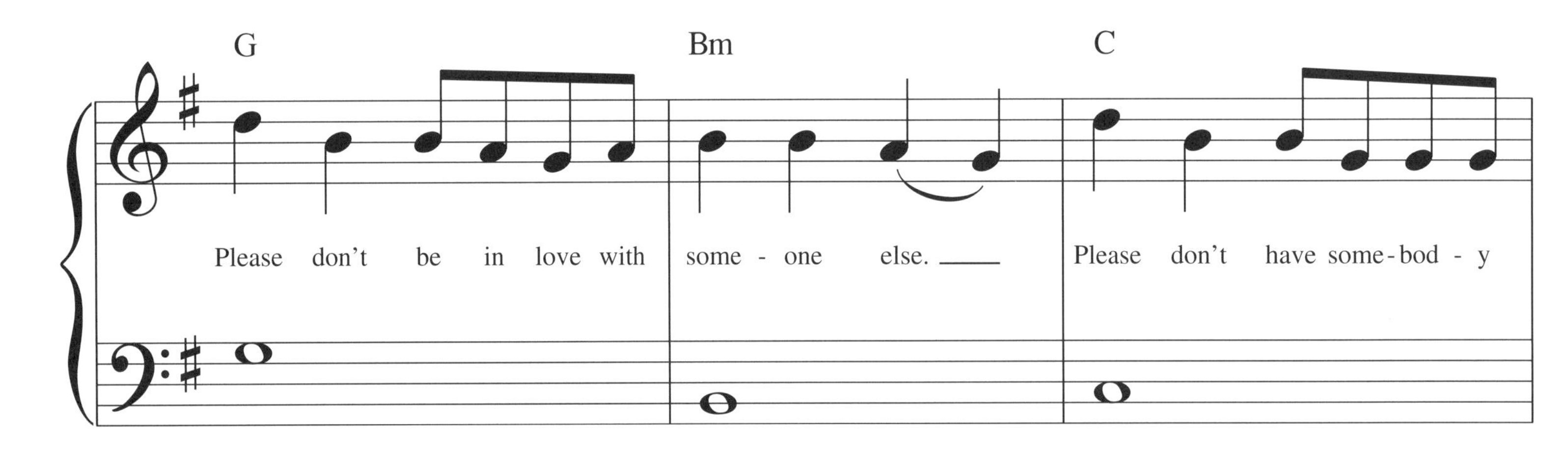
G
Bm
C
Please don't be in love with
some - one else.
Please don't have some - bod - y

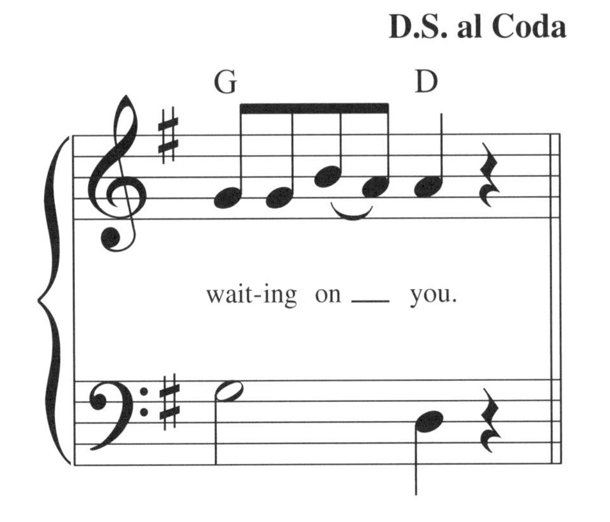
D.S. al Coda
G
D
wait - ing on you.

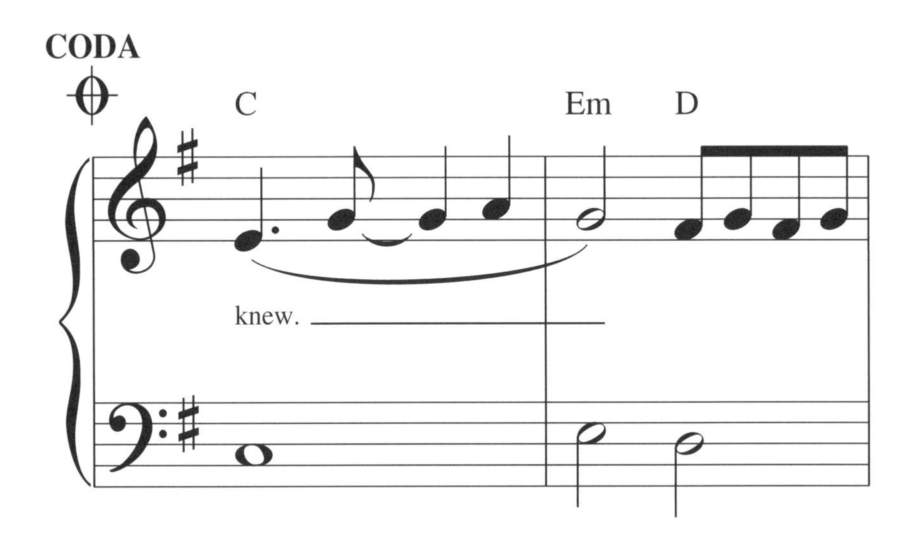
CODA
C
Em
D
knew.

C G D C
This night is flaw - less. Don't you let it go. I'm won - der -
G D C G D
struck, danc - ing 'round all a - lone. I'll spend for - ev - er won - d'ring if you
C Em D G
knew I was en - chant - ed to meet you. Please don't be in love with
Bm C G
some - one else. Please don't have some - bod - y wait - ing on you.
rit.

I ALMOST DO

Words and Music by
TAYLOR SWIFT

D(add4)
C
2
5
week.
I bet you're

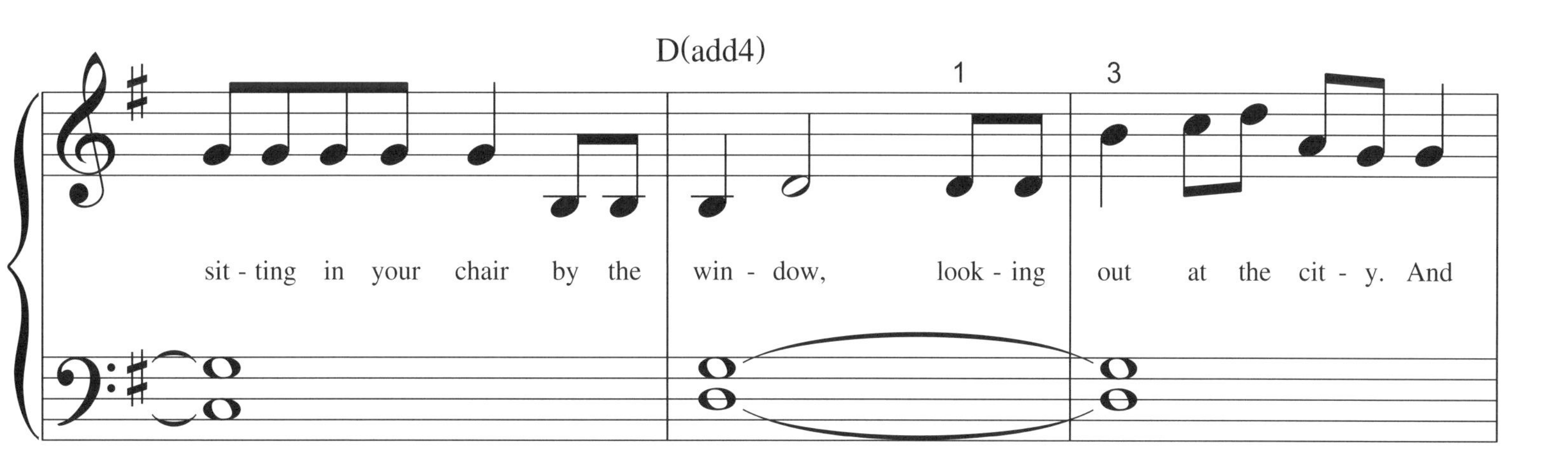
D(add4)
1
3
sit - ting in your chair by the
win - dow, look - ing
out at the cit - y. And

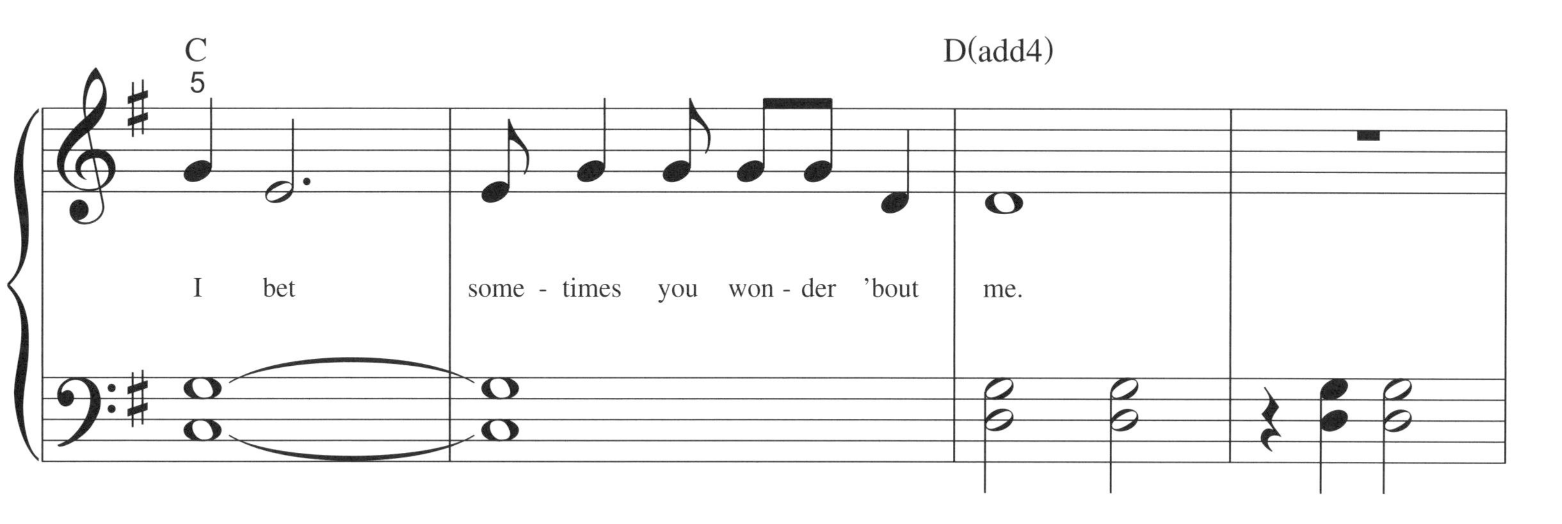
C
D(add4)
5
I bet
some - times you won - der 'bout
me.

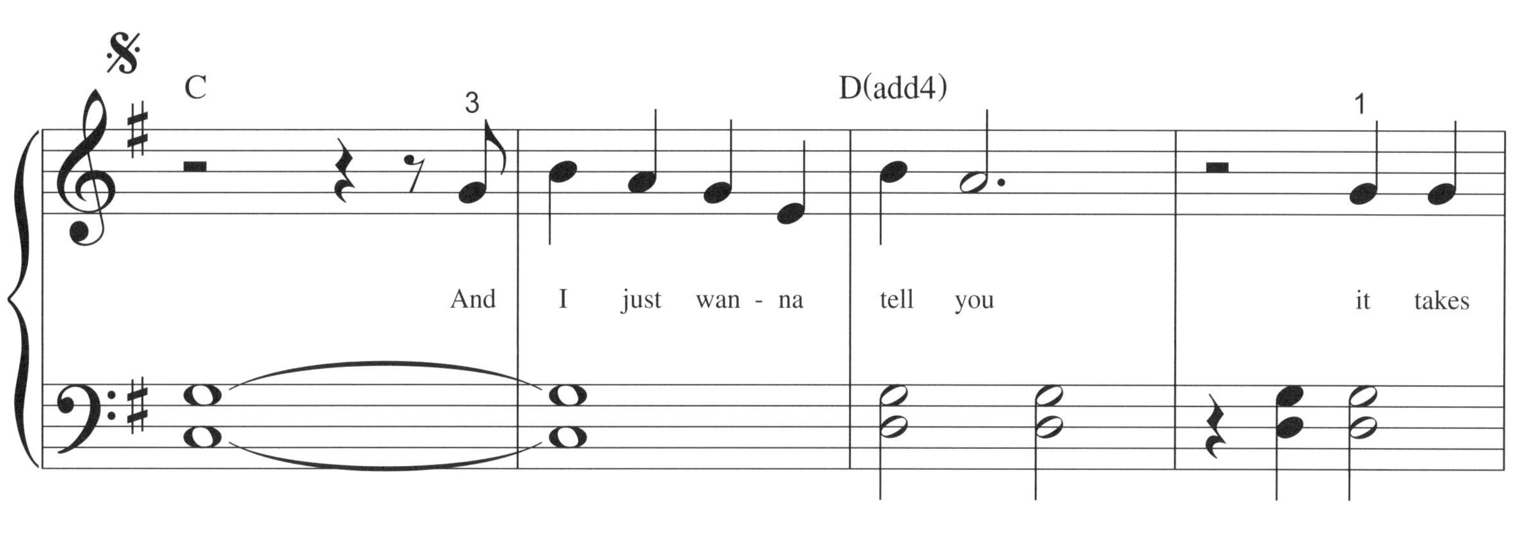
C
D(add4)
3
1
And
I just wan - na
tell you
it takes

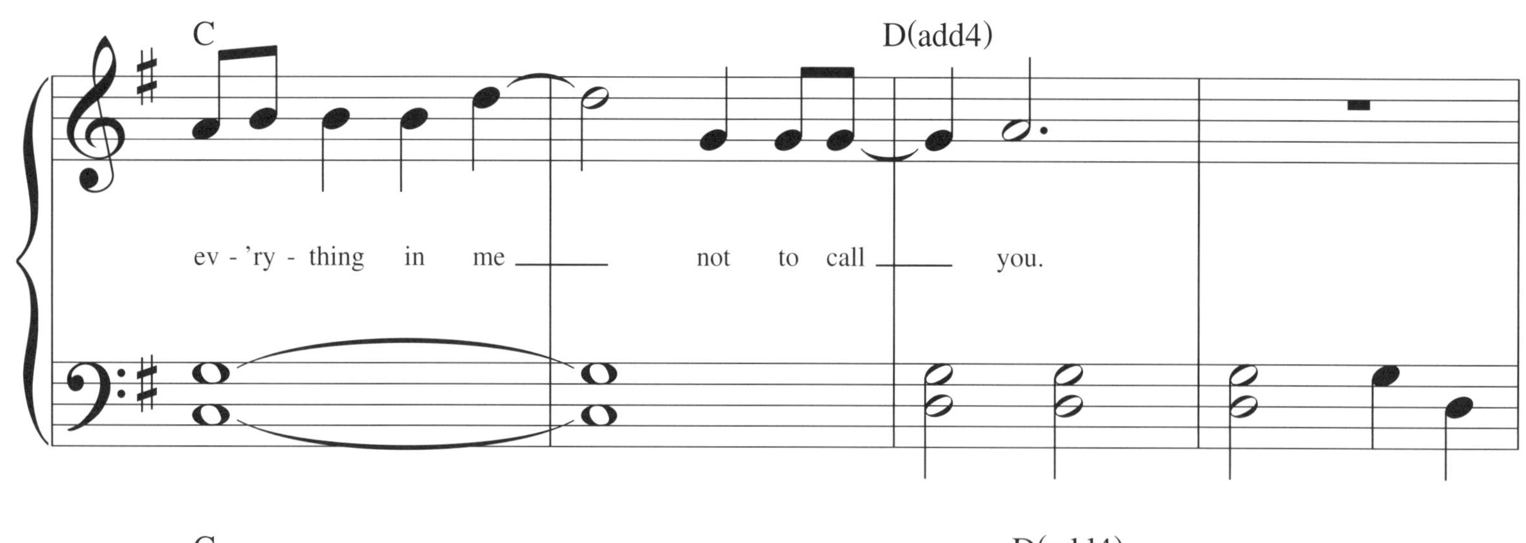
C
D(add4)
ev - 'ry - thing in me
not to call
you.

C
3
D(add4)
2
And I wish I could
run to you. And I

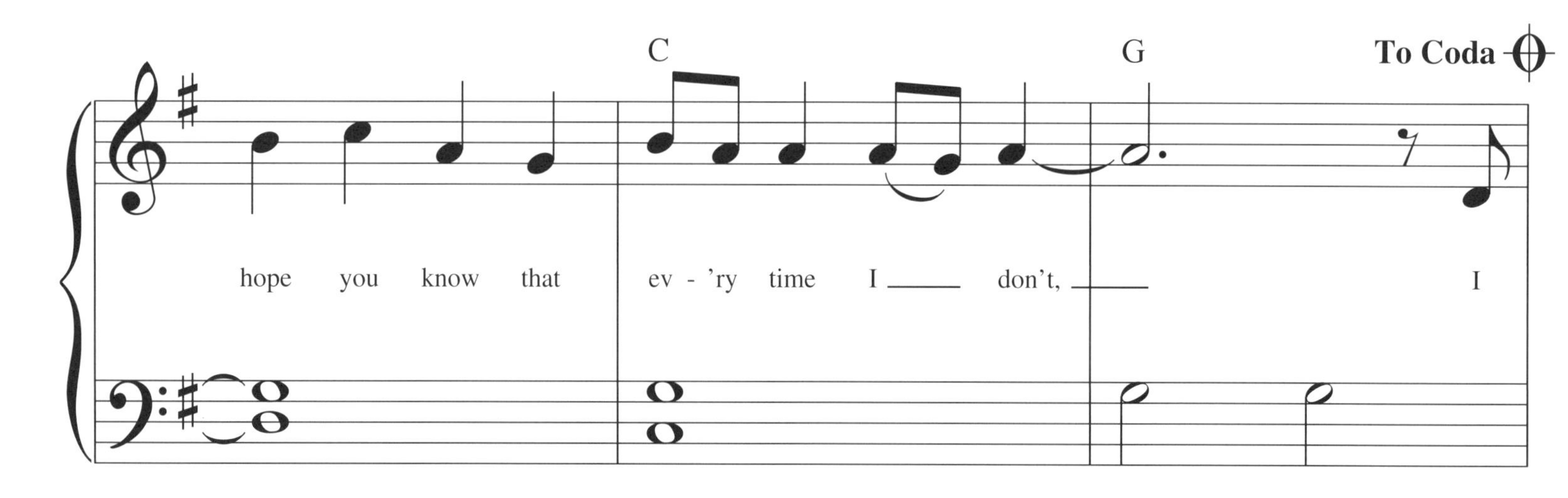
C
G
To Coda
hope you know that
ev - 'ry time I don't,
I

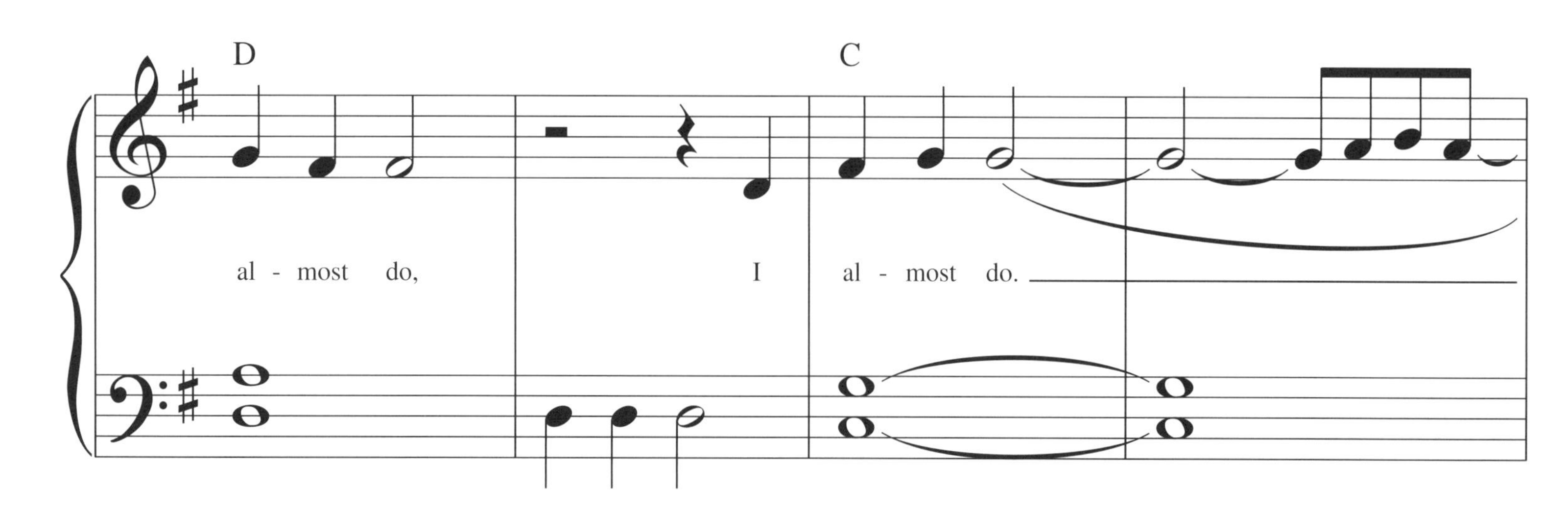
D
C
al - most do,
I
al - most do.

D
C
4
D
C
5
I bet you think I
ei - ther moved on or hate you.
D(add4)
'Cause each time you reach
C
G
2
D(add4)
out, there's no re - ply.

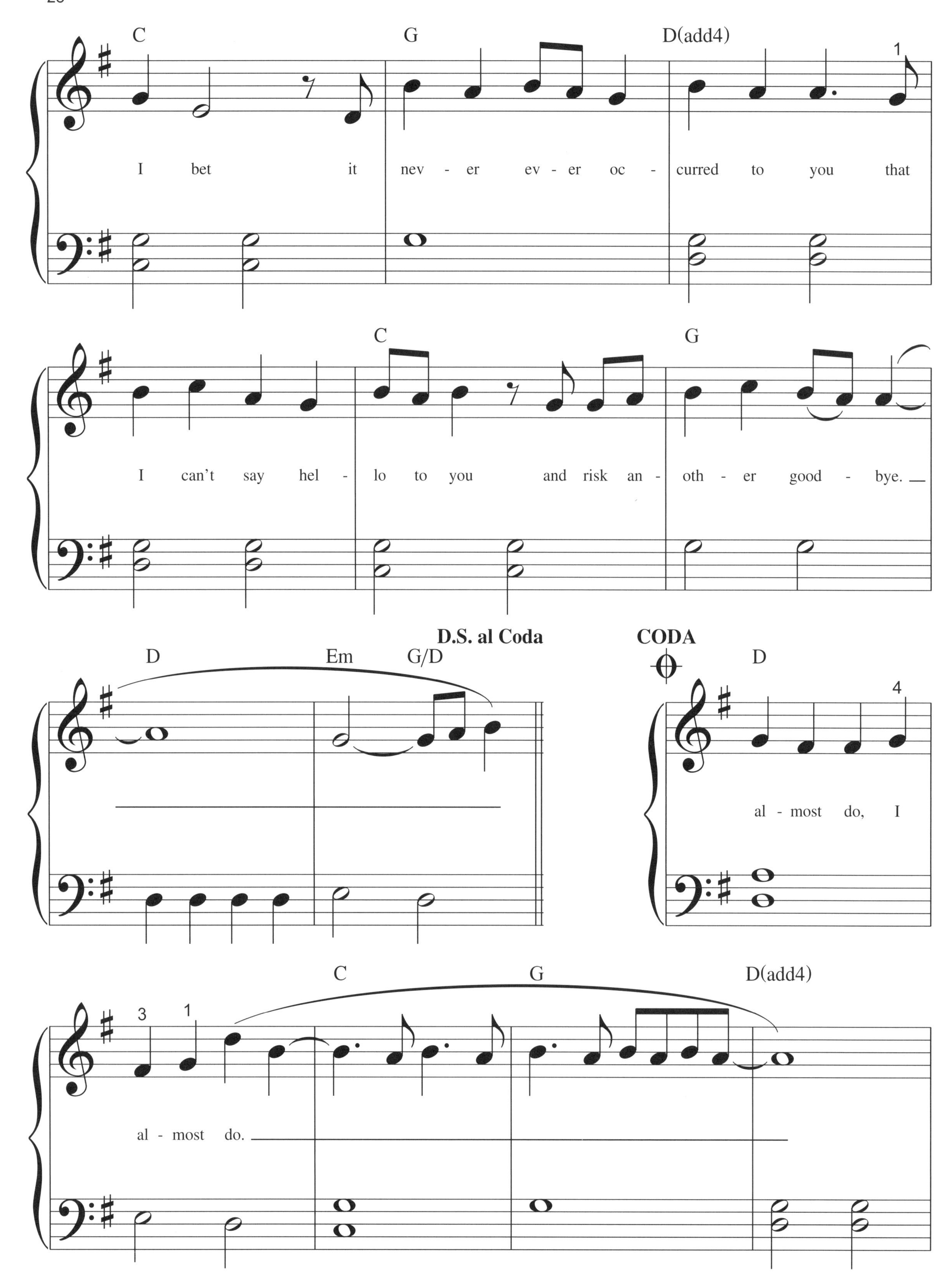
C
G
D(add4)
1
I bet it nev - er ev - er oc - curred to you that
C
G
I can't say hel - lo to you and risk an - oth - er good - bye.
D.S. al Coda
CODA
D
Em
G/D
D
4
al - most do, I
C
G
D(add4)
3
1
al - most do.

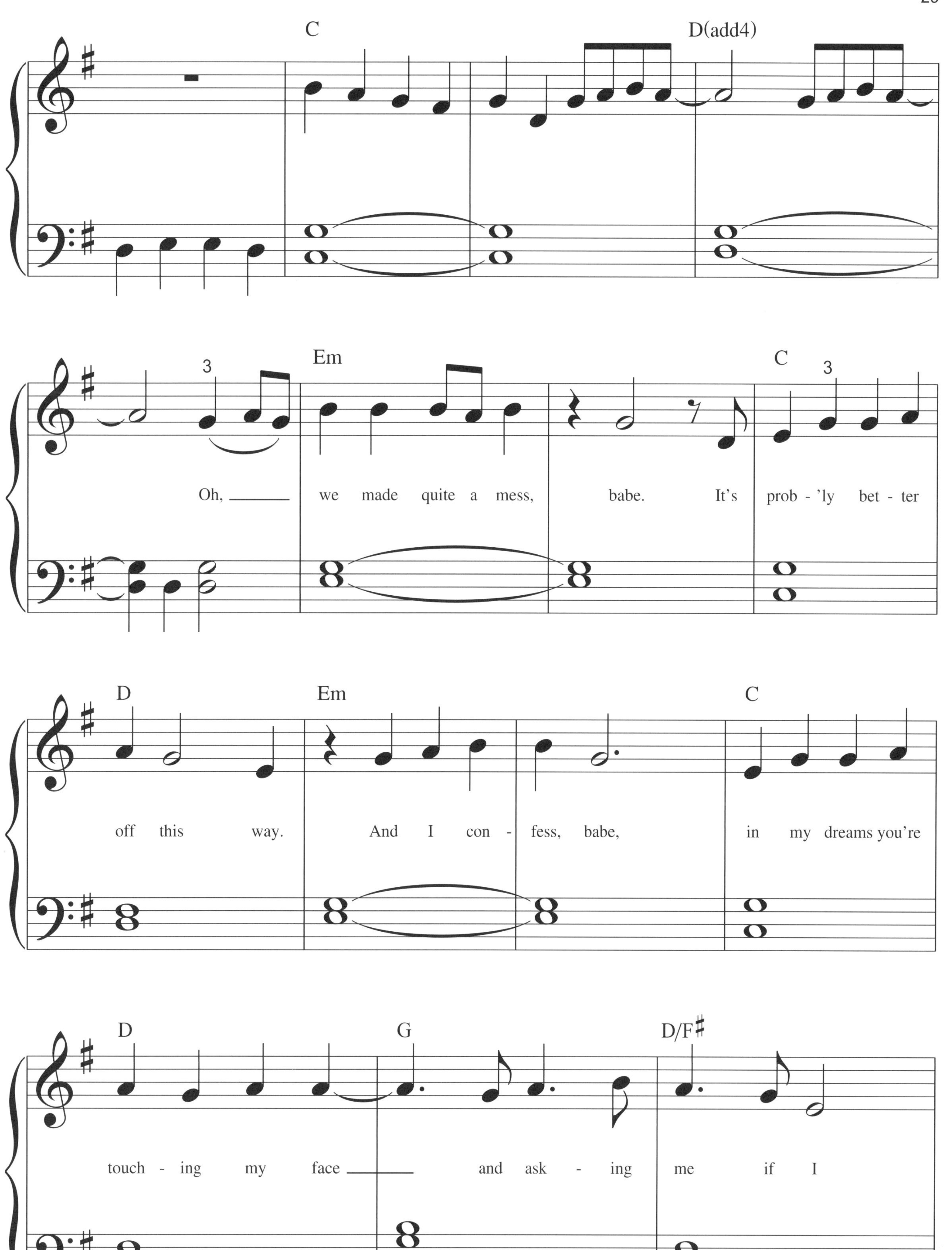
C
D(add4)
3
Em
C
3
Oh, we made quite a mess, babe. It's prob - 'ly bet - ter
D
Em
C
off this way. And I con - fess, babe, in my dreams you're
D
G
D/F♯
touch - ing my face and ask - ing me if I

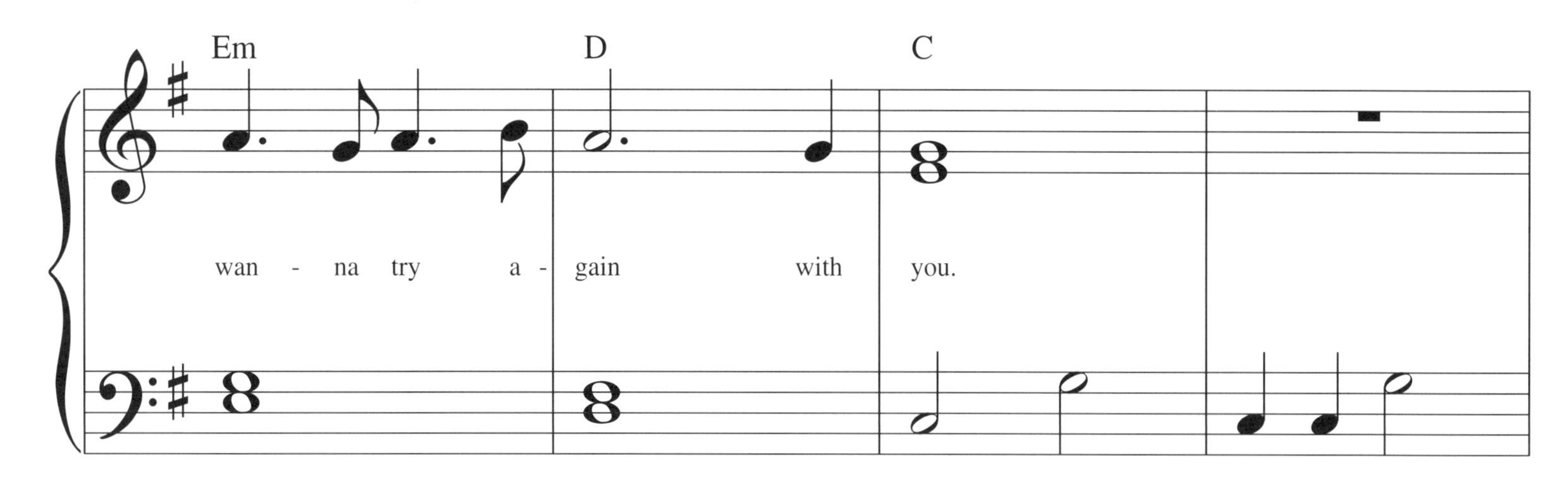
Em
D
C
wan - na try a - gain with you.

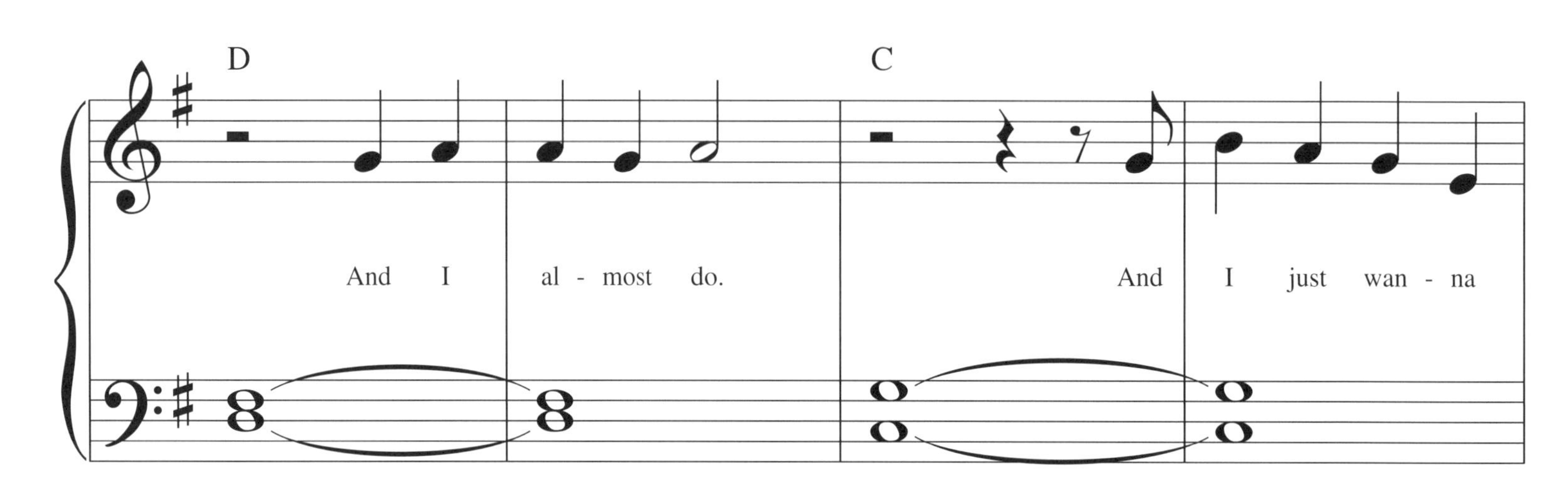
D
C
And I al - most do. And I just wan - na

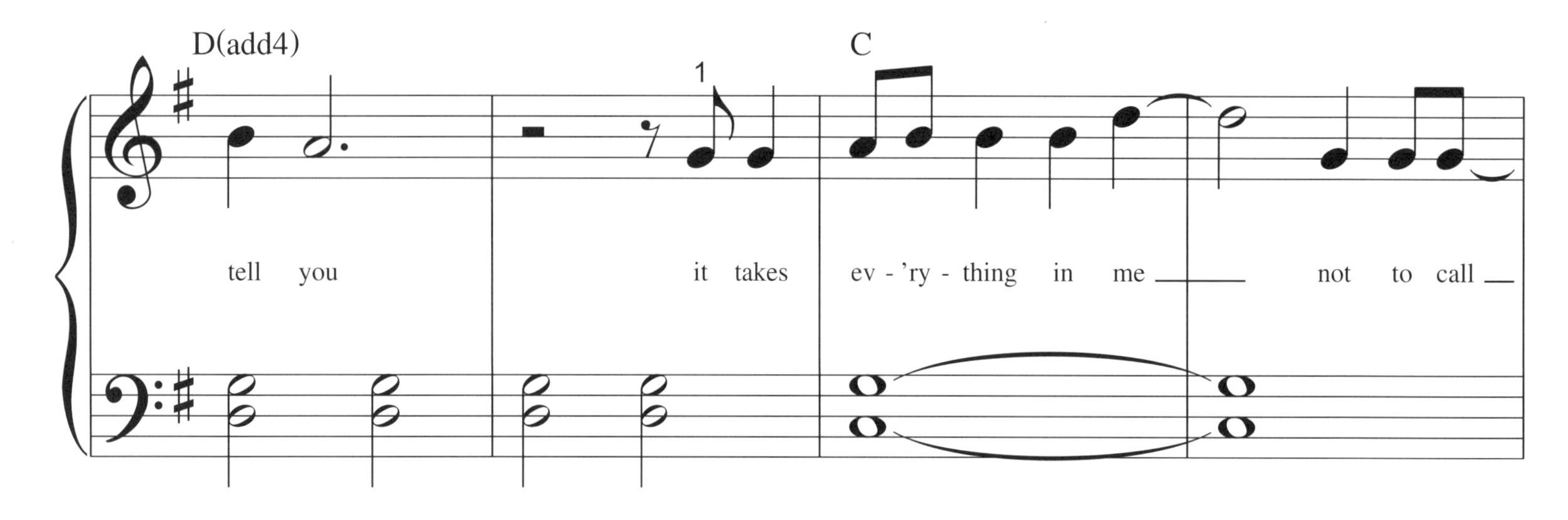
D(add4)
1
C
tell you it takes ev - 'ry - thing in me not to call

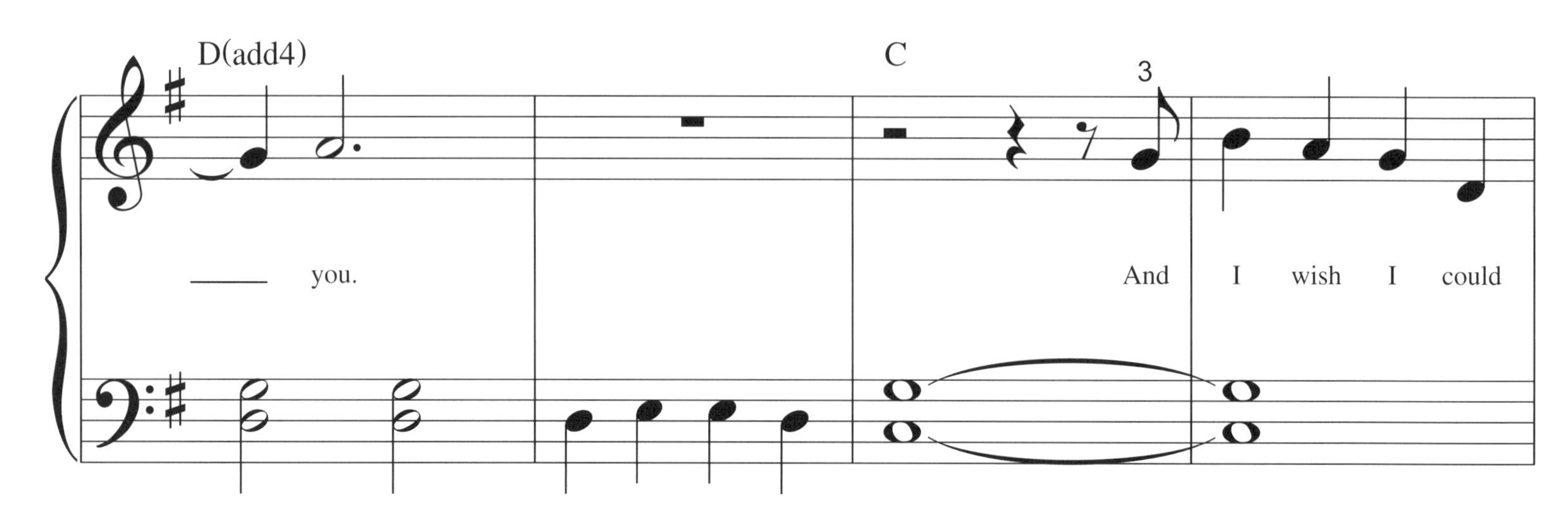
D(add4)
C
3
you. And I wish I could

D(add4)
C
run to you. And I hope you know that ev - 'ry time I don't,
G
D
C
I al - most do, I al - most do.
G
D
Em
C
D

C
D(add4)
I bet this time of night you're still up.

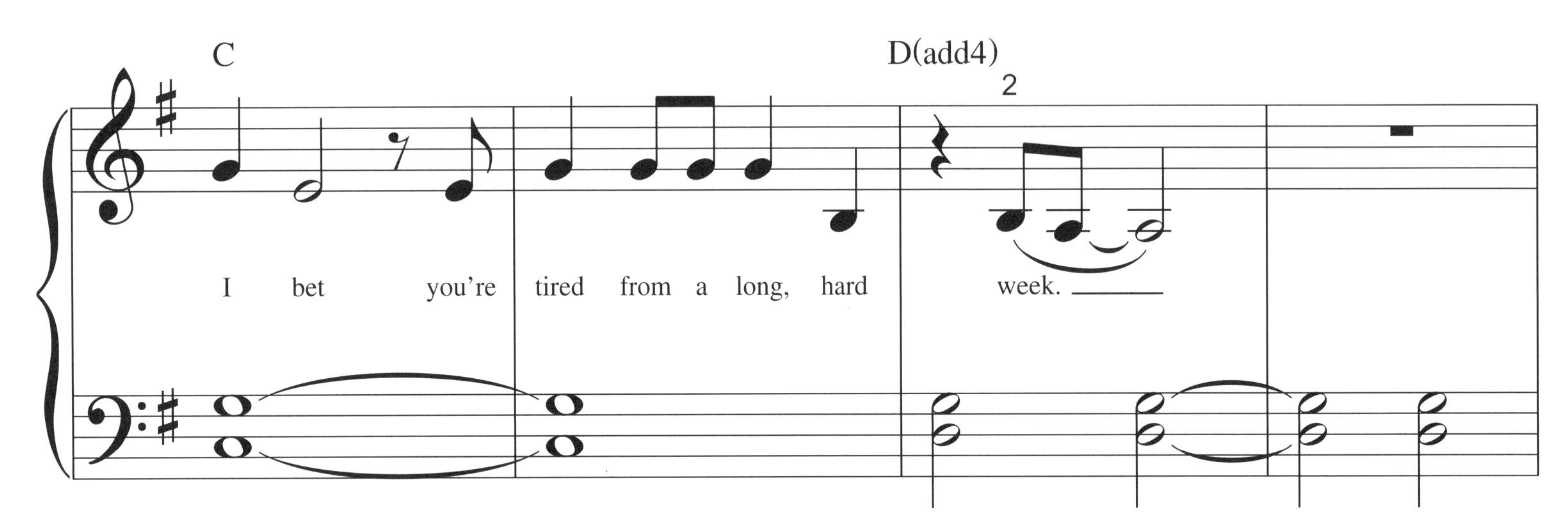
C
D(add4)
2
I bet you're tired from a long, hard week.

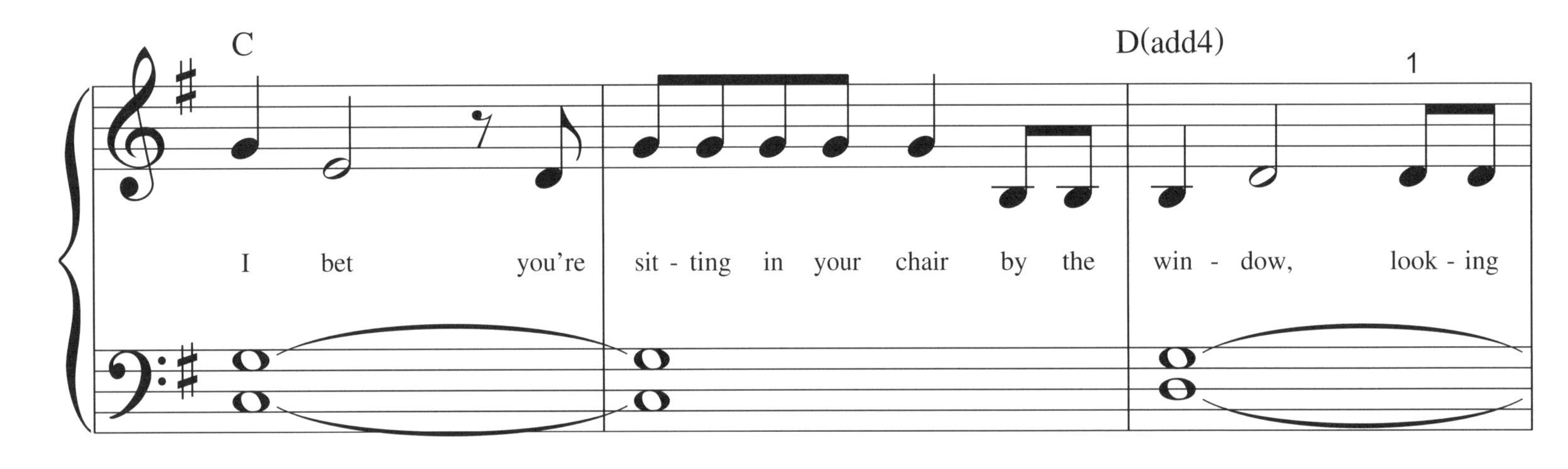
C
D(add4)
1
I bet you're sit - ting in your chair by the win - dow, look - ing

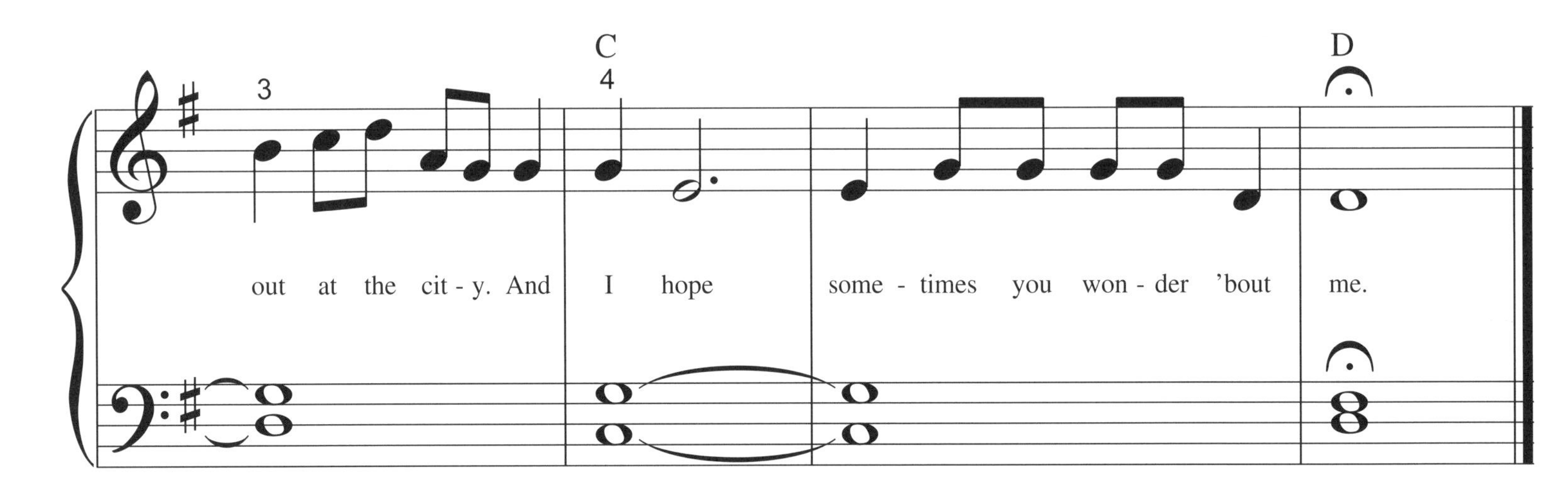
3
C
4
D
out at the cit - y. And I hope some - times you won - der 'bout me.

TODAY WAS A FAIRYTALE

from VALENTINE'S DAY

Words and Music by
TAYLOR SWIFT

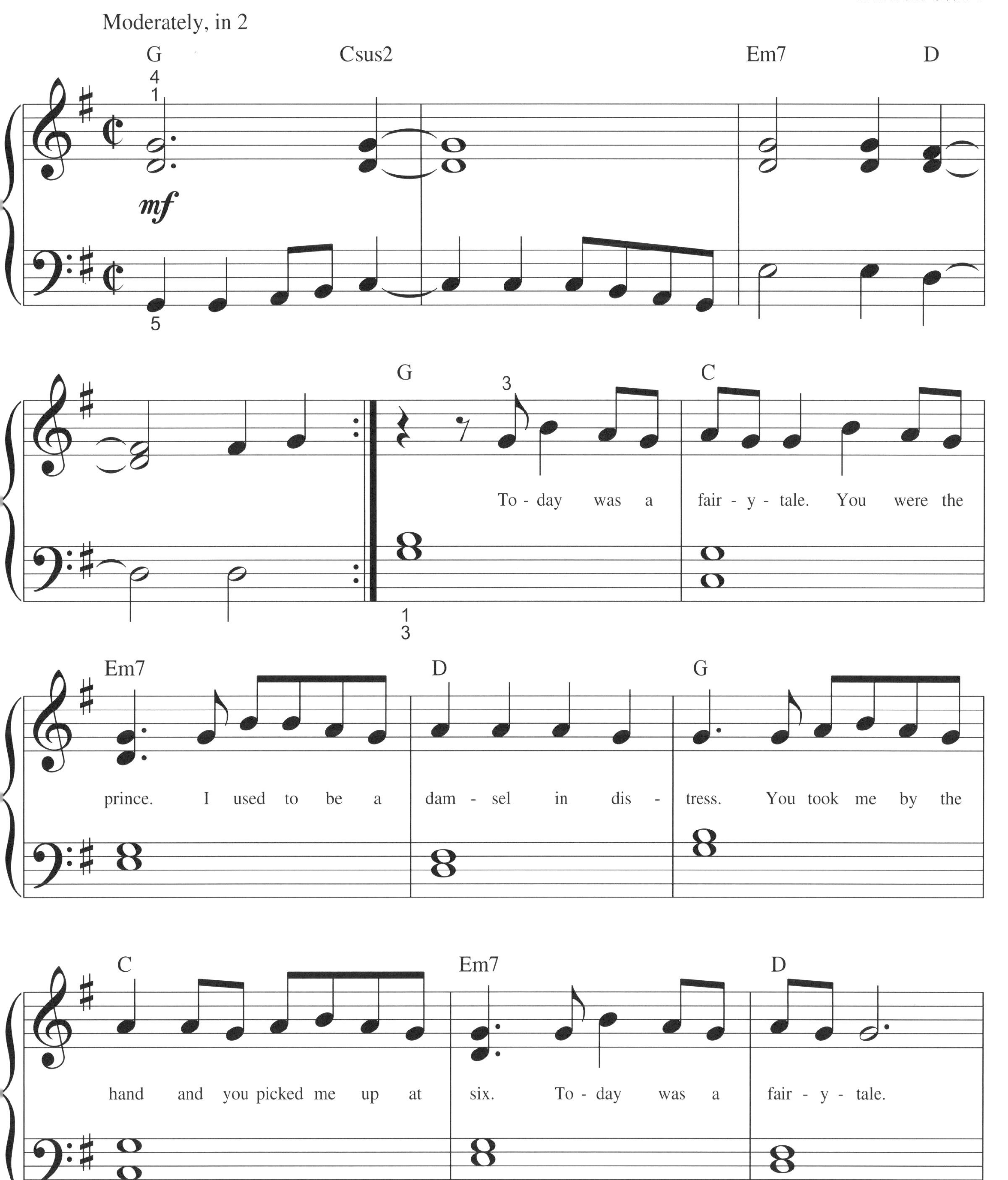

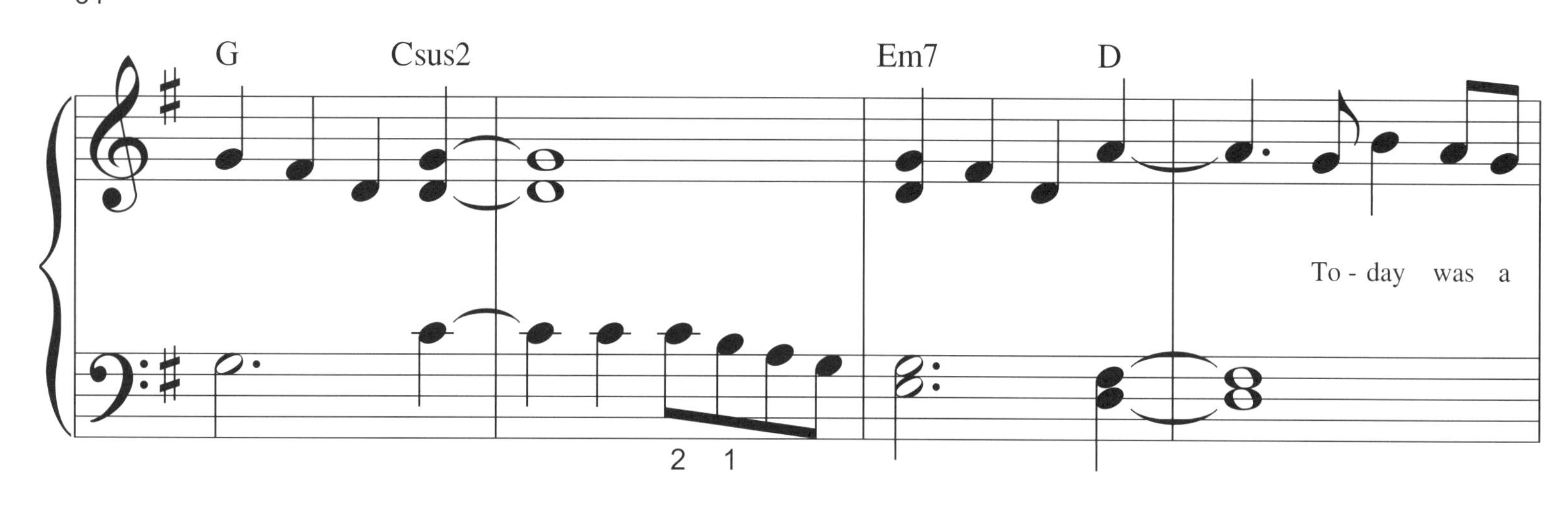
G
Csus2
Em7
D
To - day was a
2 1

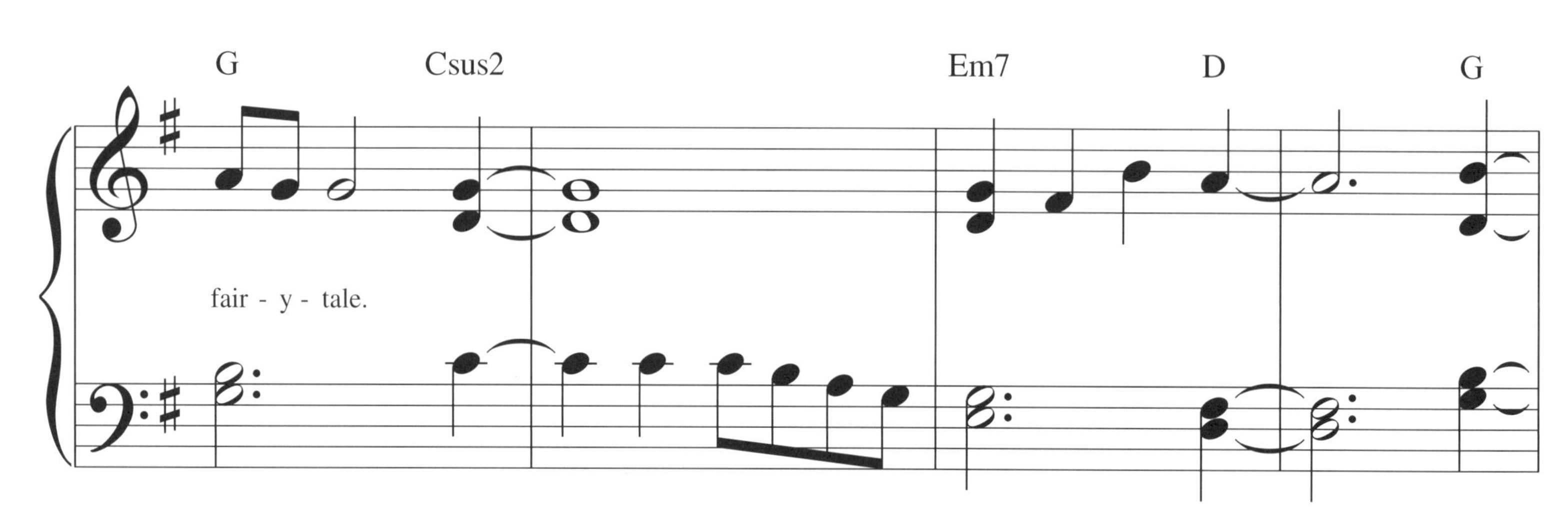
G
Csus2
Em7
D
G
fair - y - tale.

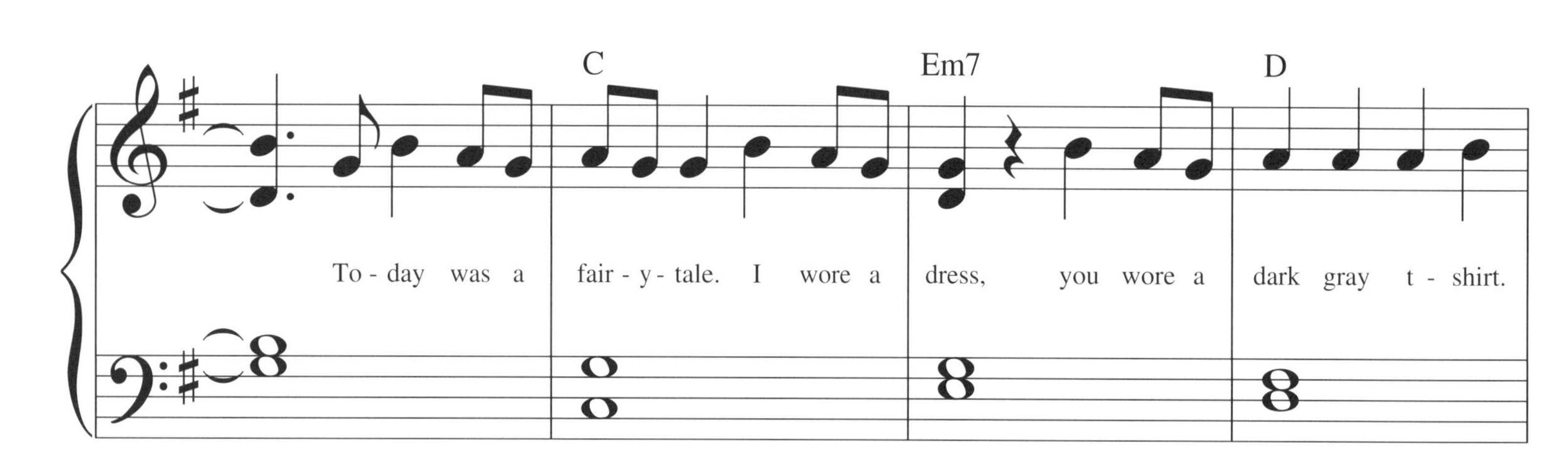
C
Em7
D
To - day was a
fair - y - tale. I wore a
dress, you wore a
dark gray t - shirt.

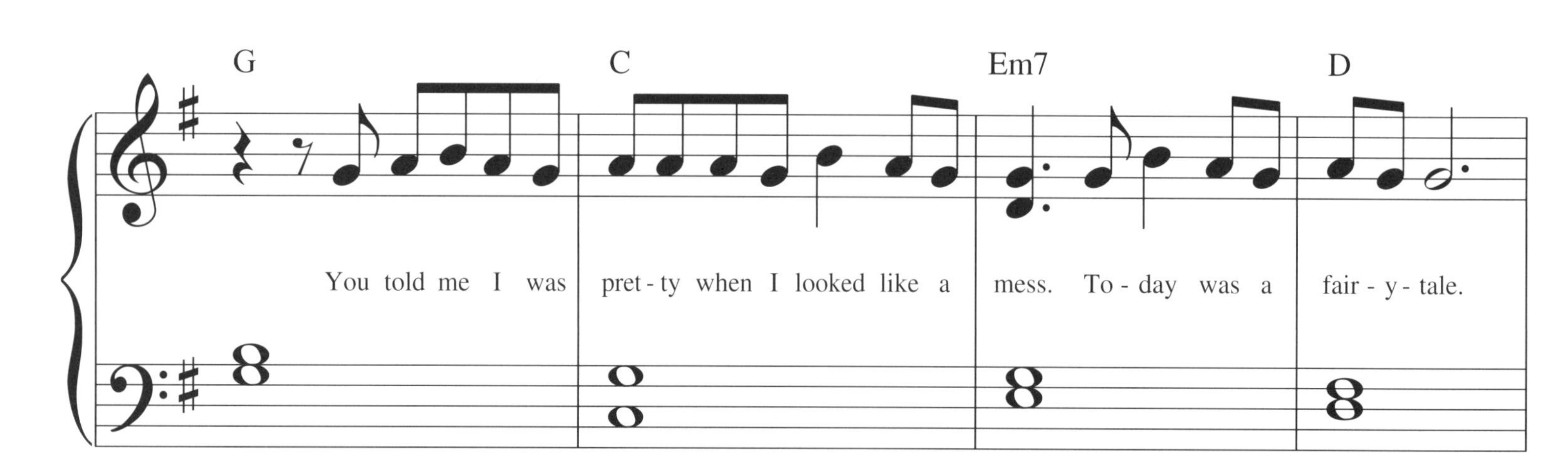
G
C
Em7
D
You told me I was
pret - ty when I looked like a
mess. To - day was a
fair - y - tale.

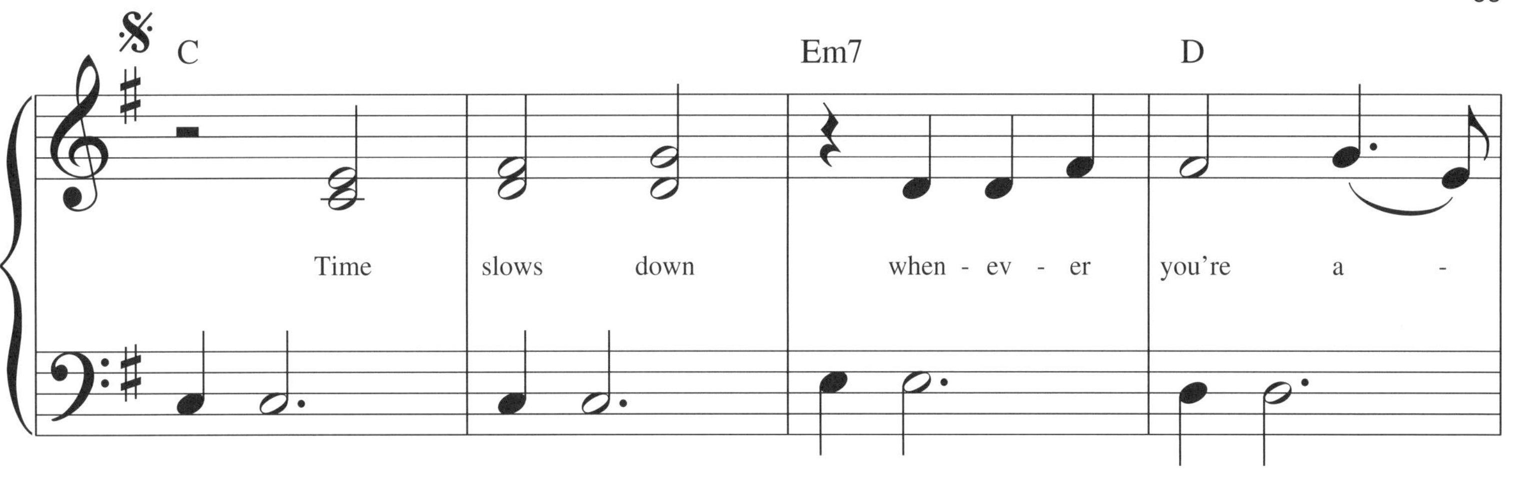
C
Em7
D
Time slows down when - ev - er you're a -

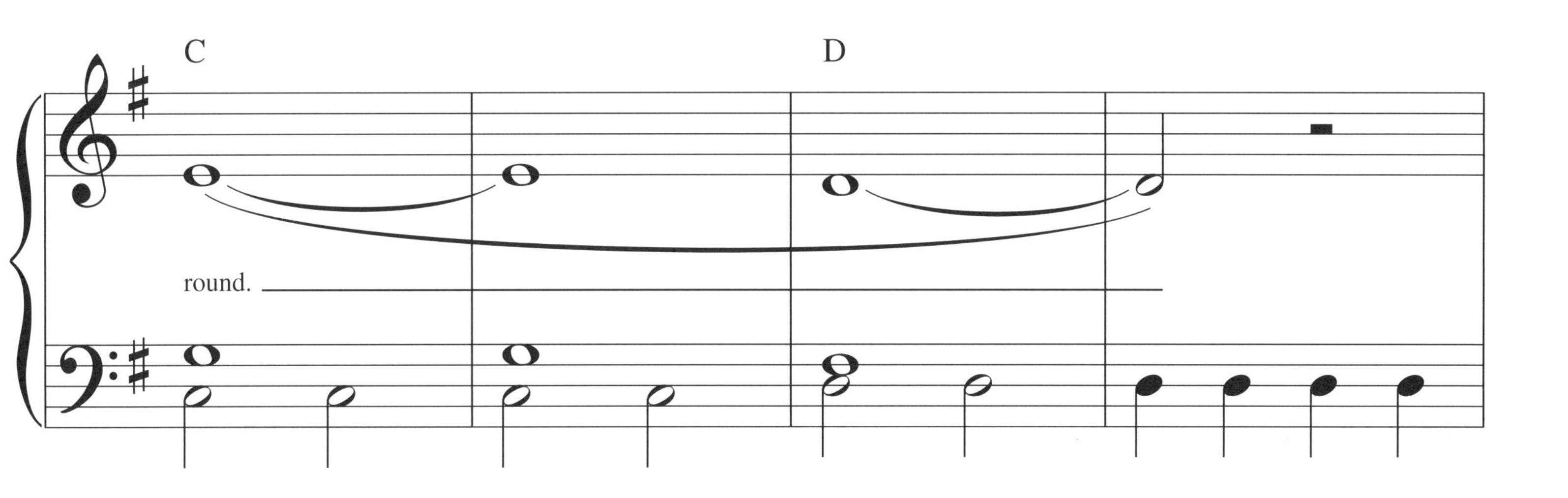
C
D
round.

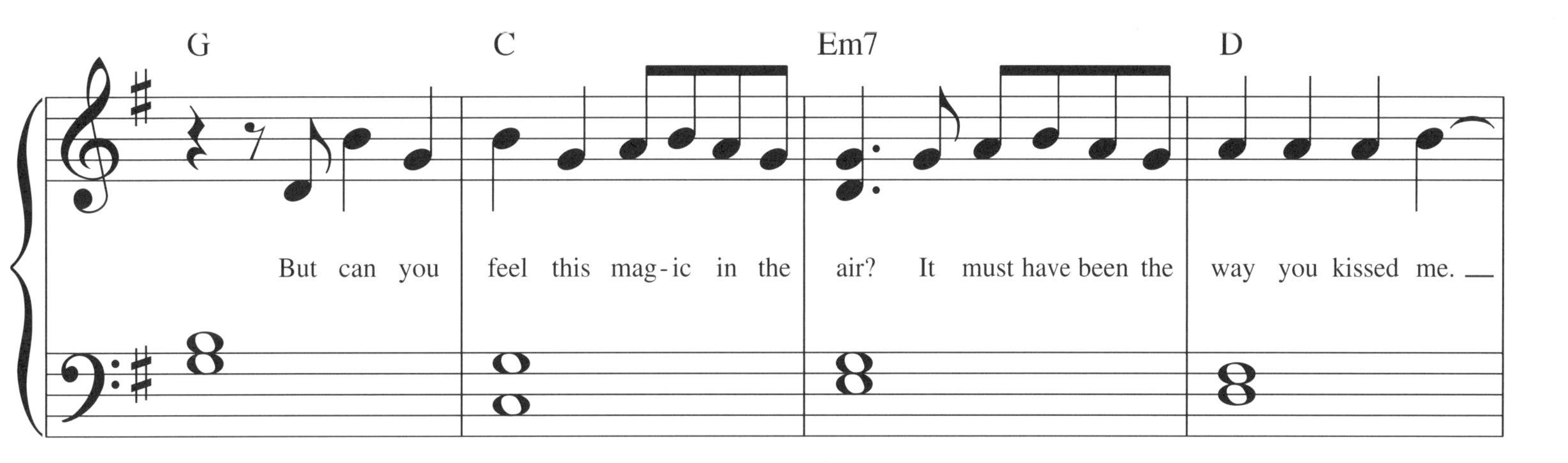
G
C
Em7
D
But can you feel this mag - ic in the air? It must have been the way you kissed me.

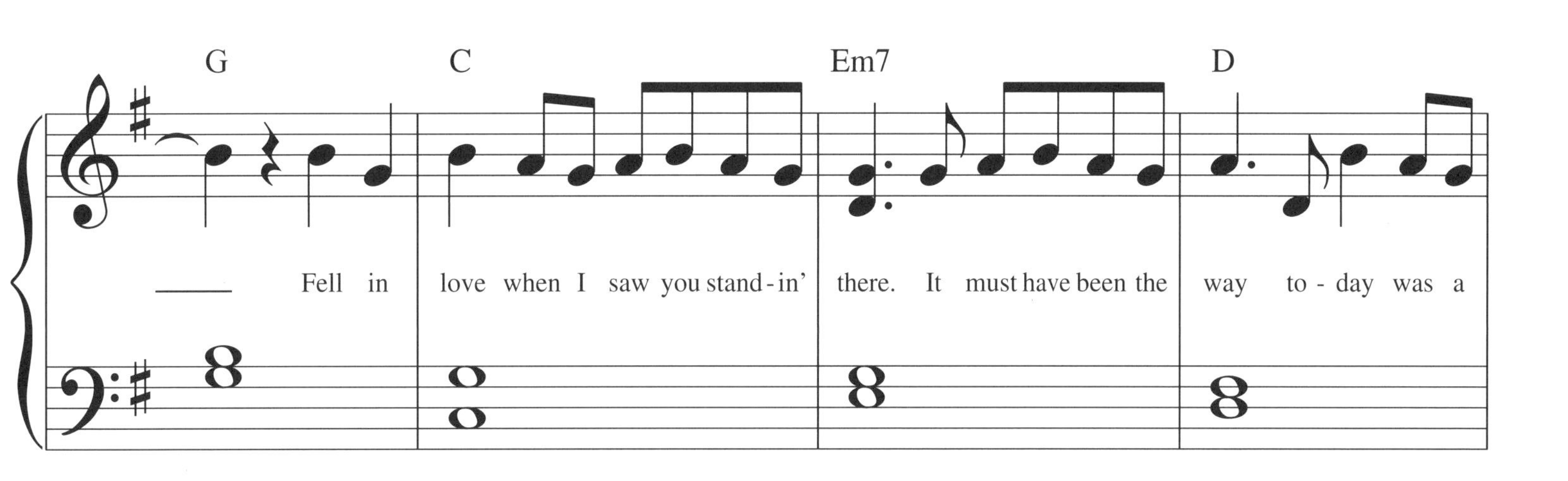
G
C
Em7
D
Fell in love when I saw you stand - in' there. It must have been the way to - day was a

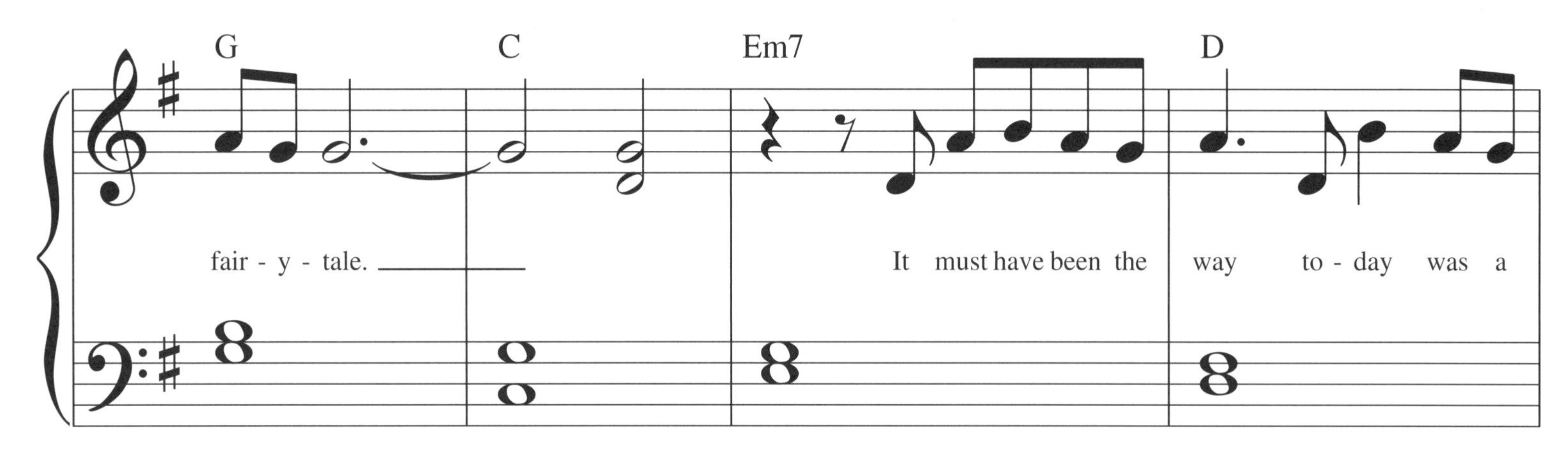
G
C
Em7
D
fair - y - tale.
It must have been the way to - day was a

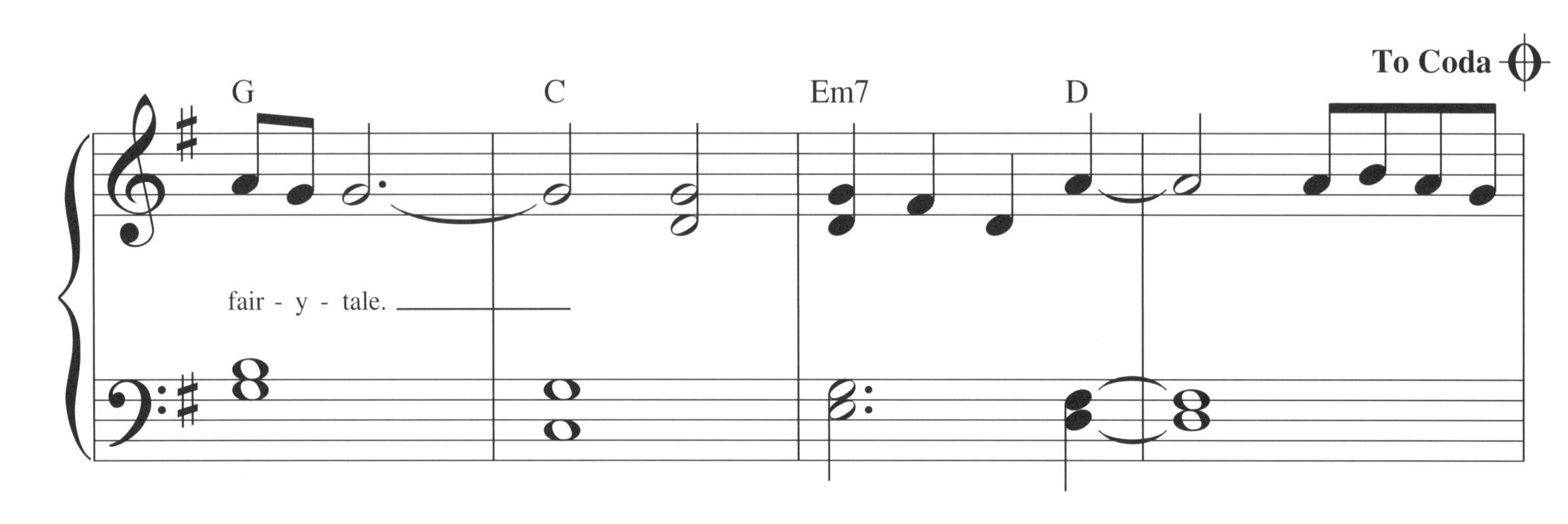
To Coda
G
C
Em7
D
fair - y - tale.

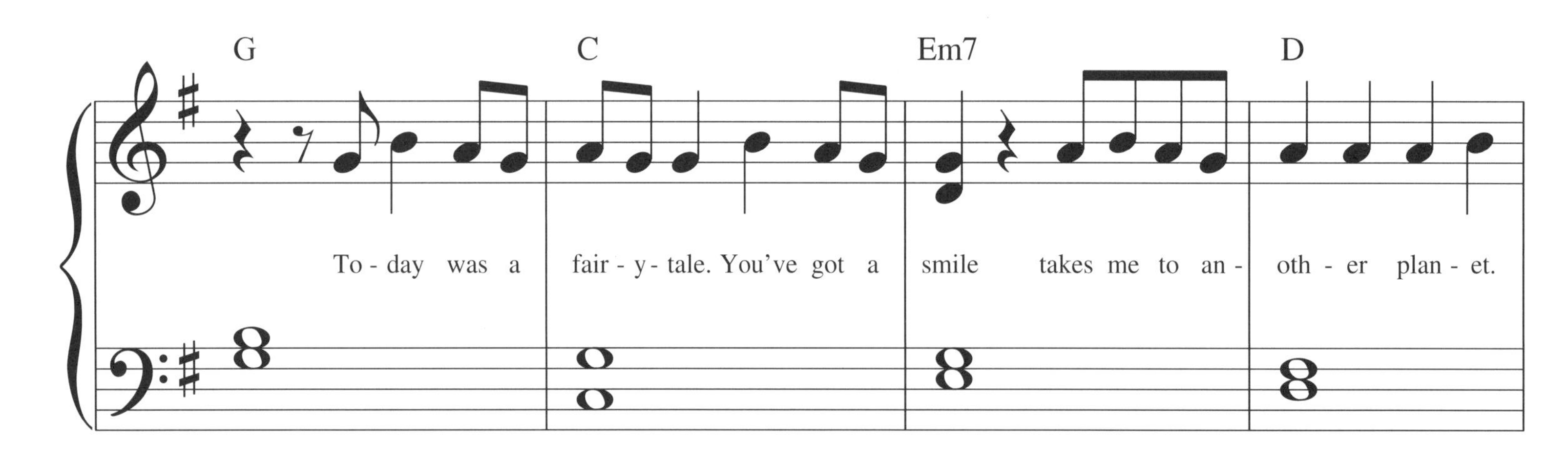
G
C
Em7
D
To - day was a fair - y - tale. You've got a smile takes me to an - oth - er plan - et.

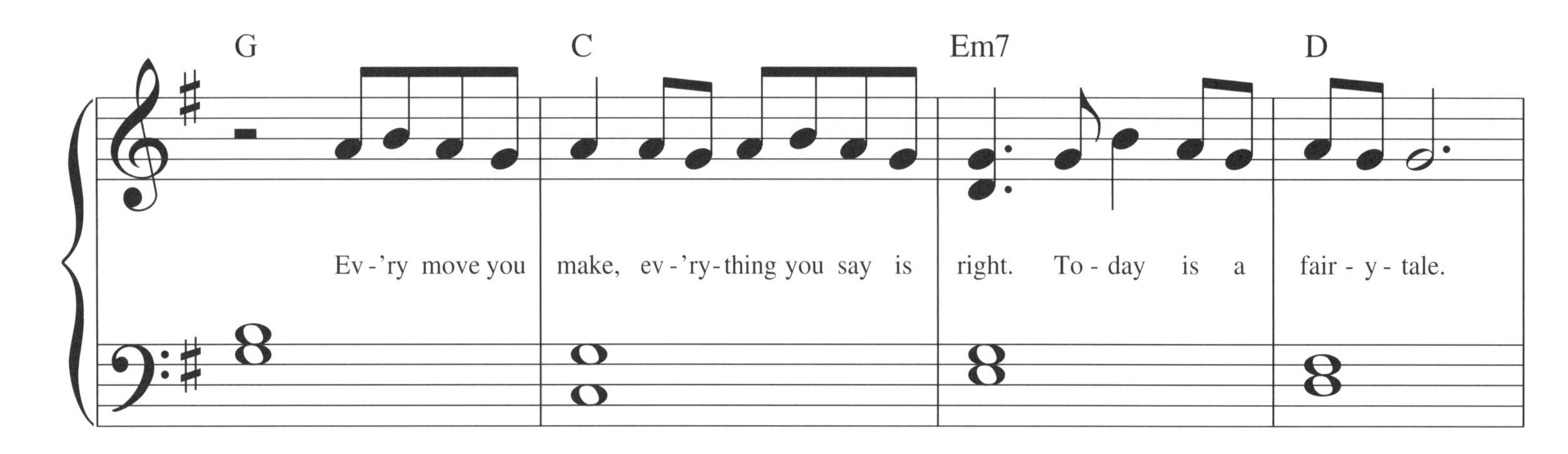
G
C
Em7
D
Ev - 'ry move you make, ev - 'ry - thing you say is right. To - day is a fair - y - tale.

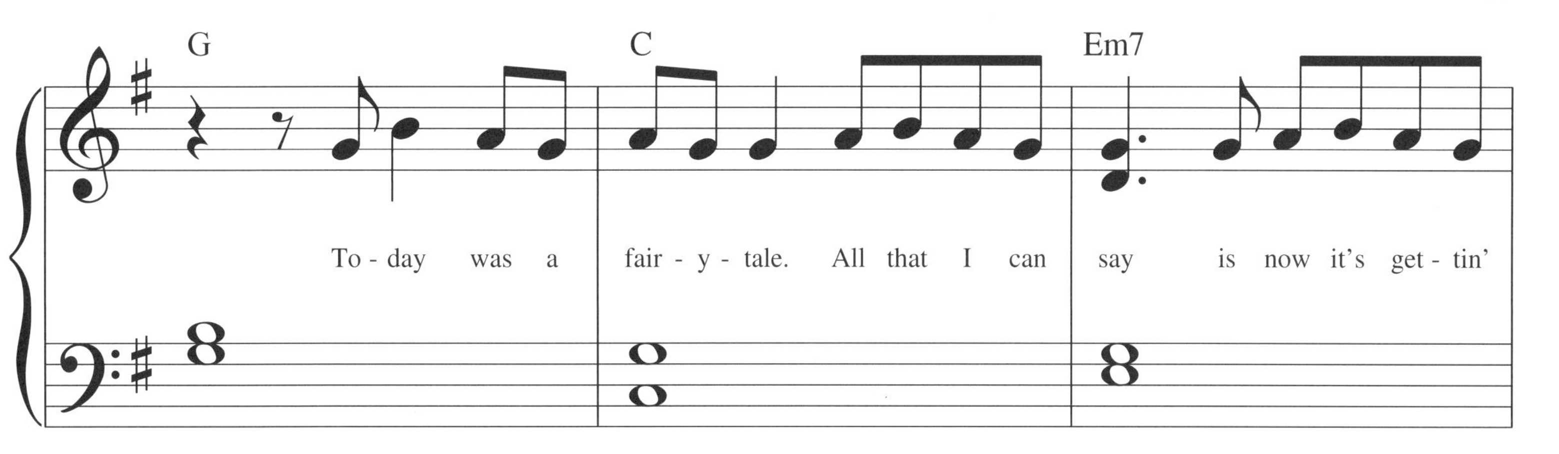
G
C
Em7
To - day was a fair - y - tale. All that I can say is now it's get - tin'

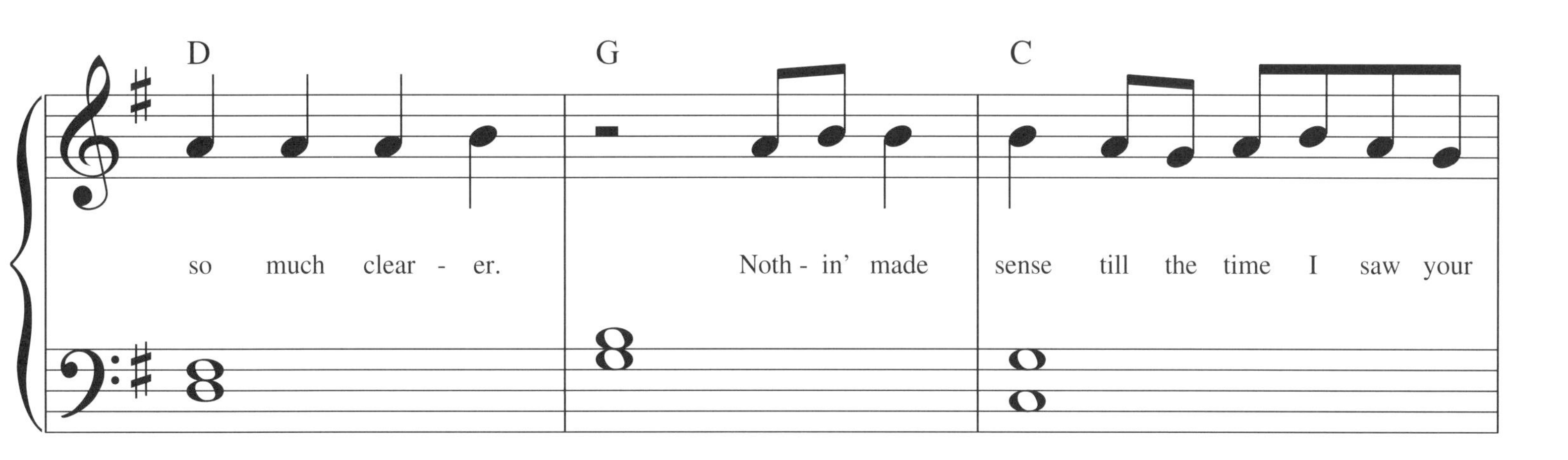
D
G
C
so much clear - er. Noth - in' made sense till the time I saw your

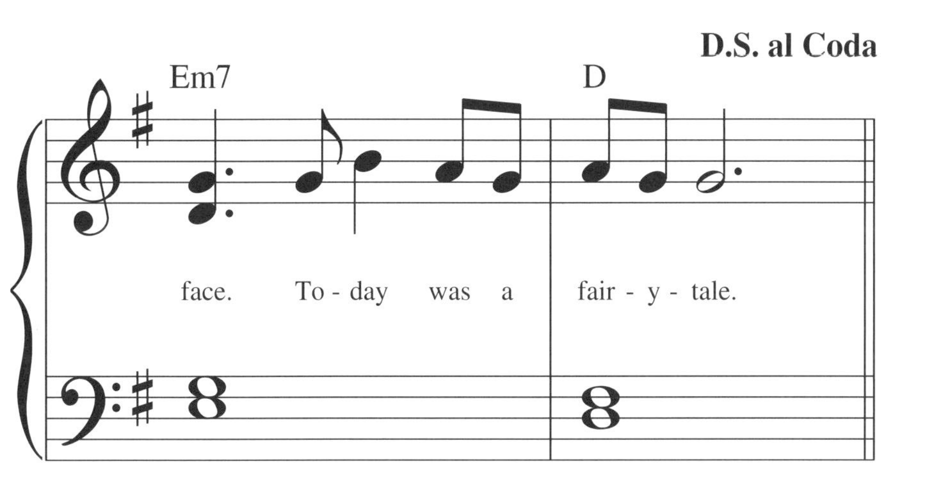
D.S. al Coda
Em7
D
face. To - day was a fair - y - tale.

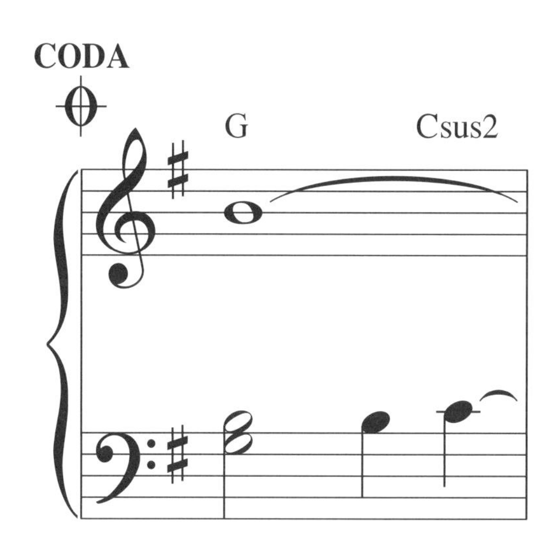
CODA
G
Csus2

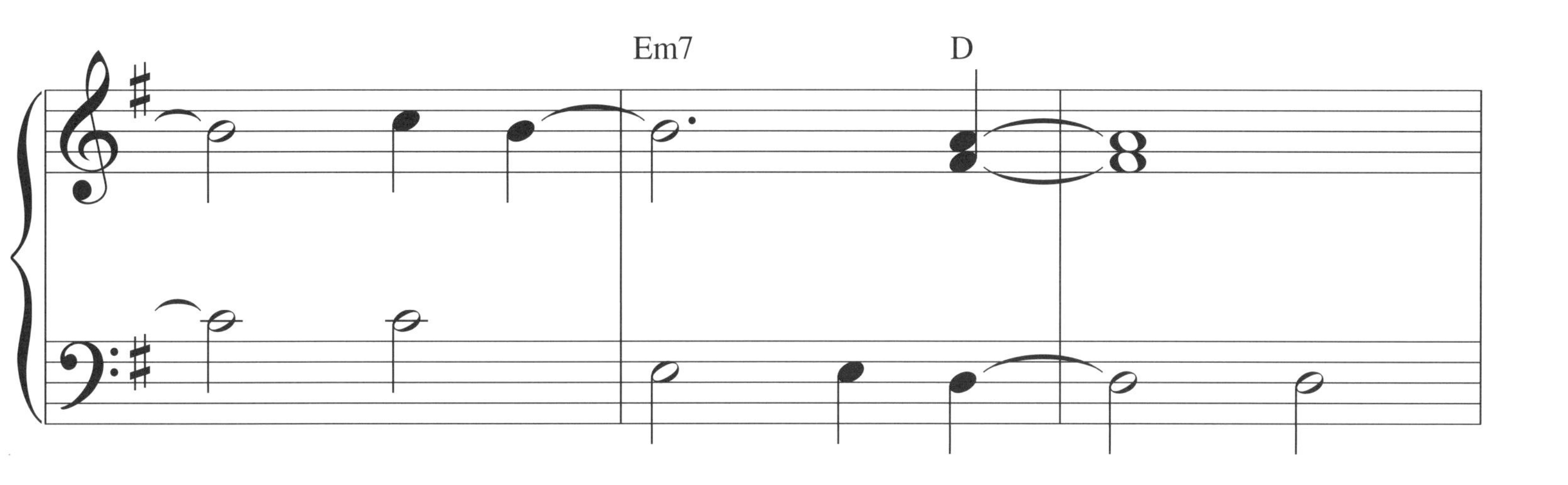
Em7
D

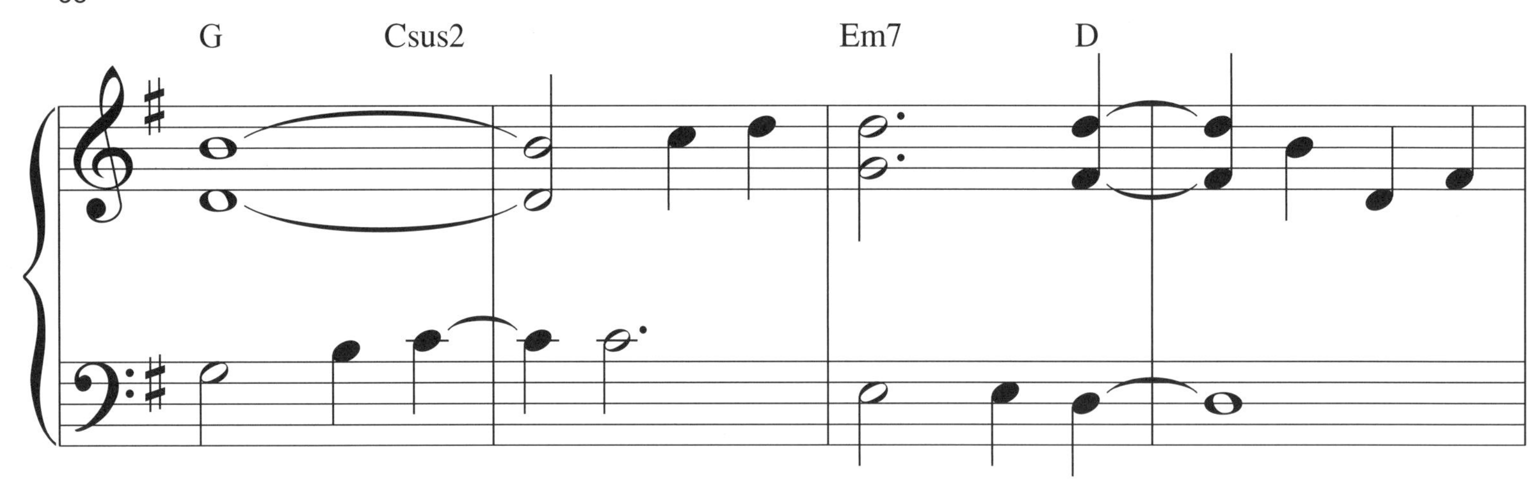
G
Csus2
Em7
D

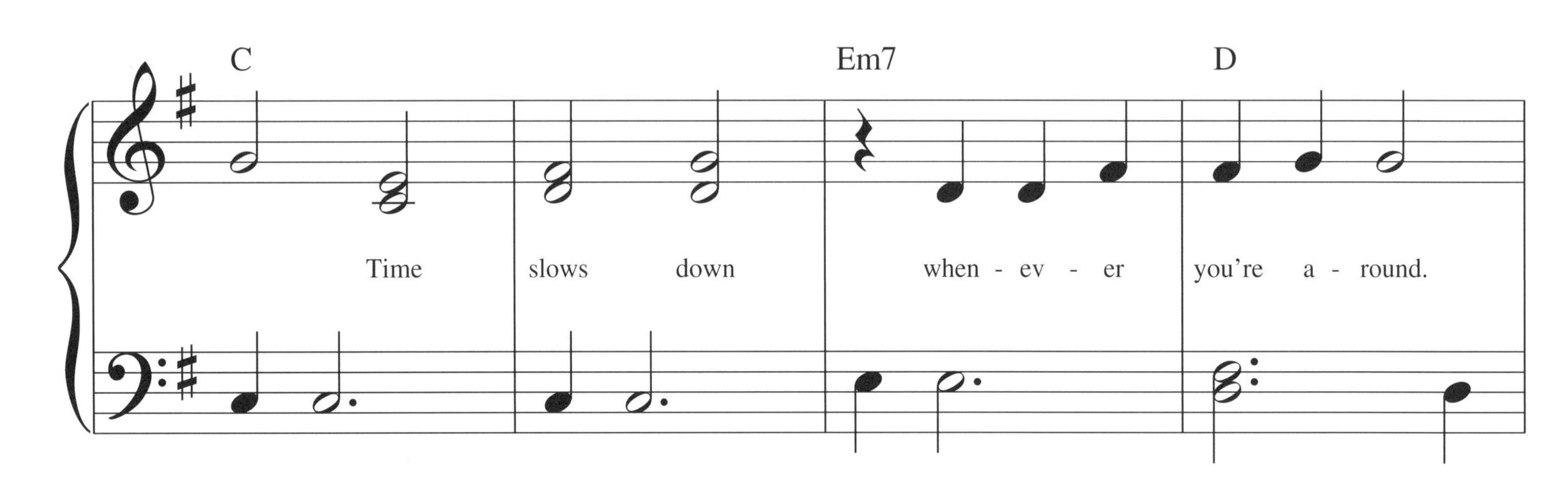
C
Em7
D
Time slows down when - ev - er you're a - round.

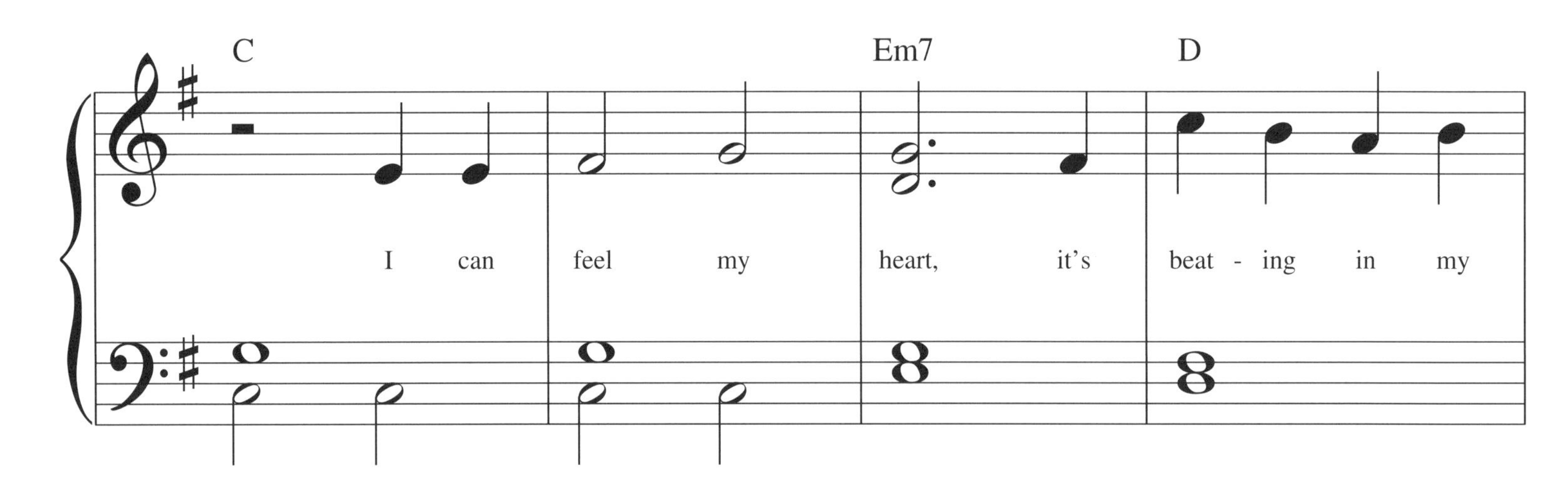
C
Em7
D
I can feel my heart, it's beat - ing in my

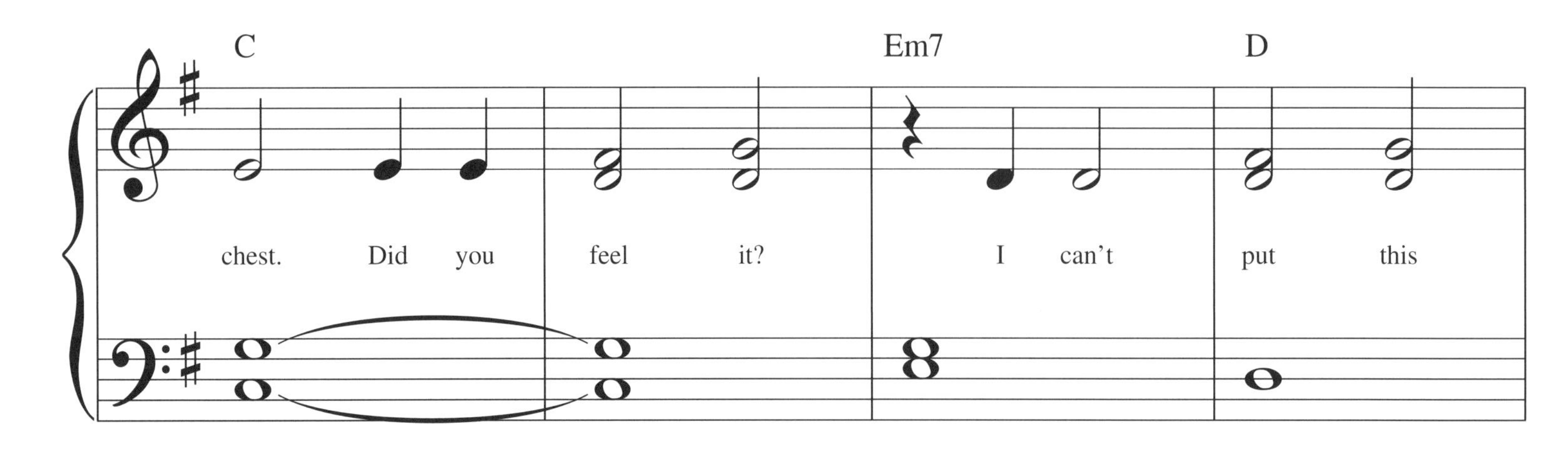
C
Em7
D
chest. Did you feel it? I can't put this

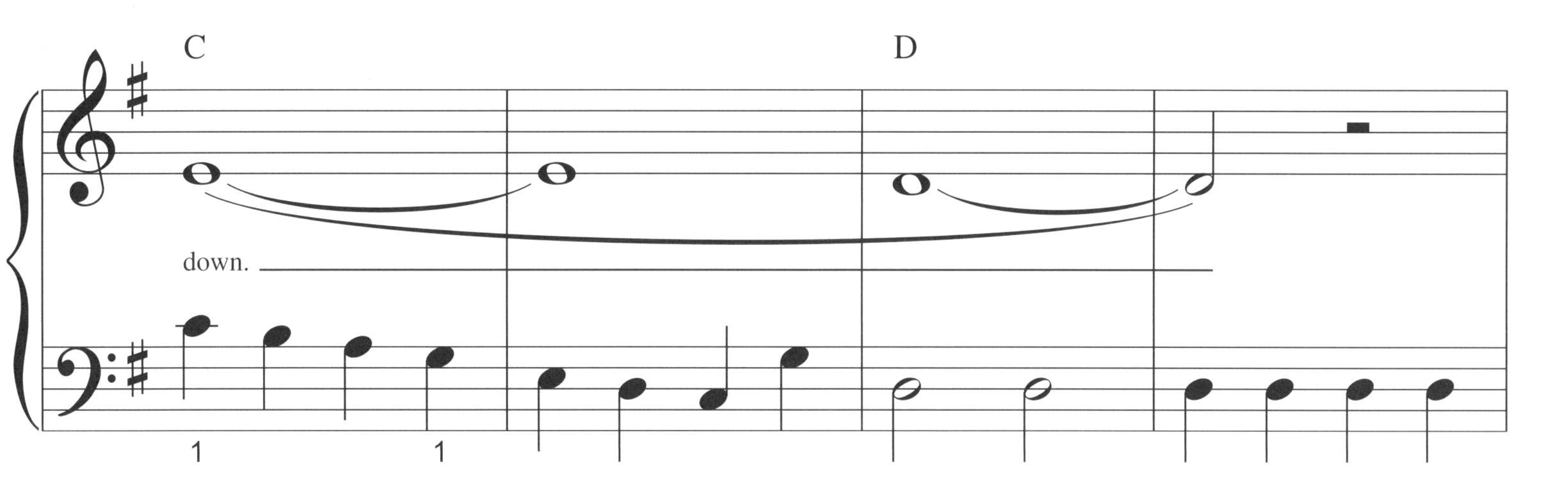
C
D
down.
1
1

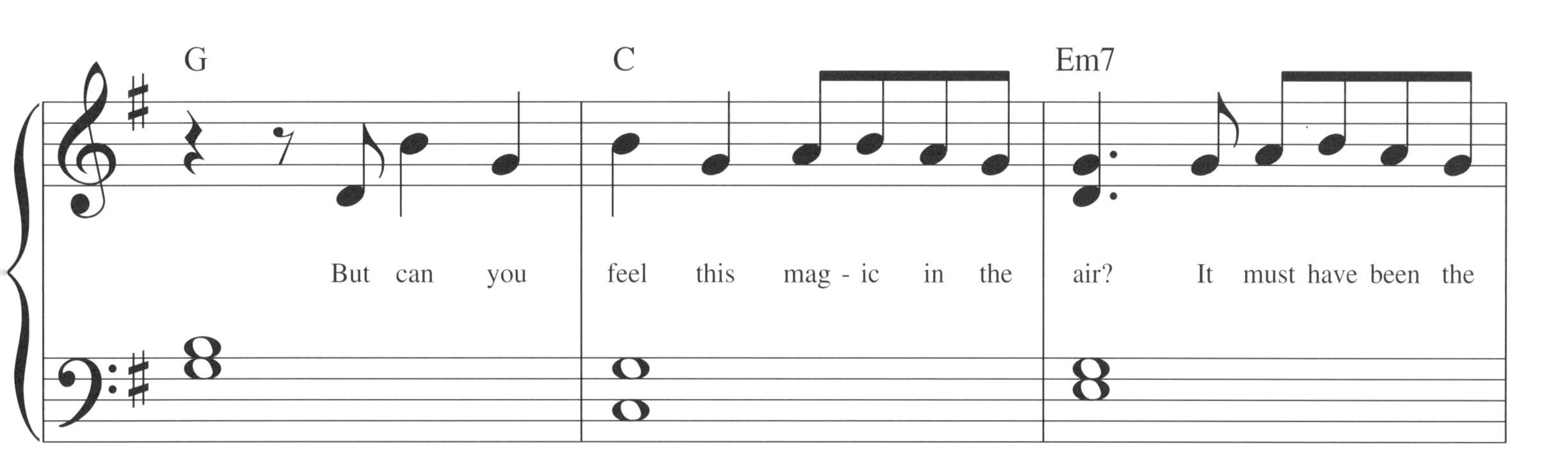
G
C
Em7
But can you
feel this mag - ic in the
air? It must have been the

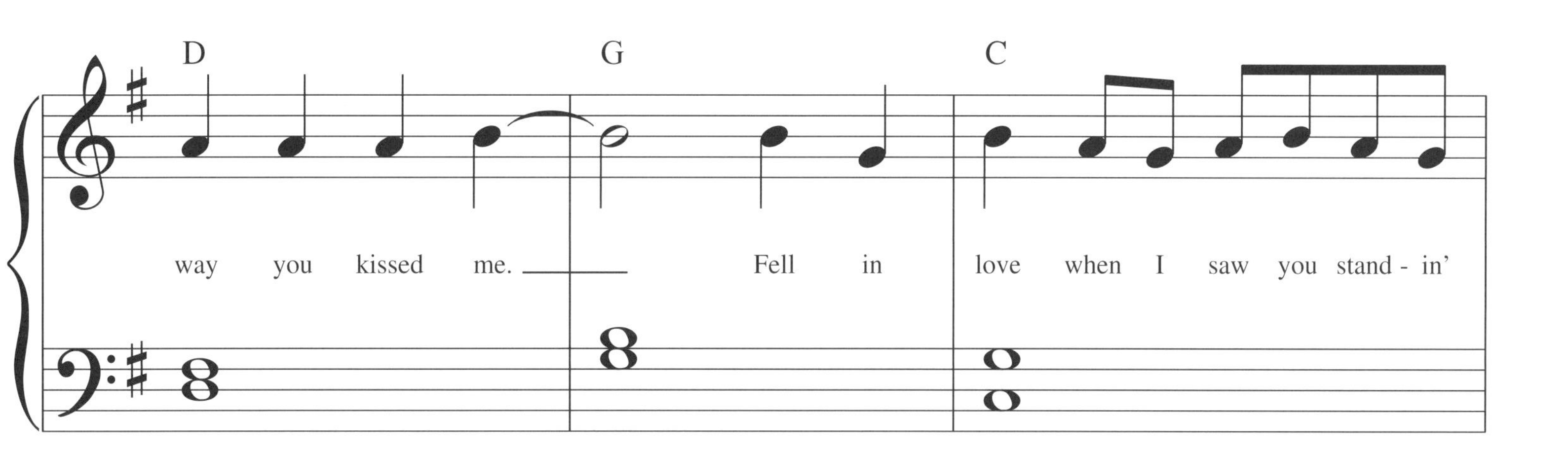
D
G
C
way you kissed me.
Fell in
love when I saw you stand - in'

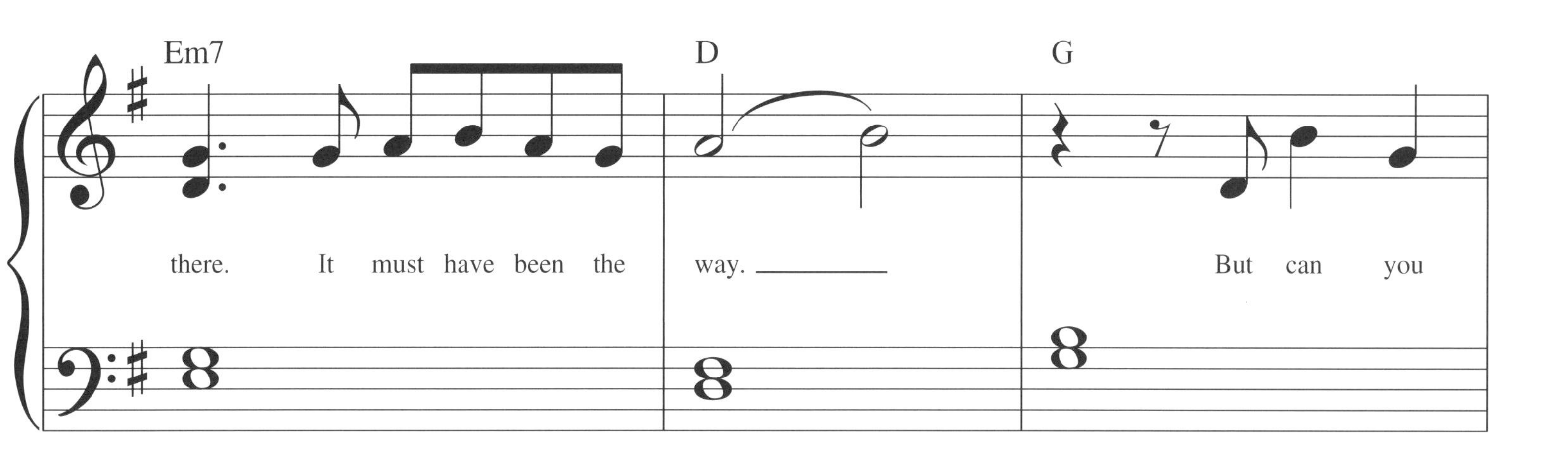
Em7
D
G
there. It must have been the
way.
But can you

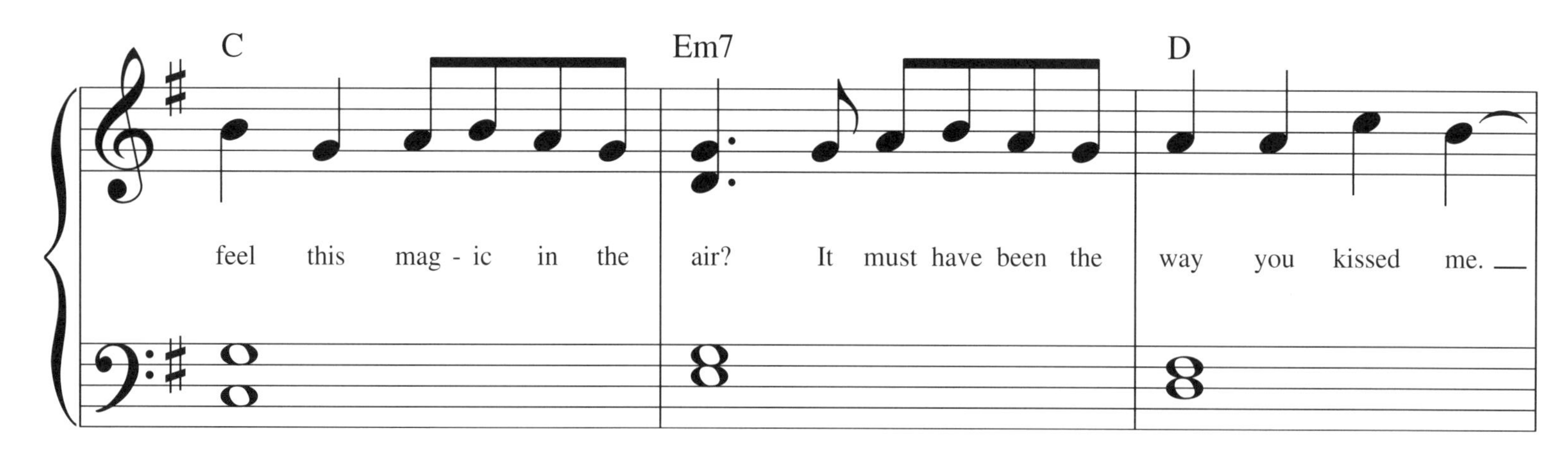
C
Em7
D
feel this mag - ic in the
air? It must have been the
way you kissed me.

G
C
Em7
Fell in
love when I saw you stand - in'
there, it must have been the

D
G
Csus2
way to - day was a
fair - y - tale.

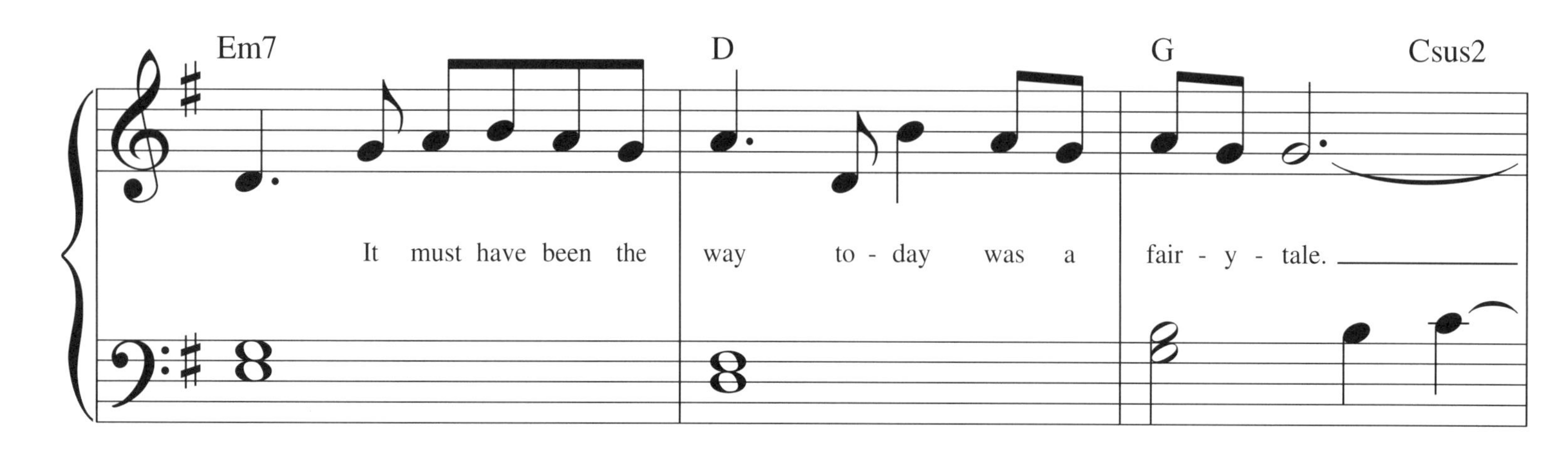
Em7
D
G
Csus2
It must have been the
way to - day was a
fair - y - tale.

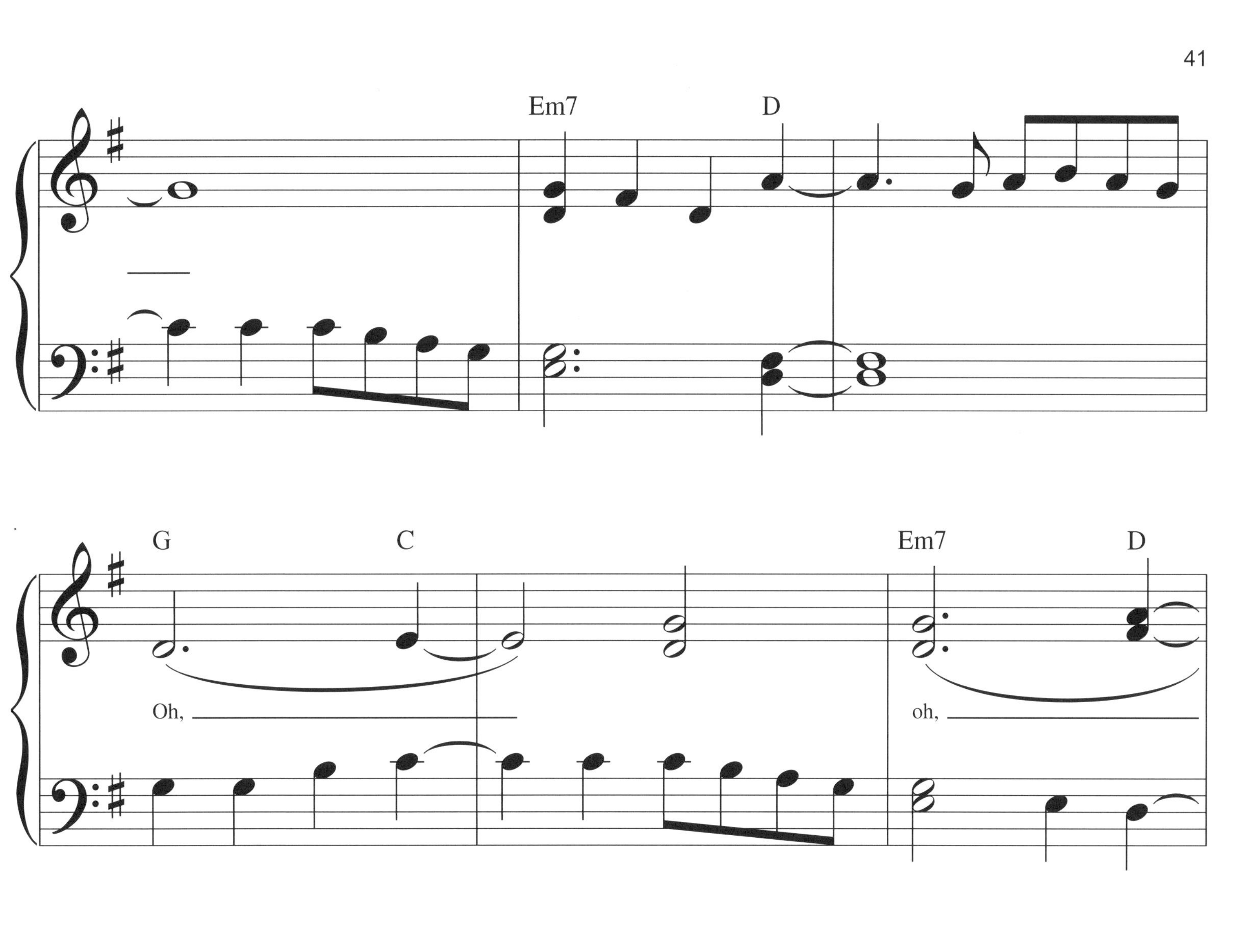
Em7
D
G
C
Em7
D
Oh,
oh,

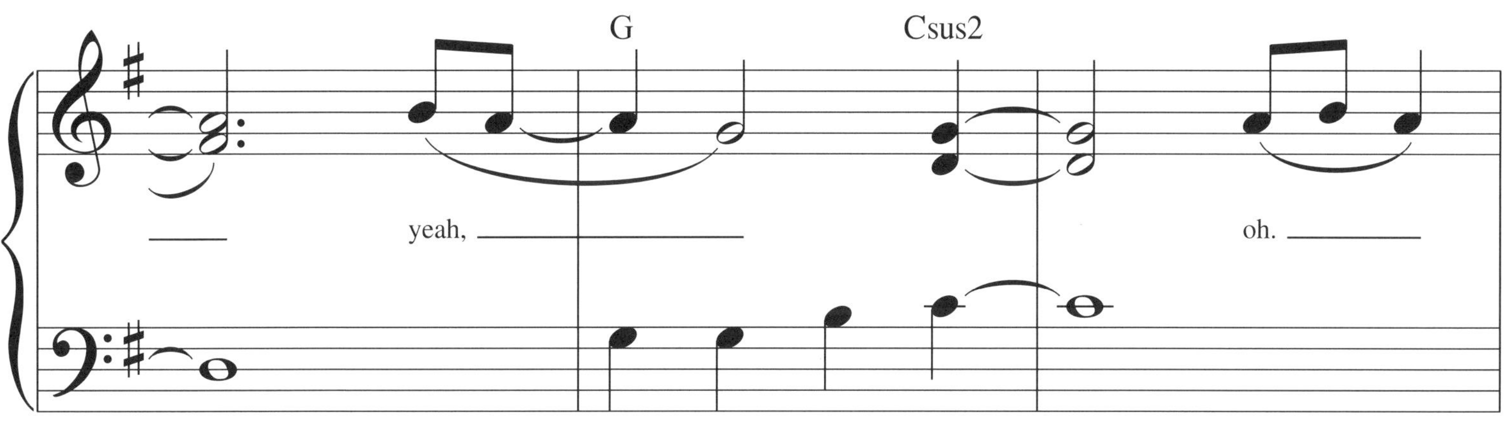
G
Csus2
yeah,
oh.

Em7
D
G
To - day was a fair - y - tale.

I KNEW YOU WERE TROUBLE

Words and Music by TAYLOR SWIFT,
SHELLBACK and MAX MARTIN

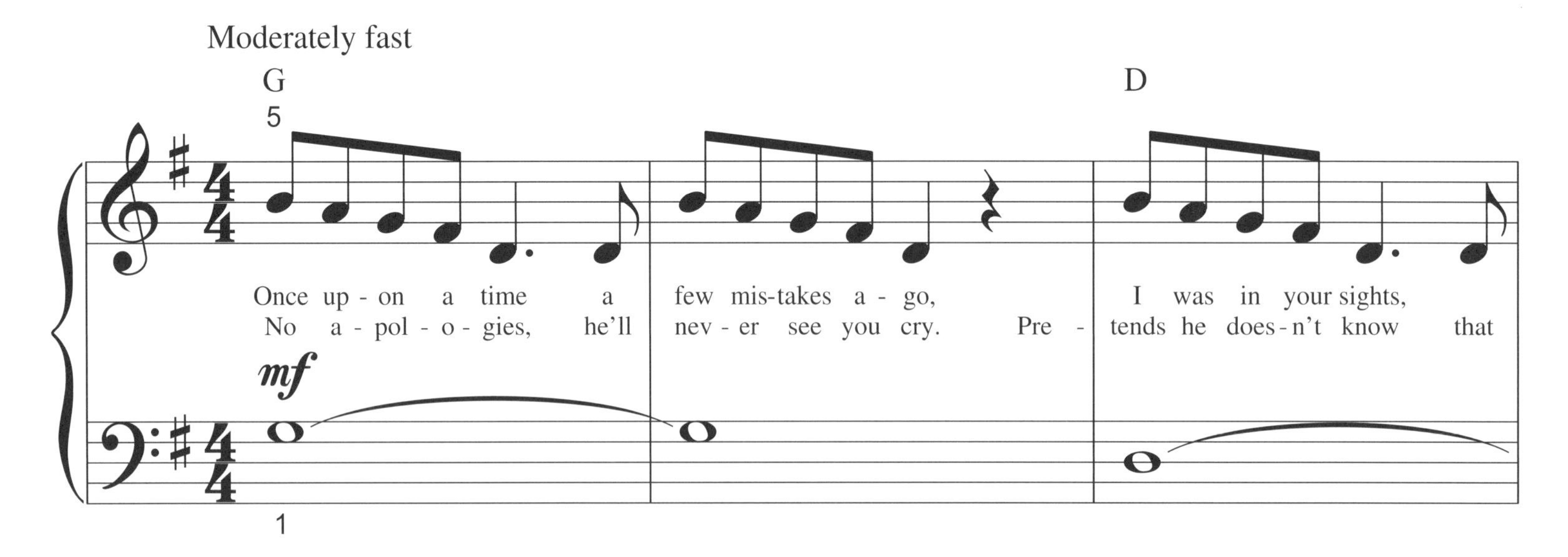

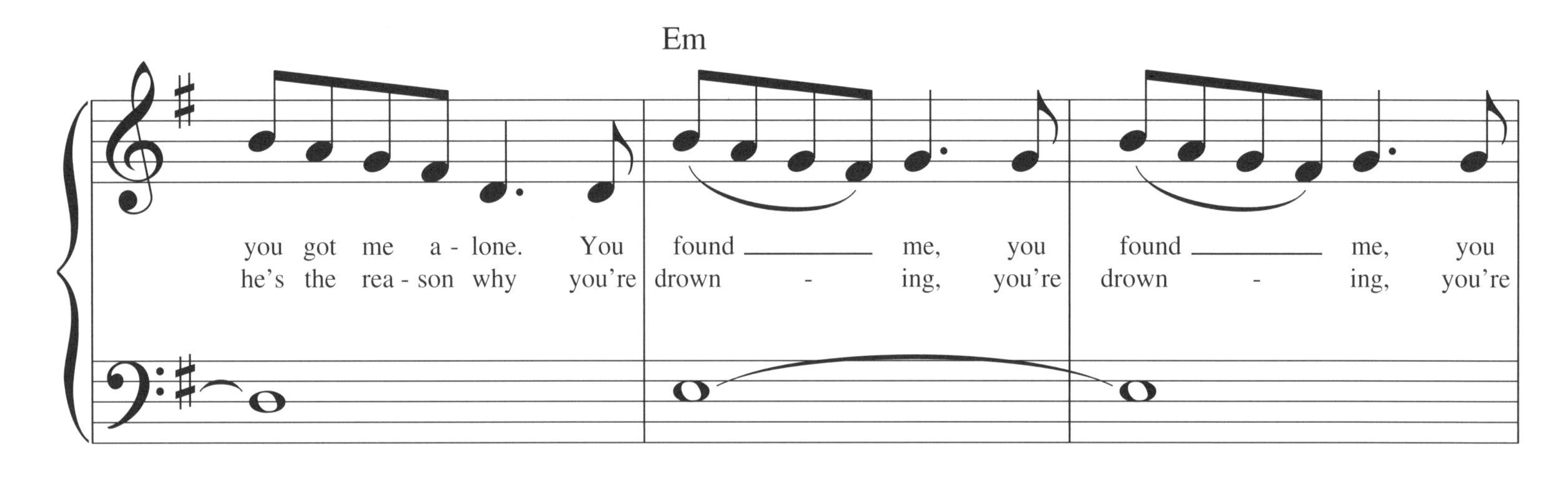

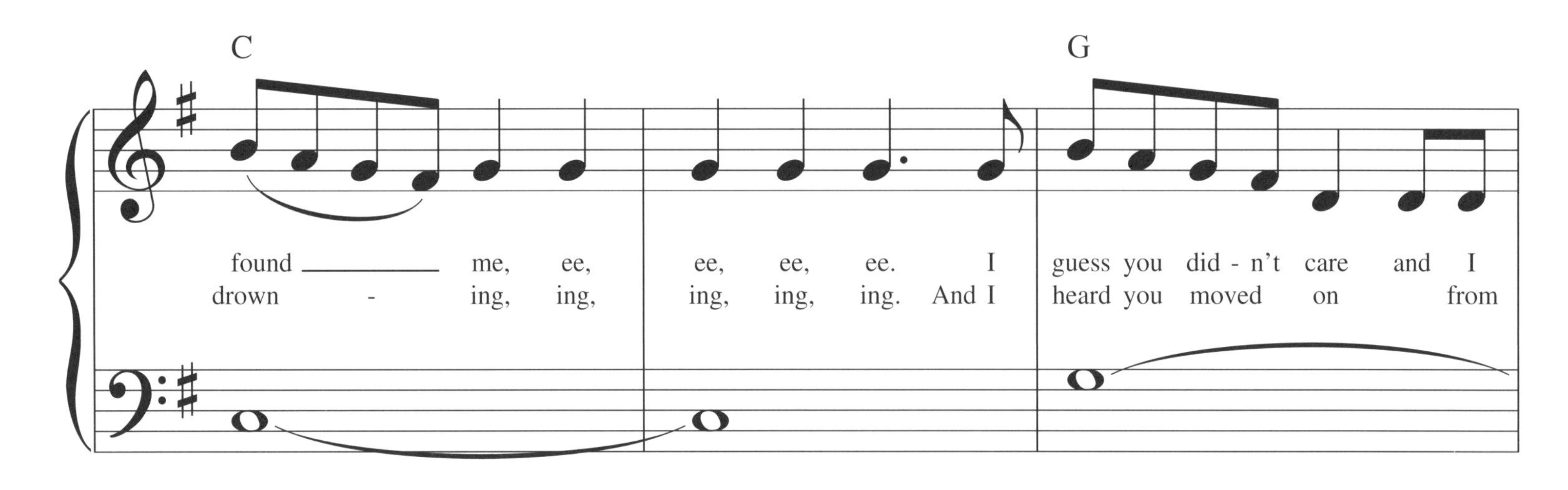

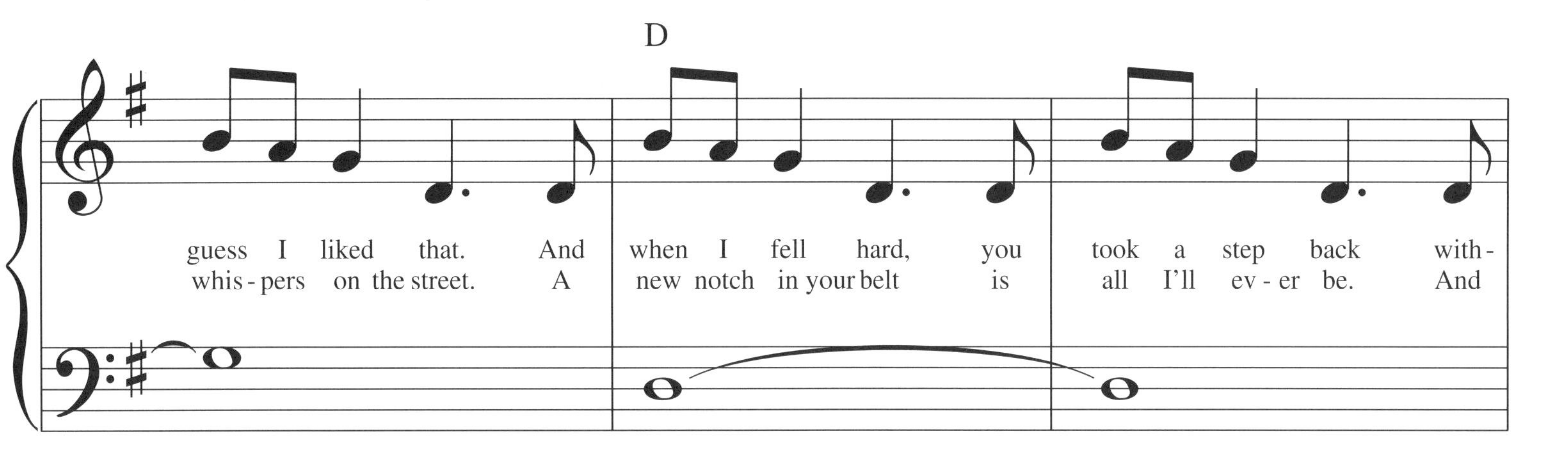
D
guess I liked that. And when I fell hard, you took a step back with-
whis-pers on the street. A new notch in your belt is all I'll ev-er be. And

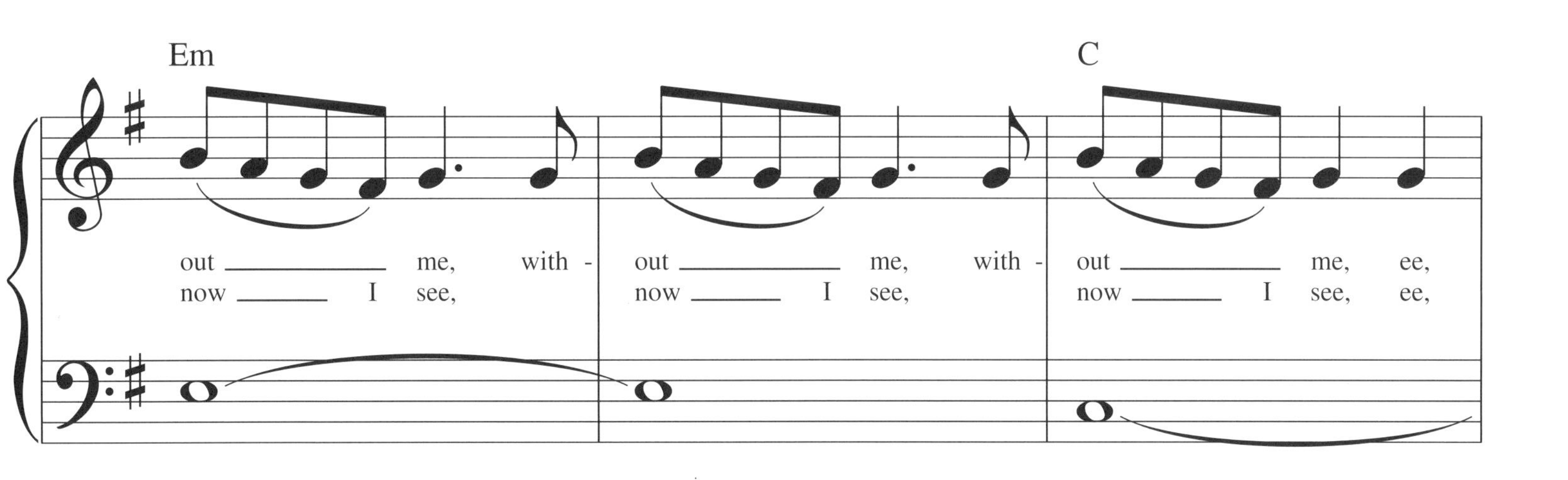
Em
C
out me, with - out me, with - out me, ee,
now I see, now I see, now I see, ee,

G
4
ee, ee, ee. And he's long
ee, ee, ee. He was long

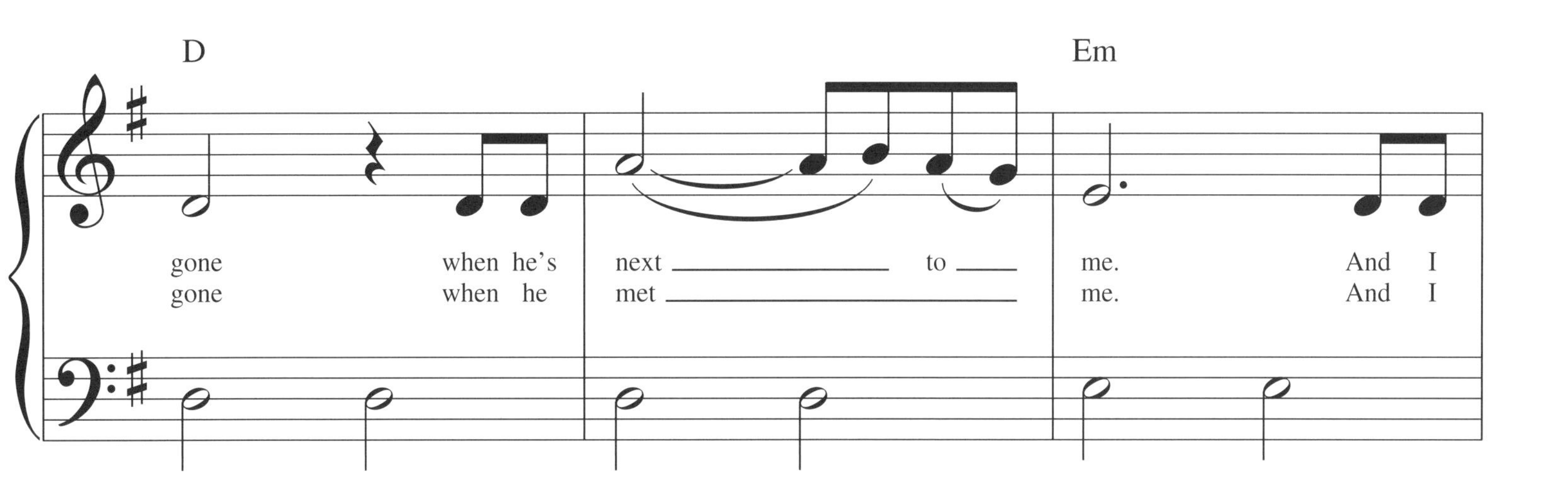
D
Em
gone when he's next to me. And I
gone when he met me. And I

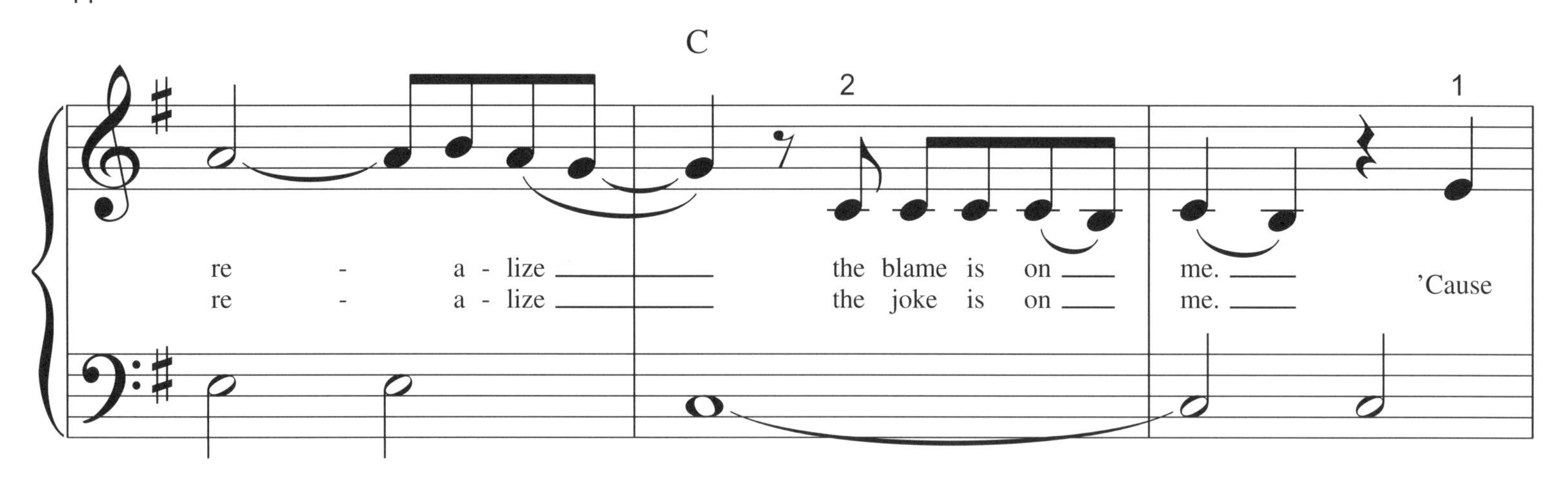
C
2
1
re - a - lize the blame is on me. 'Cause
re - a - lize the joke is on me.

Em
C
D
1
I knew you were trou - ble when you walked in, so

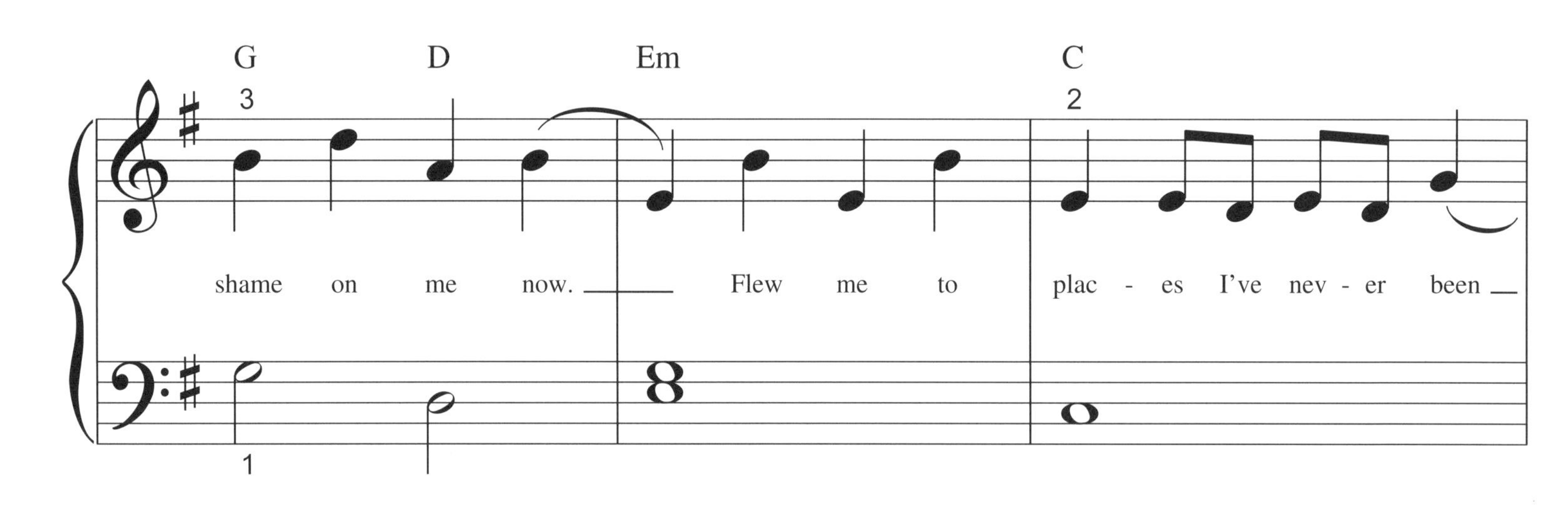
G
D
Em
C
3
2
1
shame on me now. Flew me to plac - es I've nev - er been

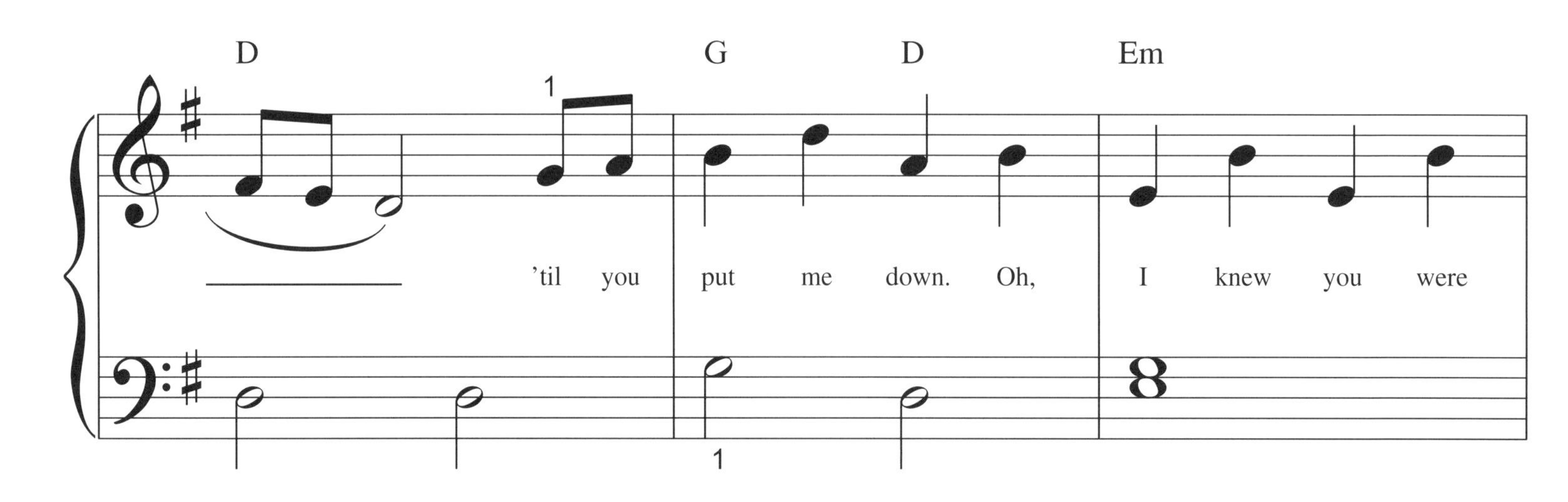
D
G
D
Em
1
1
'til you put me down. Oh, I knew you were

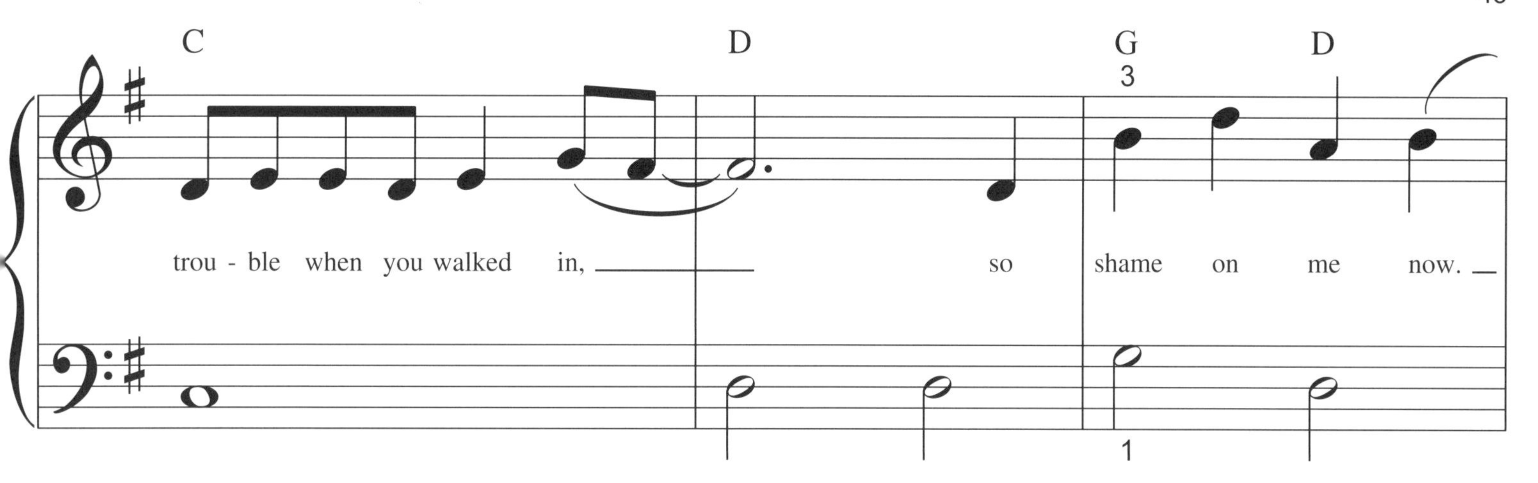
C
D
G
D
3
trou - ble when you walked in,
so
shame on me now.
1

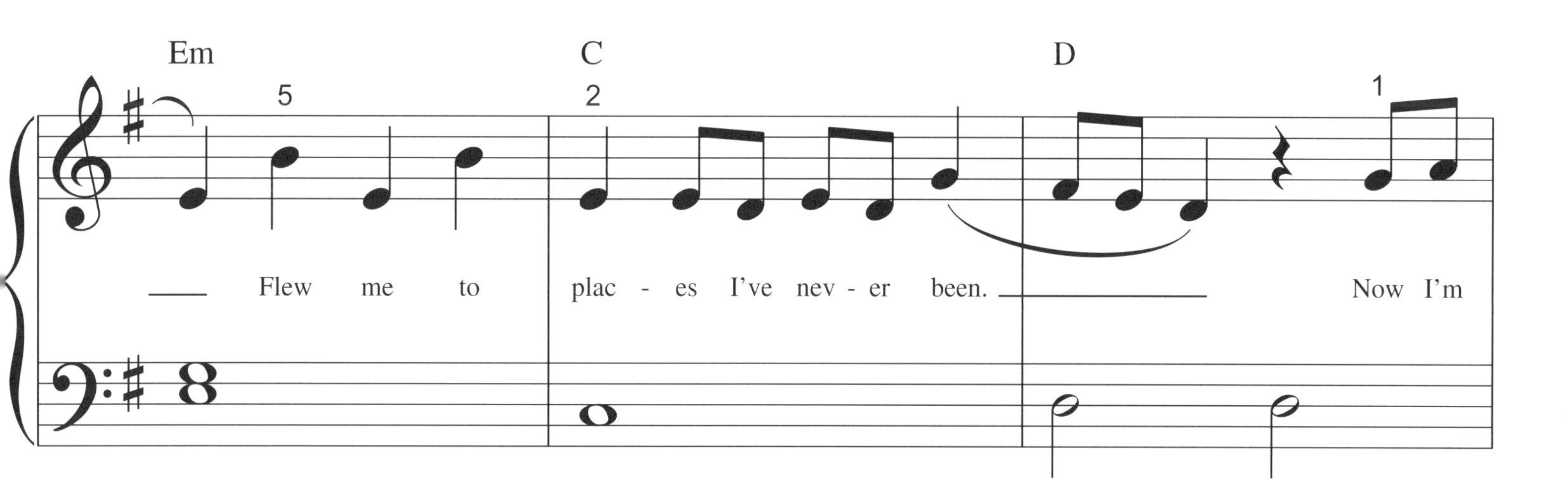
Em
C
D
5
2
1
Flew me to
plac - es I've nev - er been.
Now I'm

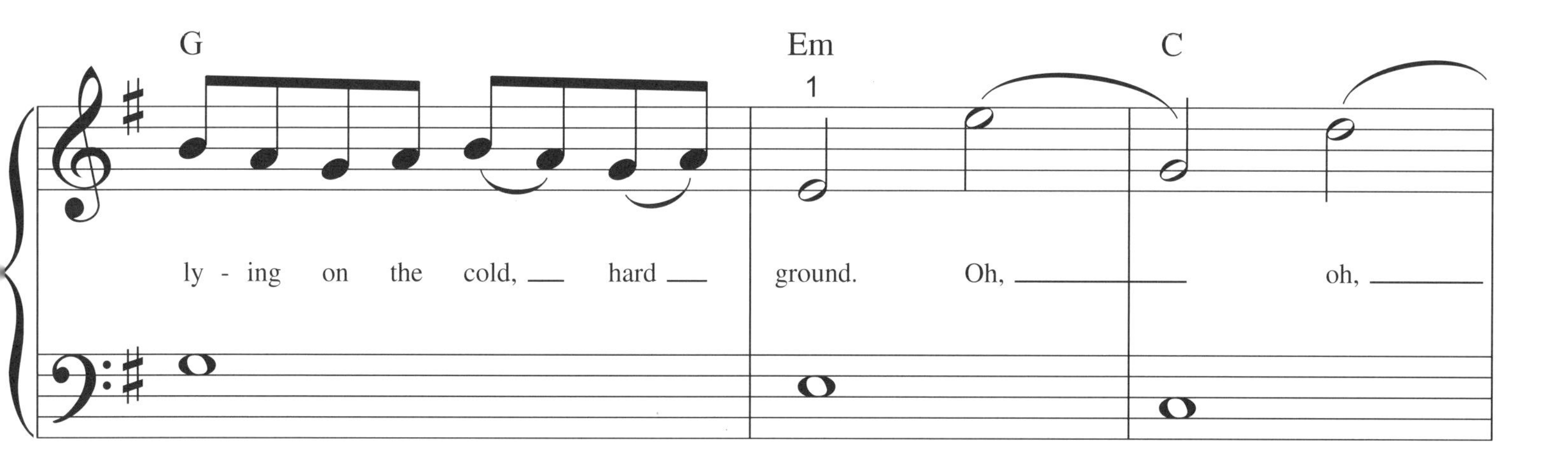
G
Em
C
1
ly - ing on the cold, hard
ground. Oh,
oh,

D
Em
3
trou - ble,
trou - ble, trou - ble.
Oh,

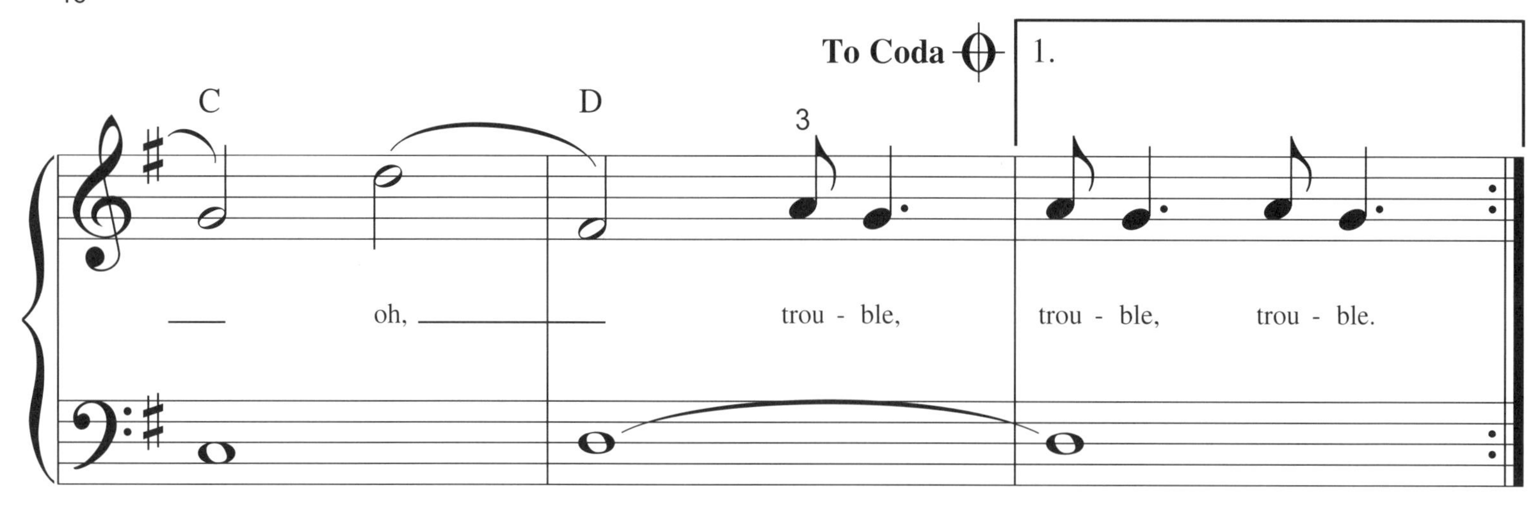
To Coda
1.
C
D
3
oh,
trou - ble,
trou - ble,
trou - ble.

2.
C
trou - ble,
trou - ble. And the
sad - dest
fear
comes

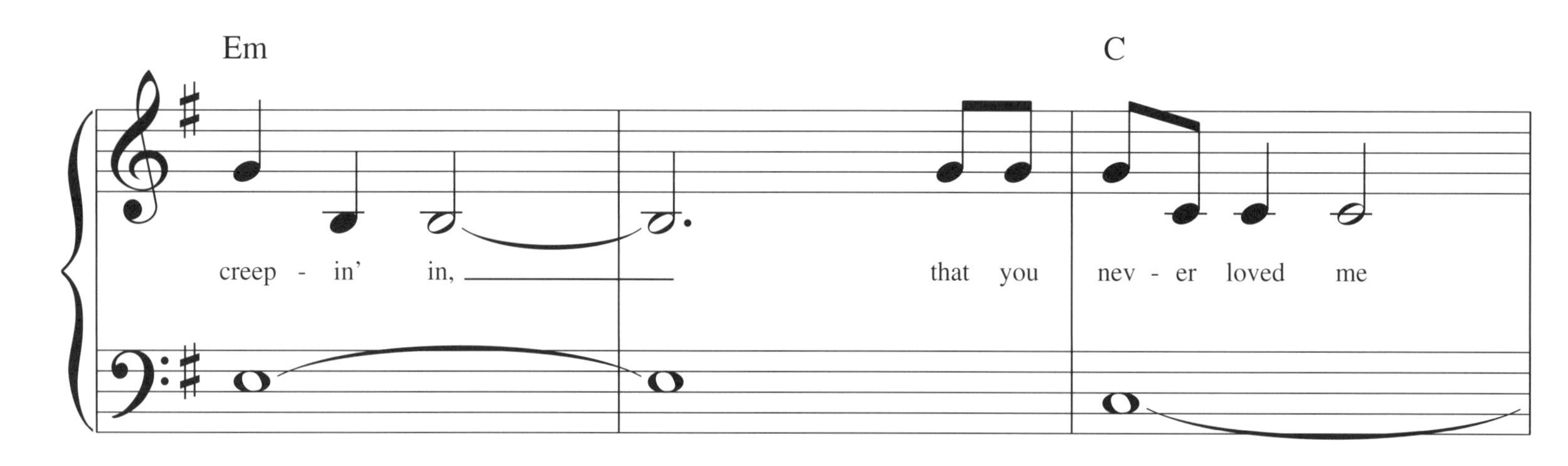
Em
C
creep - in'
in,
that you
nev - er
loved
me

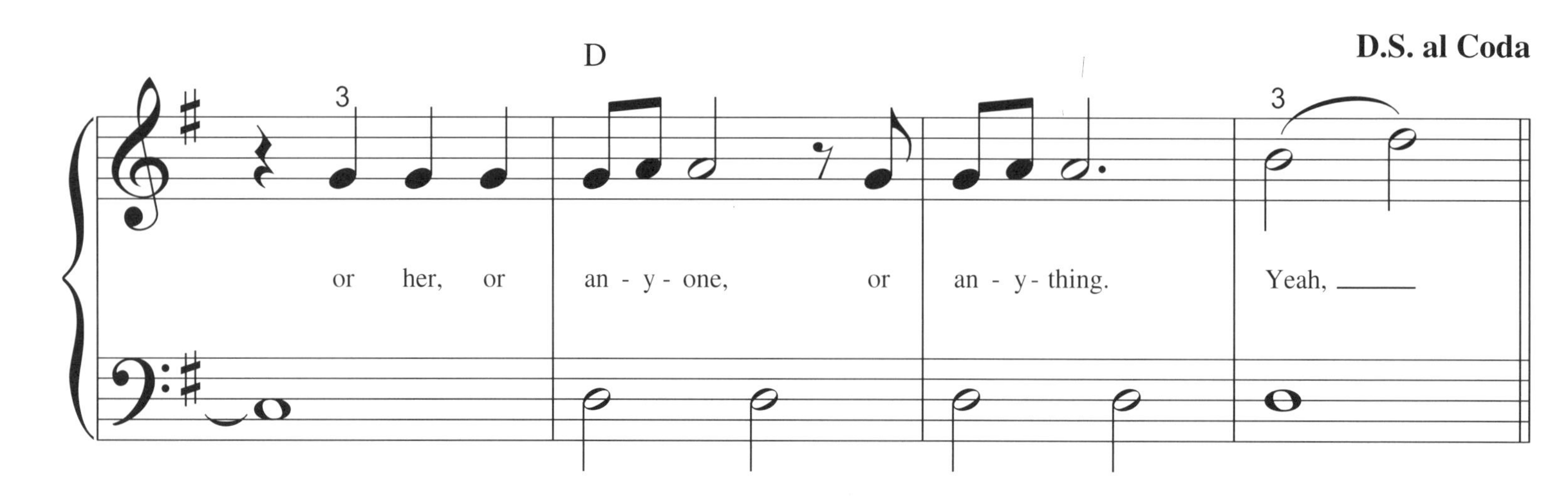
D
D.S. al Coda
3
3
or
her,
or
an - y - one,
or
an - y - thing.
Yeah,

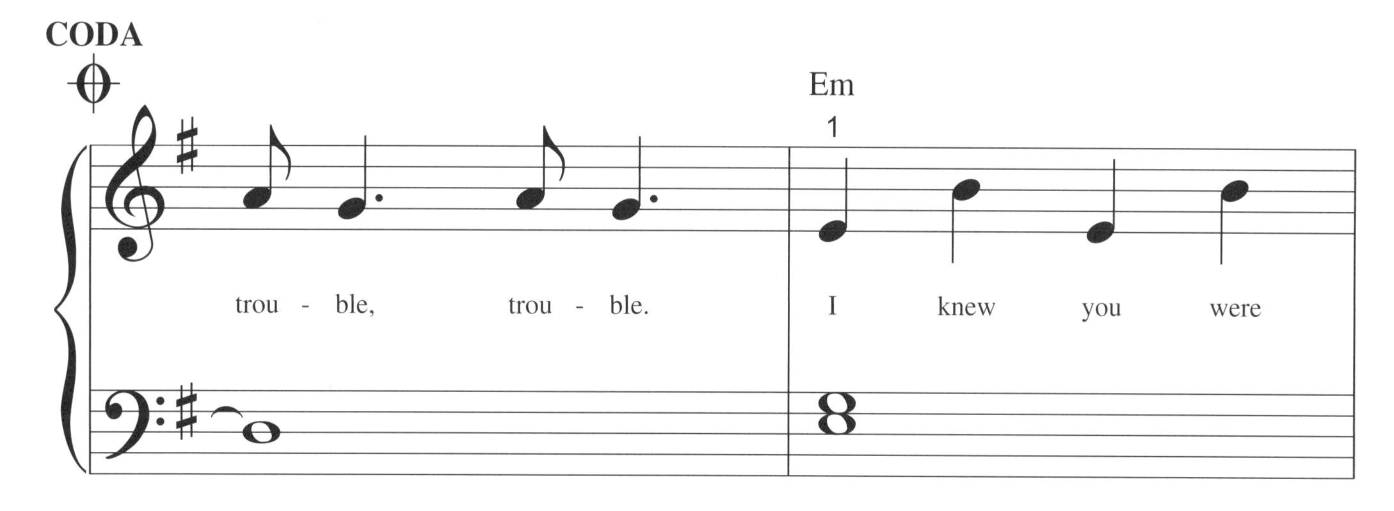
CODA
Em
1
trou - ble, trou - ble. I knew you were

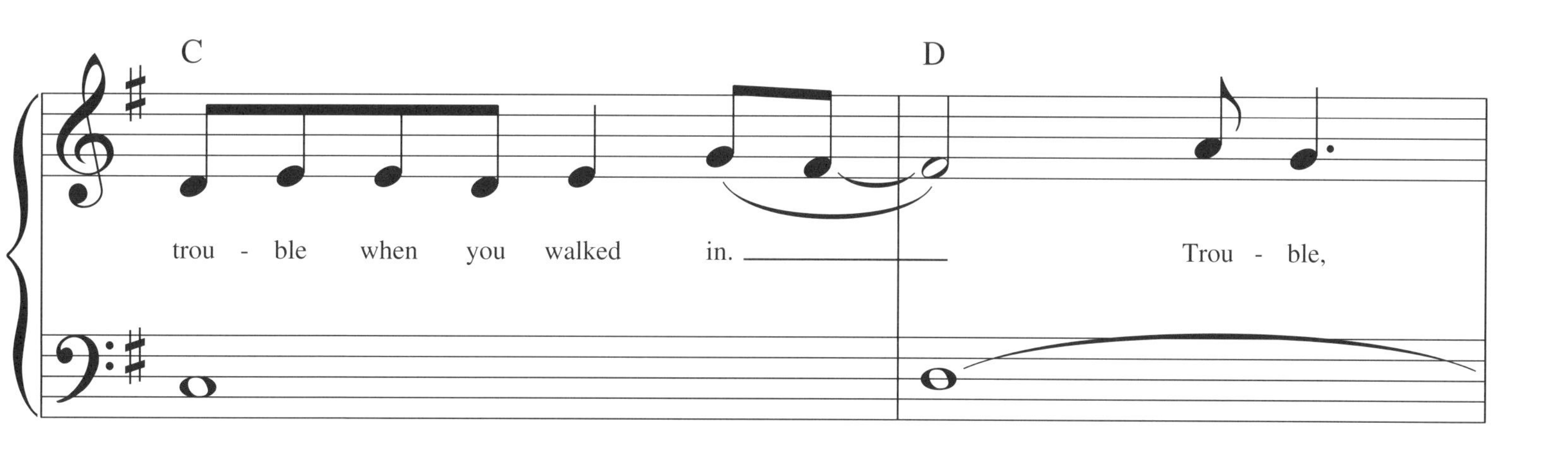
C
D
trou - ble when you walked in.
Trou - ble,

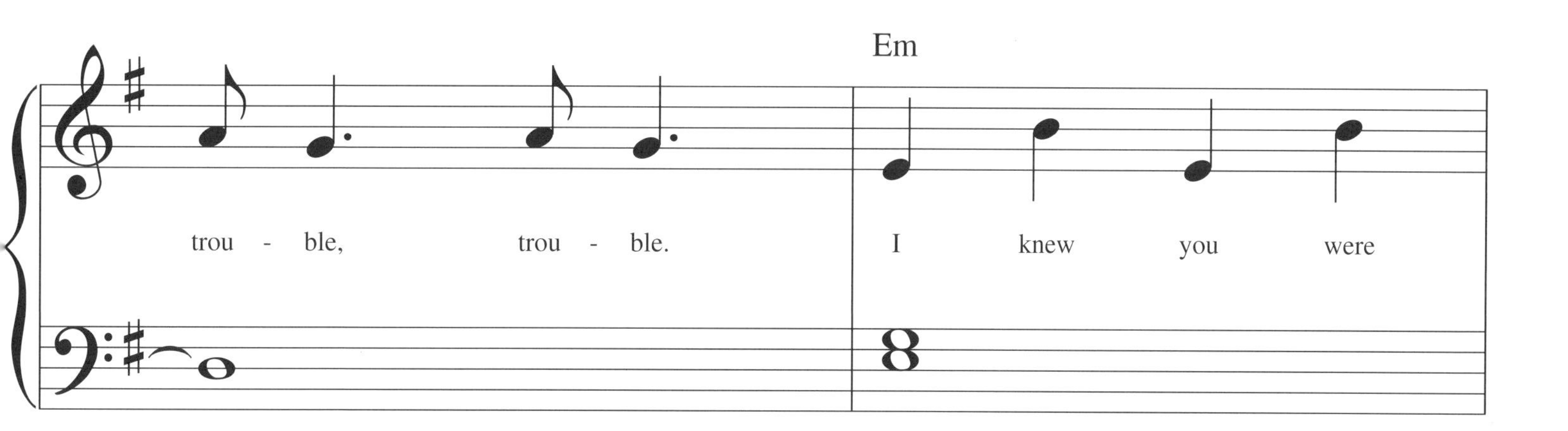
Em
trou - ble, trou - ble. I knew you were

C
D
N.C.
trou - ble when you walked in.
Trou - ble, trou - ble, trou - ble.

MEAN

Words and Music by
TAYLOR SWIFT

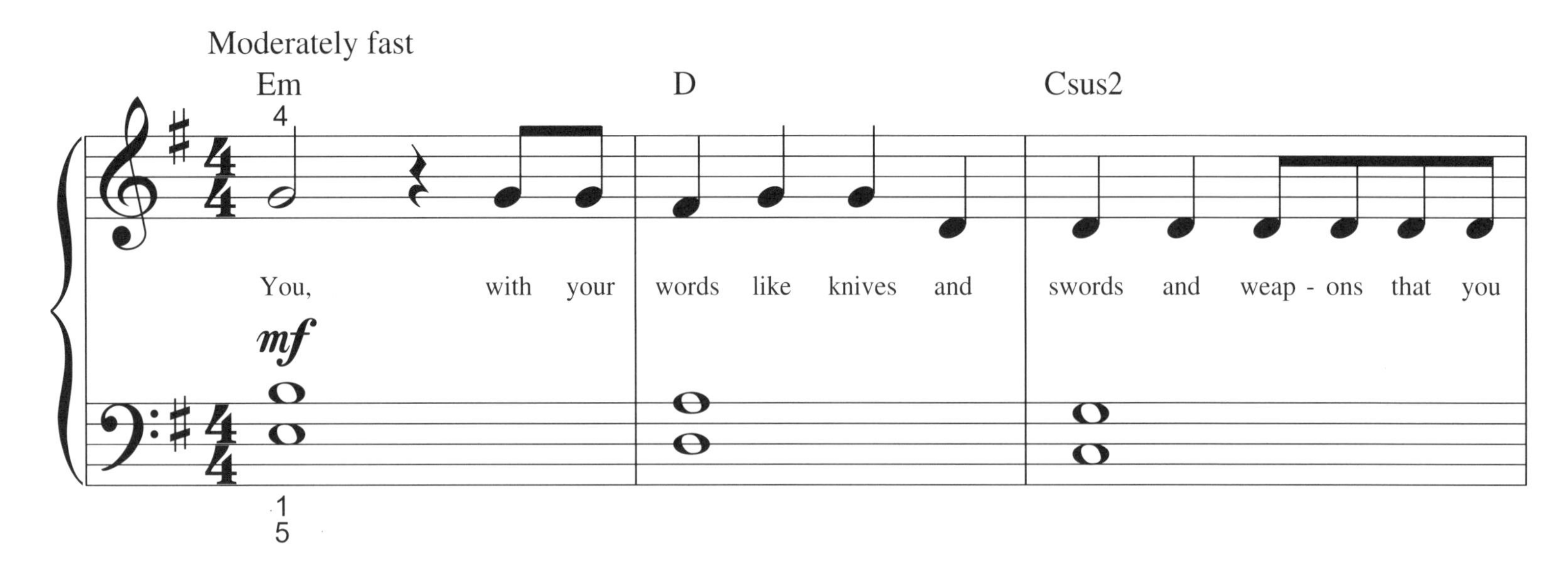

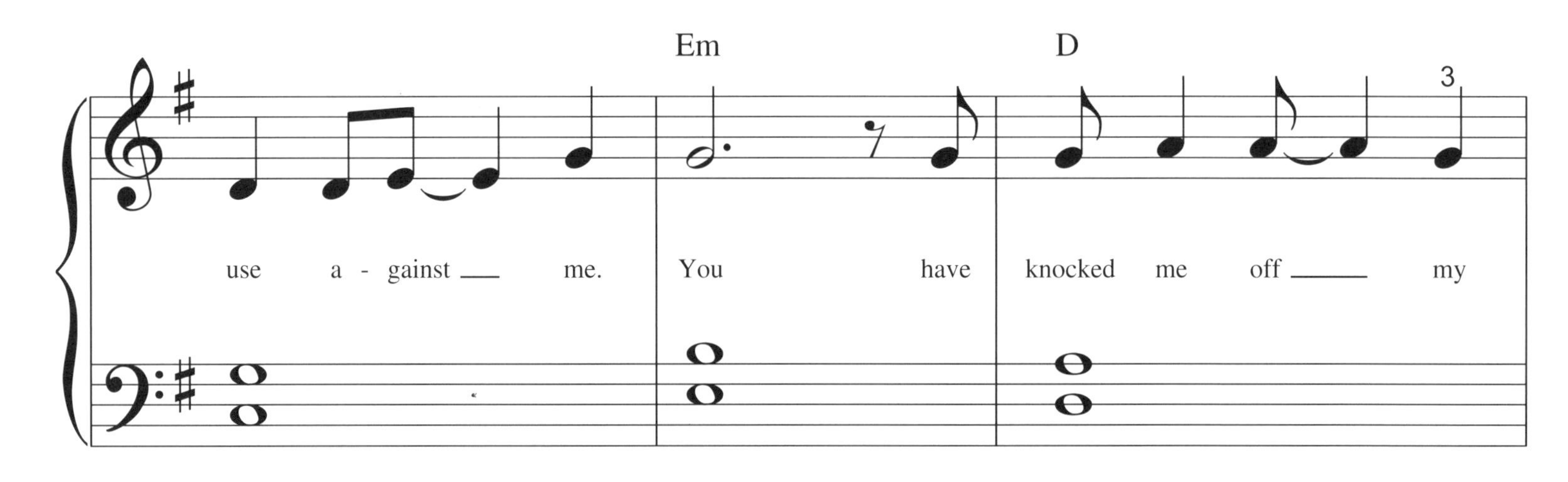

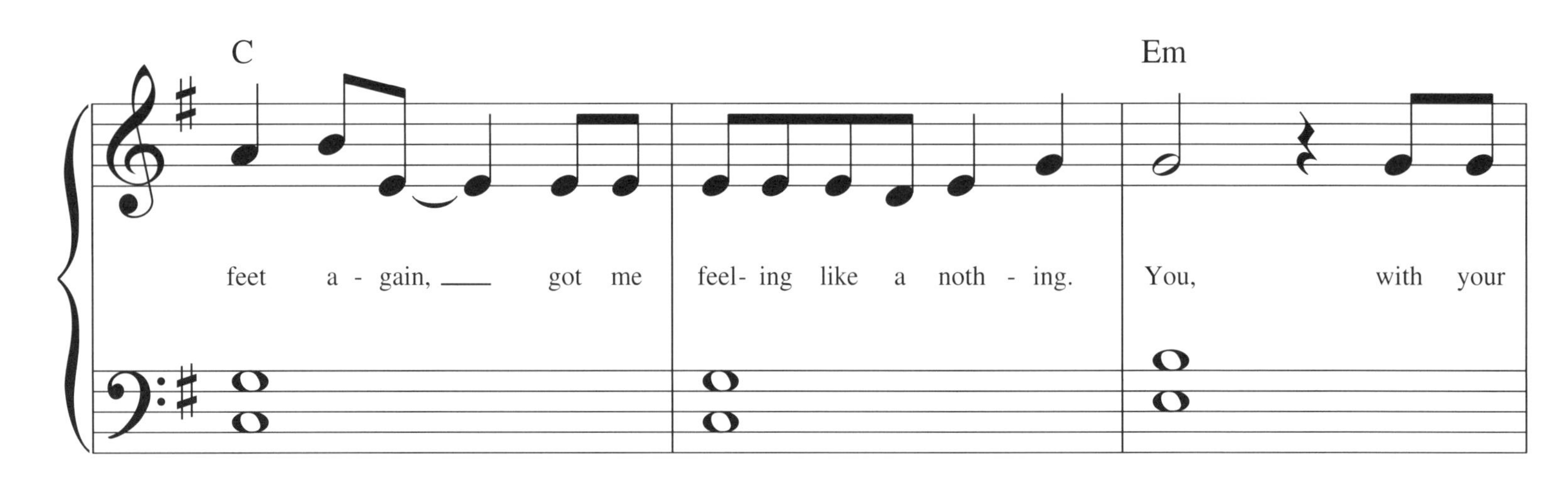

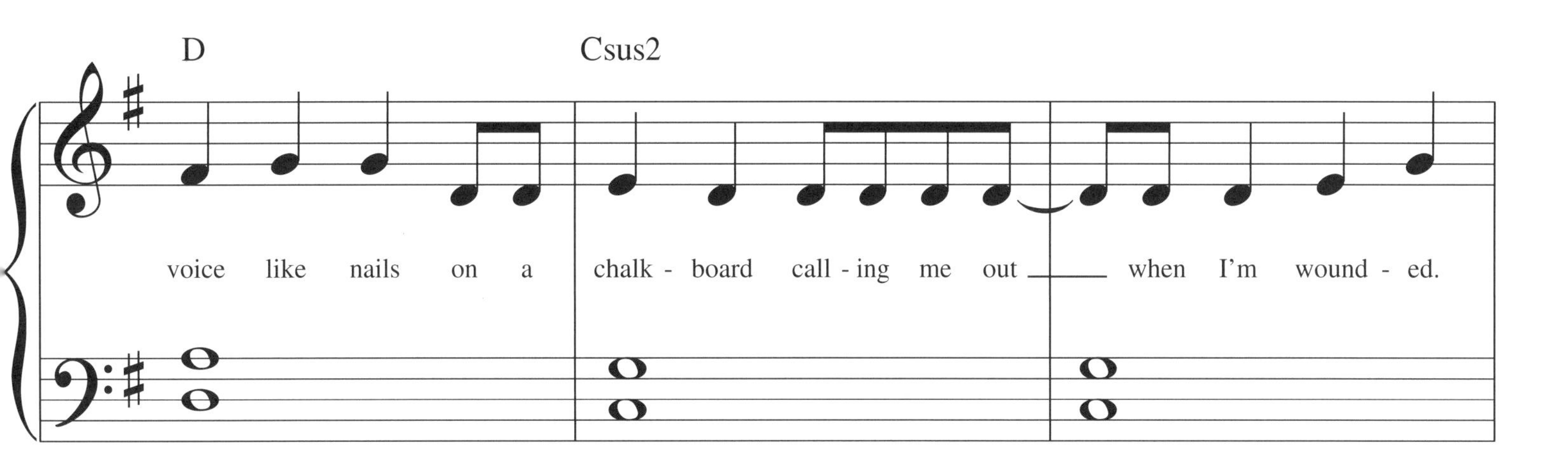
D
Csus2
voice like nails on a chalk - board call - ing me out when I'm wound - ed.

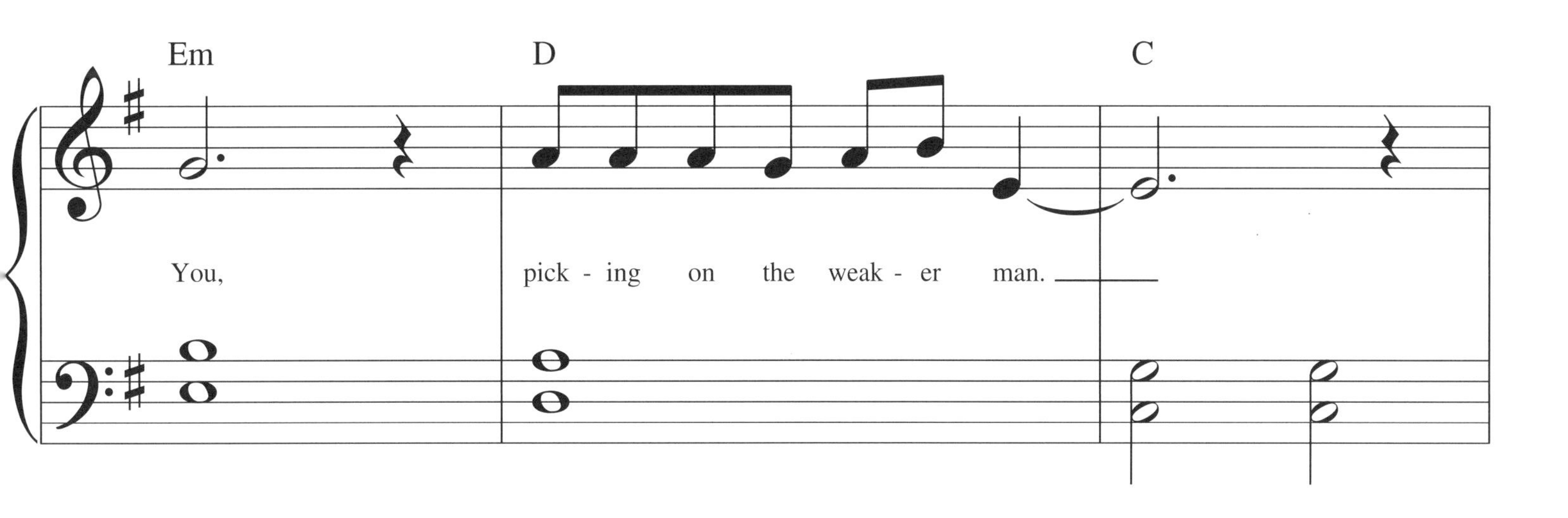
Em
D
C
You, pick - ing on the weak - er man.

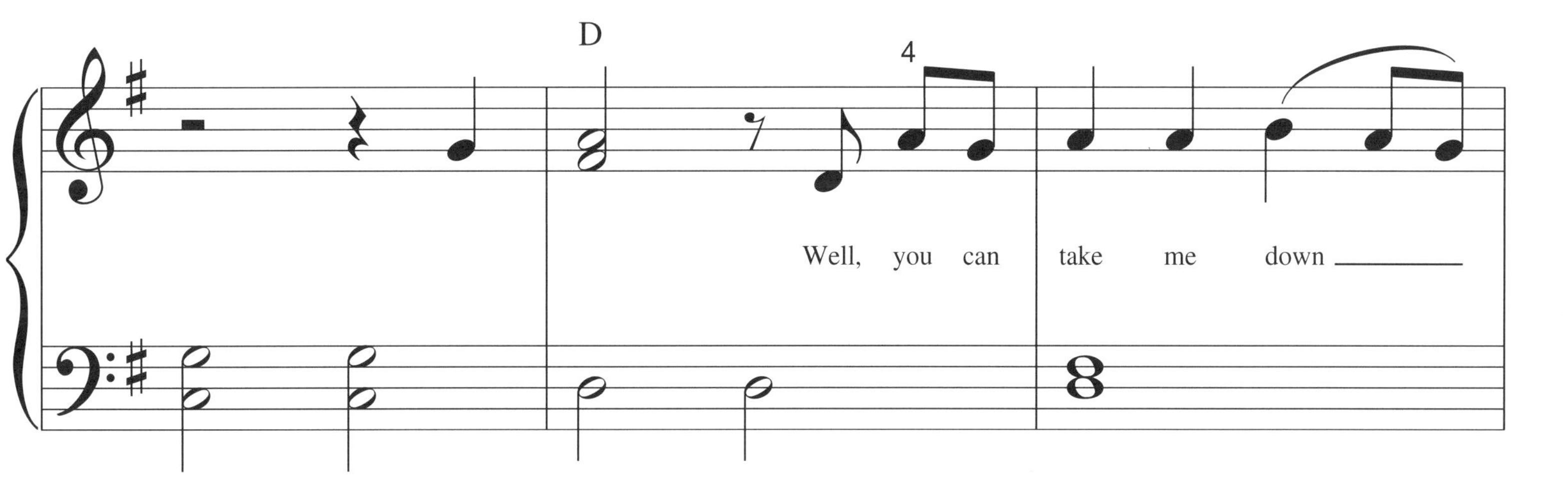
D
4
Well, you can take me down

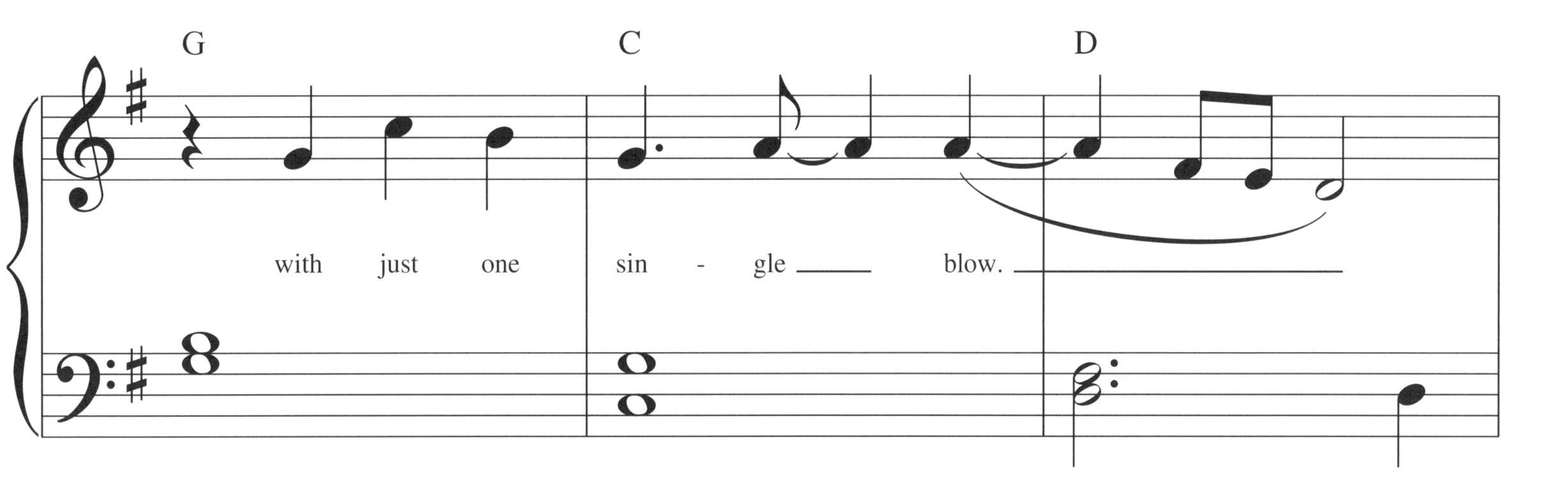
G
C
D
with just one sin - gle blow.

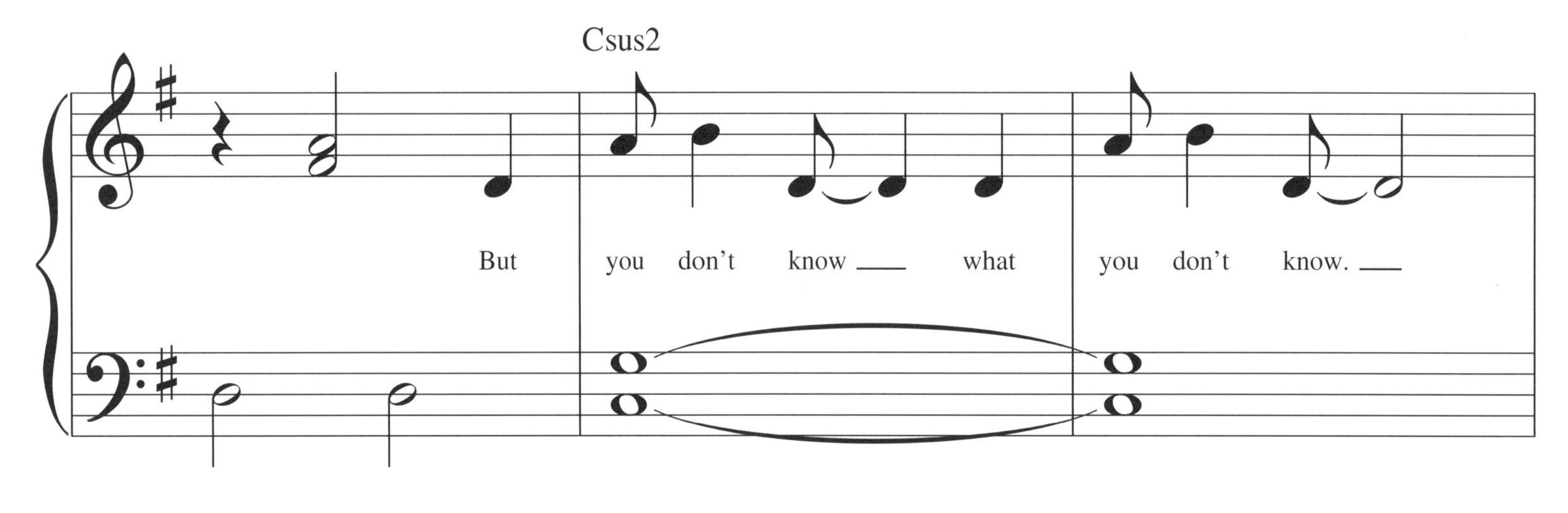
Csus2
But you don't know what you don't know.

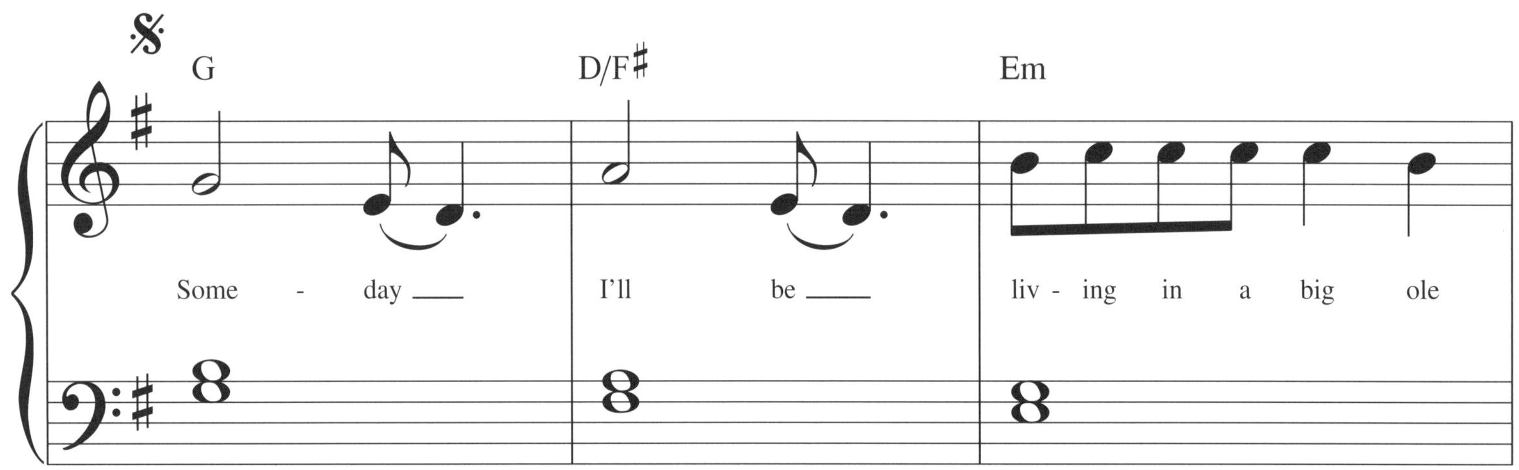
G
D/F♯
Em
Some - day I'll be liv - ing in a big ole

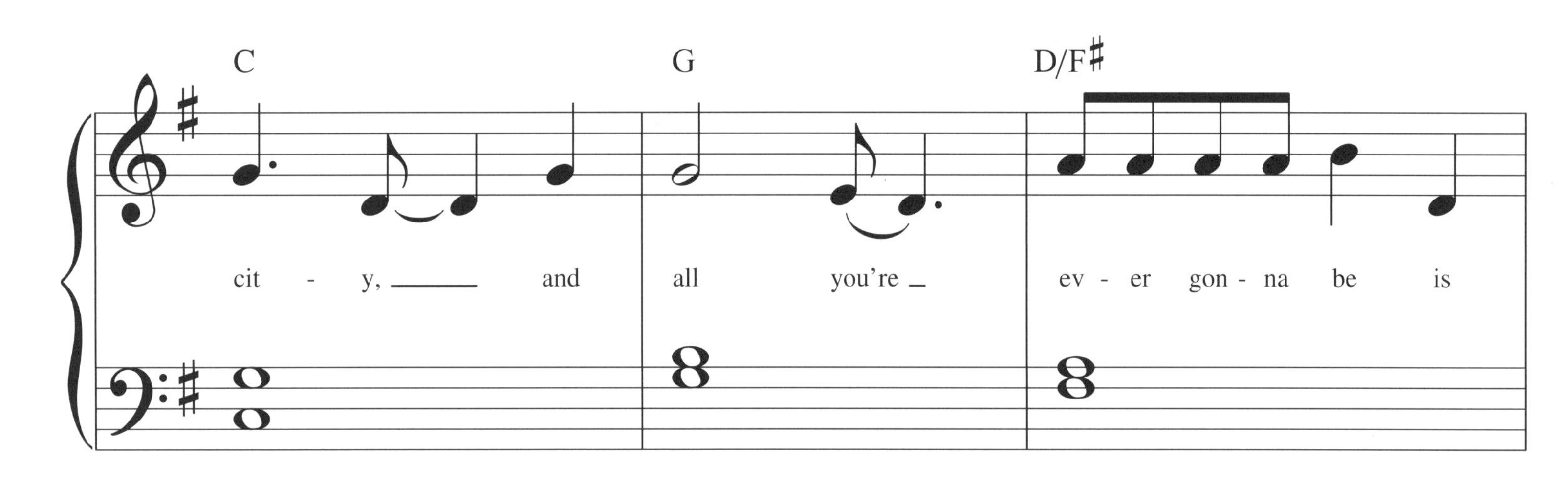
C
G
D/F♯
cit - y, and all you're ev - er gon - na be is

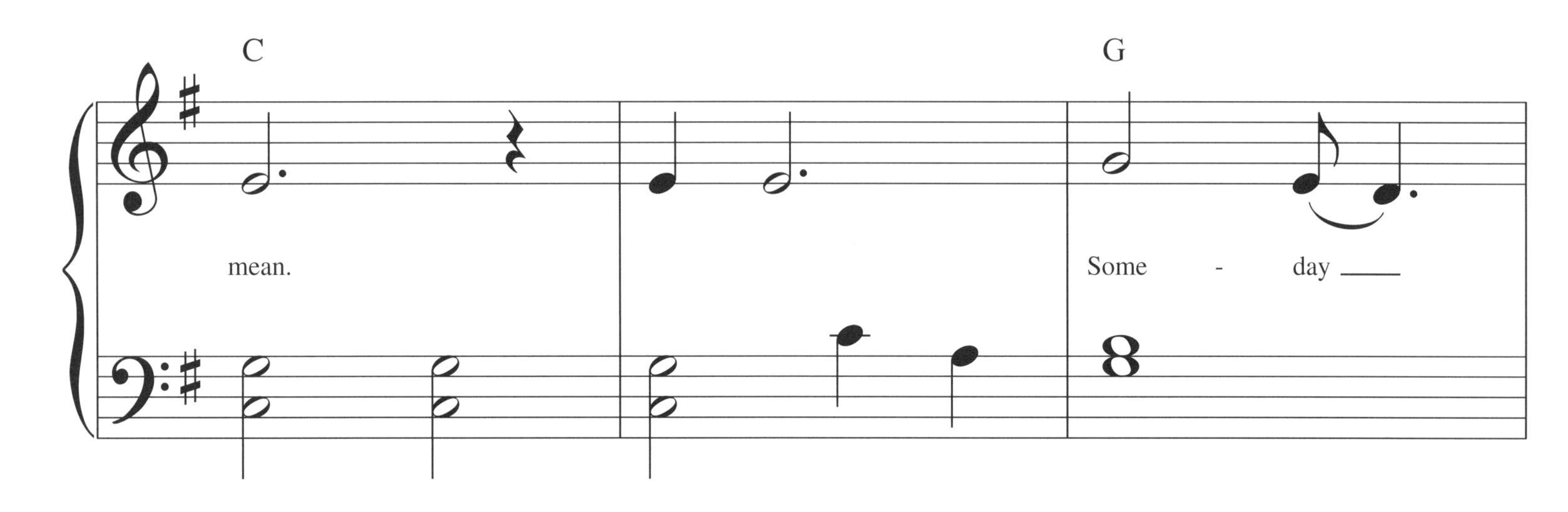
C
G
mean.
Some - day

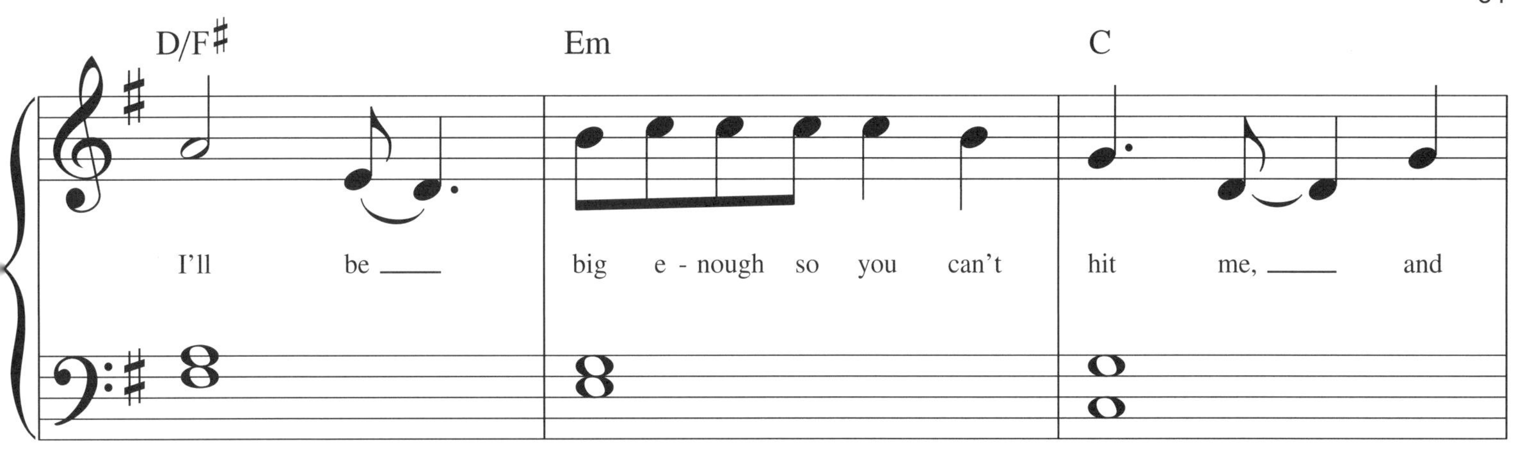
D/F♯
Em
C
I'll be big e - nough so you can't hit me, and

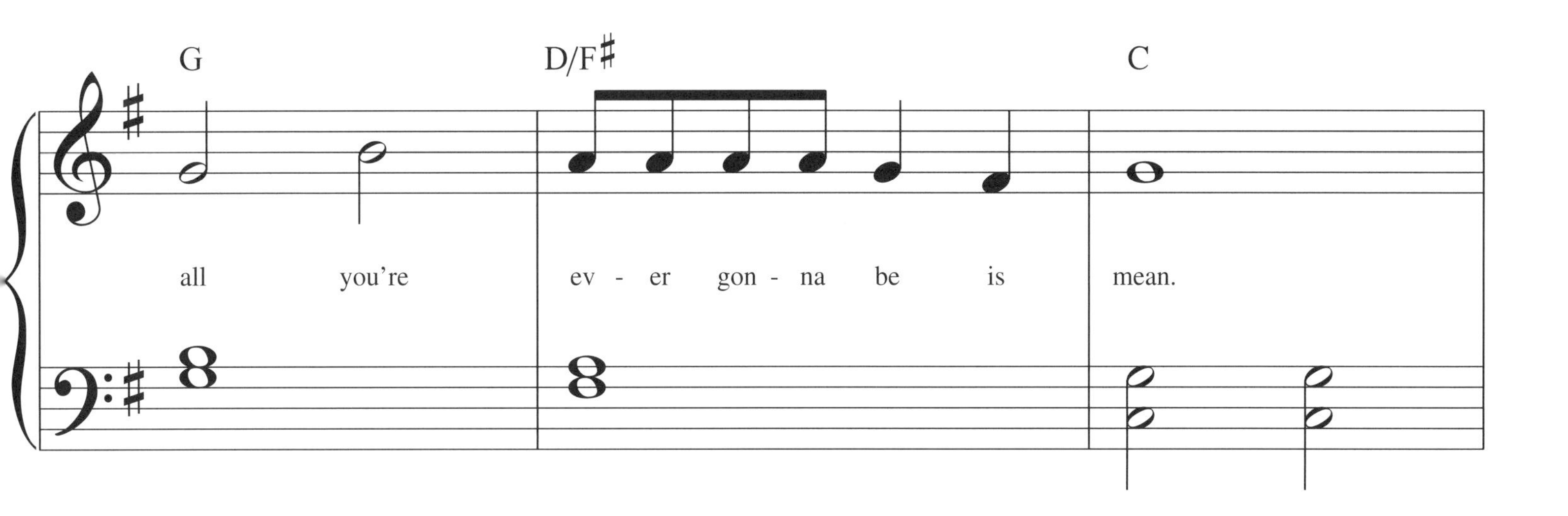
G
D/F♯
C
all you're ev - er gon - na be is mean.

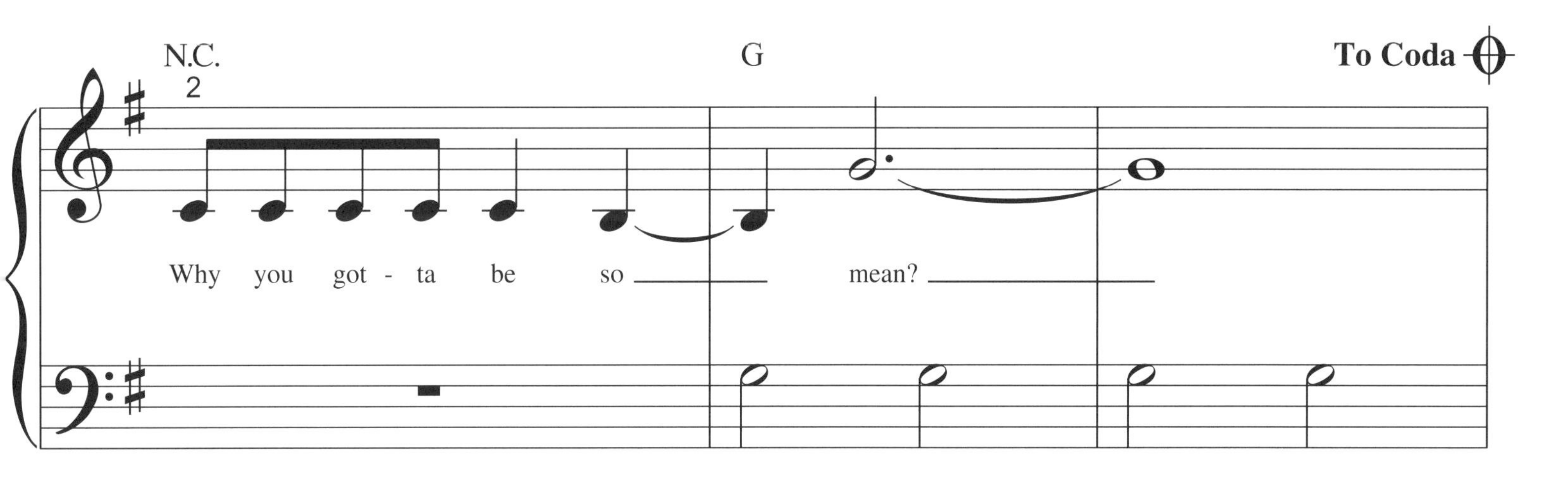
N.C.
G
To Coda
Why you got - ta be so mean?

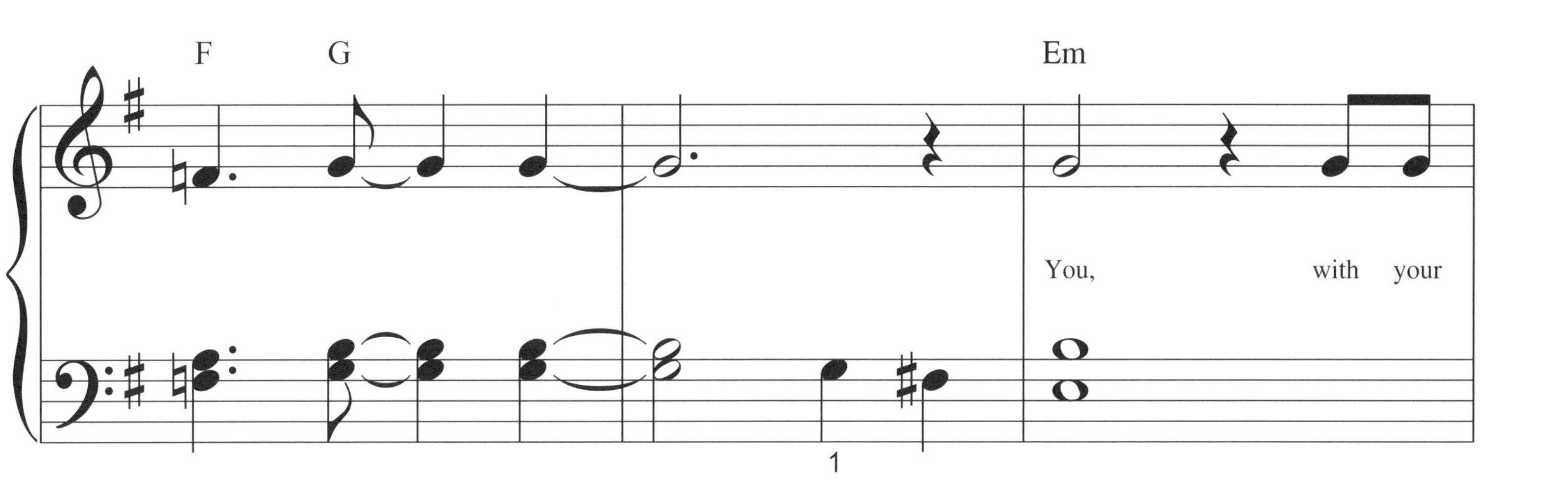
F
G
Em
You, with your

D
Csus2
switch - ing sides and your wild - fire lies and your hu - mil - i - a - tion.

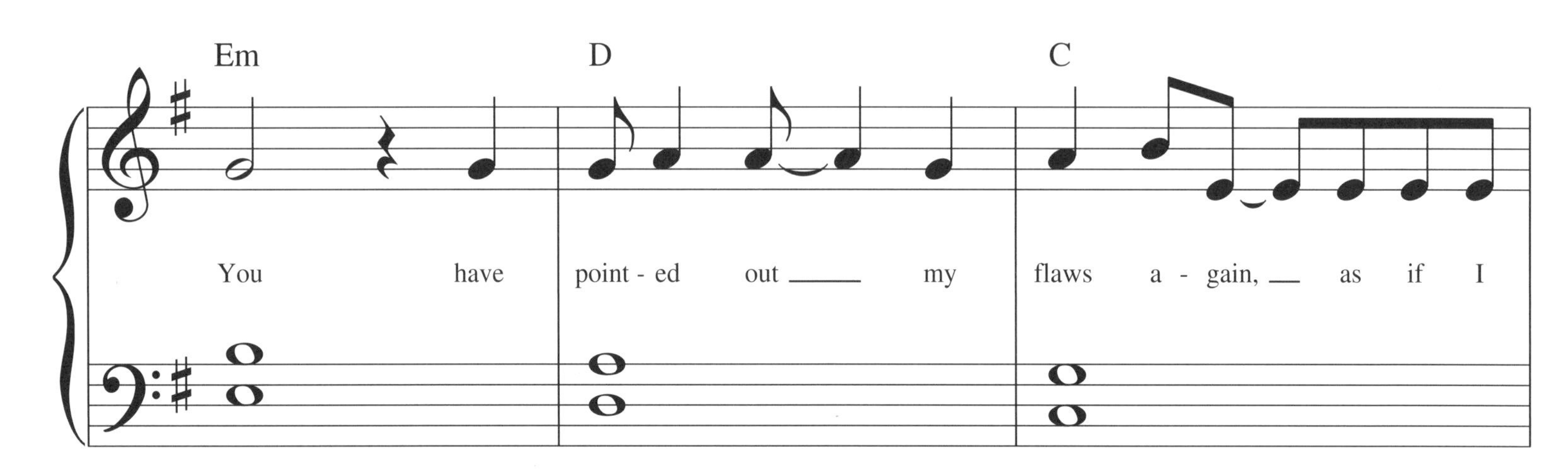
Em
D
C
You have point - ed out my flaws a - gain, as if I

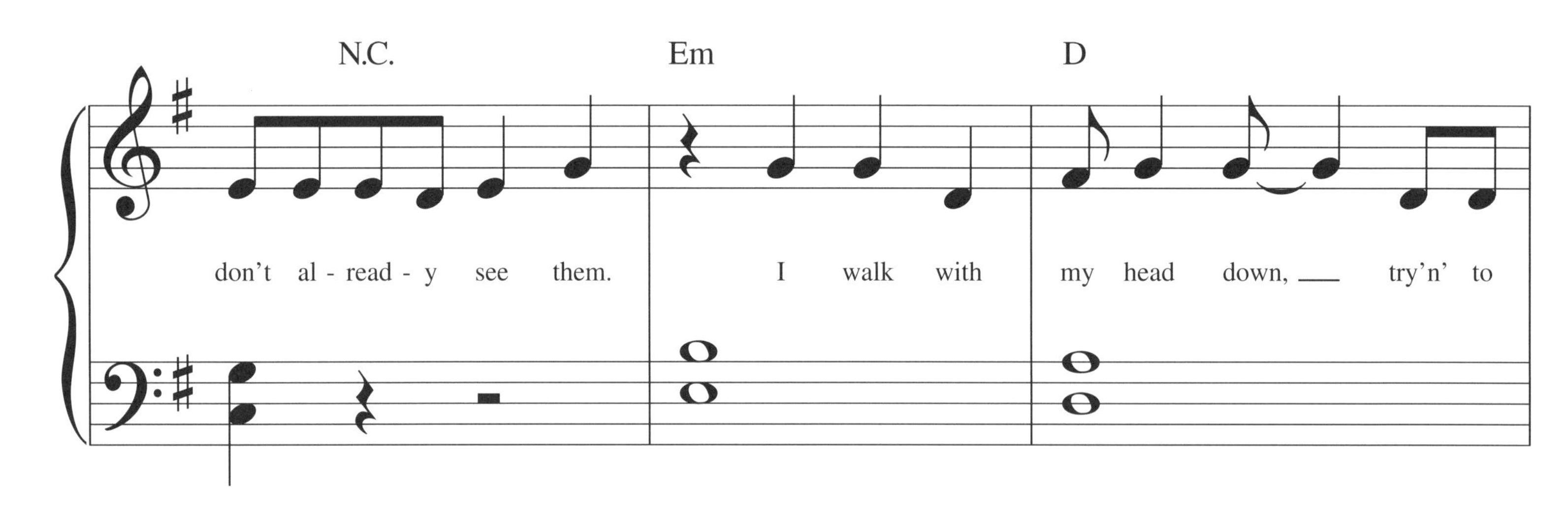
N.C.
Em
D
don't al - read - y see them. I walk with my head down, try'n' to

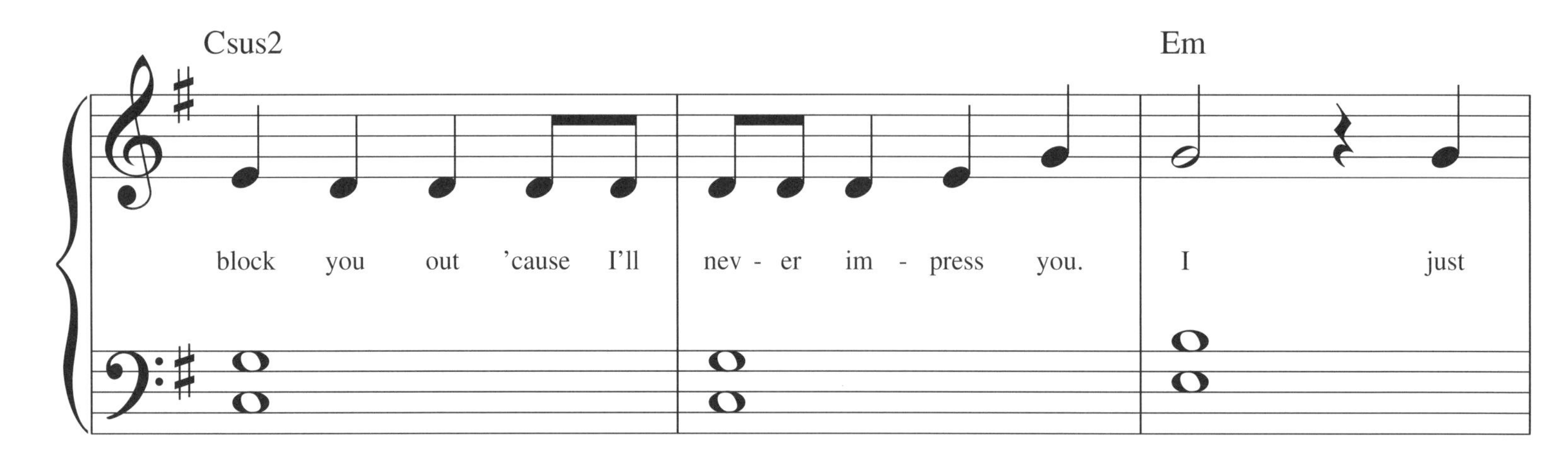
Csus2
Em
block you out 'cause I'll nev - er im - press you. I just

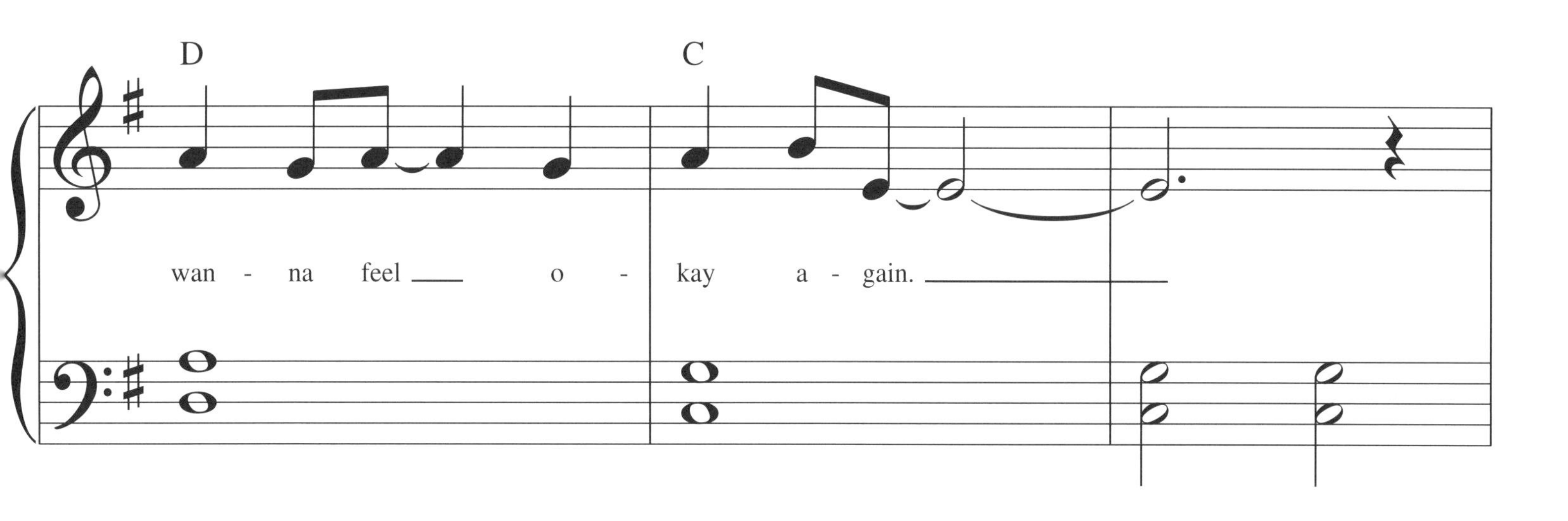
D
C
wan - na feel ___ o - kay a - gain. ___

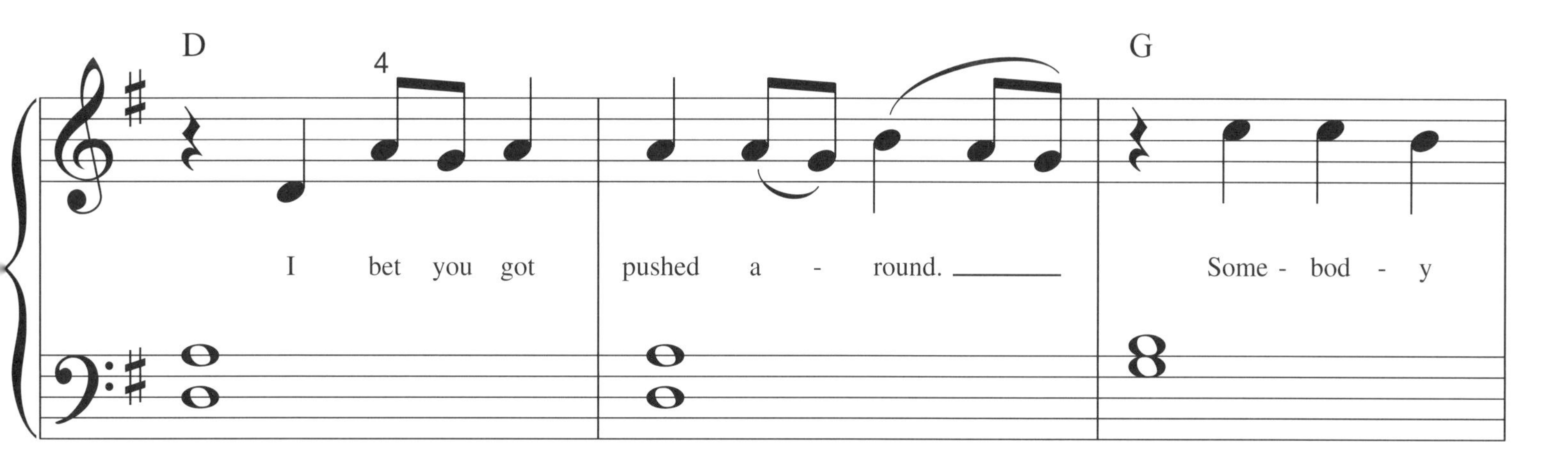
D
4
G
I bet you got pushed a - round. ___ Some - bod - y

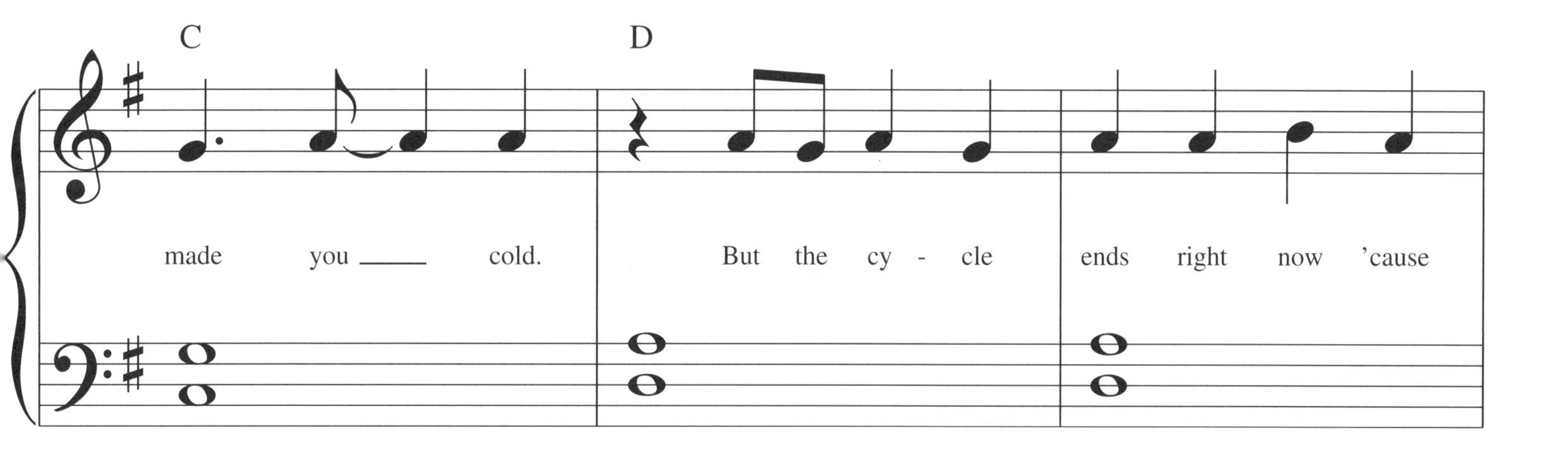
C
D
made you ___ cold. But the cy - cle ends right now 'cause

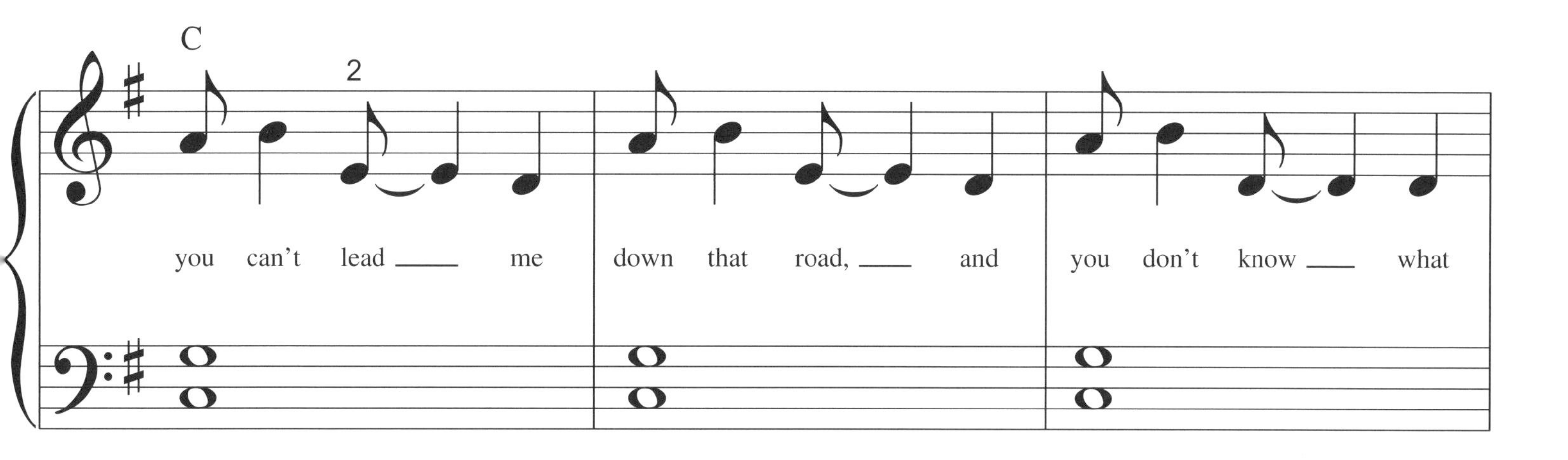
C
2
you can't lead ___ me down that road, ___ and you don't know ___ what

D.S. al Coda
CODA
F
G
you don't know.
D
And I can
see you years from
now in a bar,
G
C
D
talk - ing o - ver a
foot - ball game
with that same big,

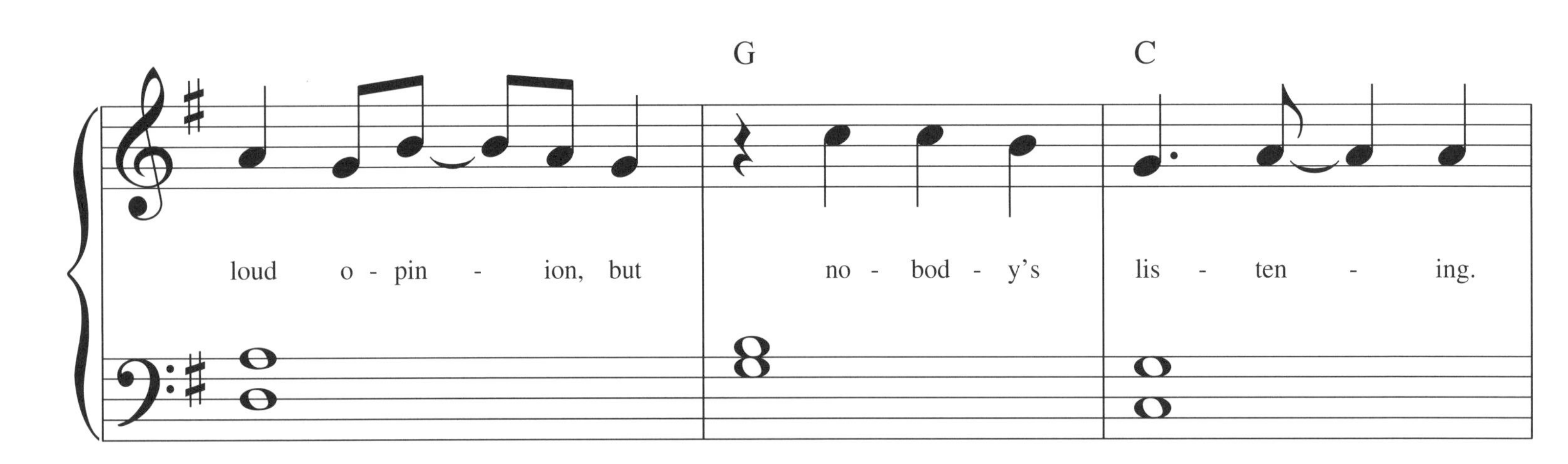
G
C
loud o - pin - ion, but
no - bod - y's
lis - ten - ing.

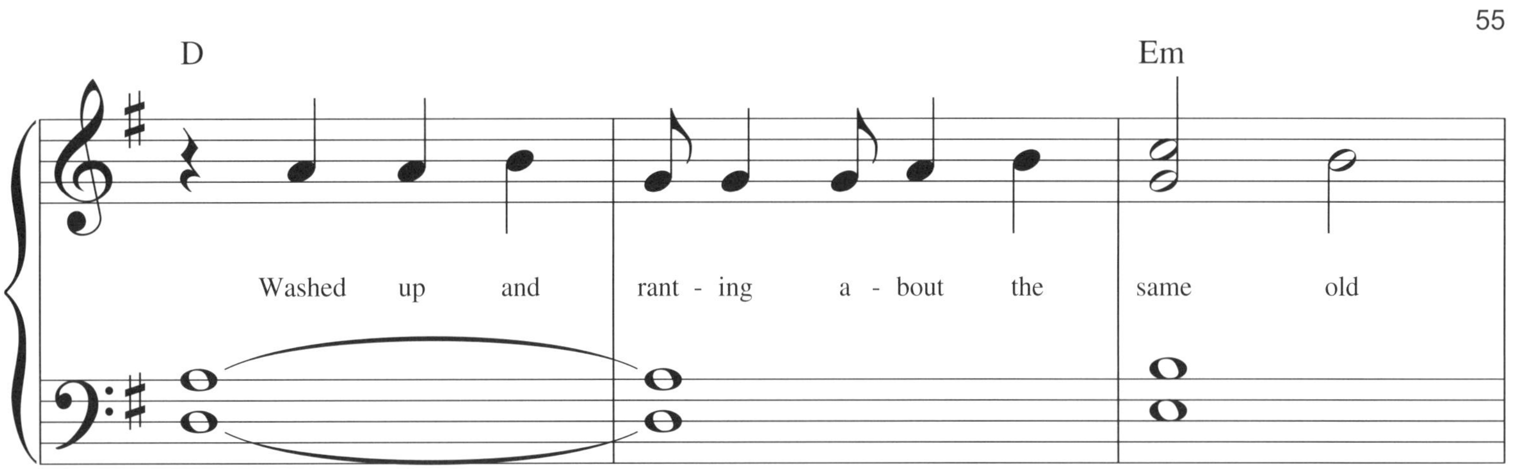
D
Em
Washed up and rant - ing a - bout the same old

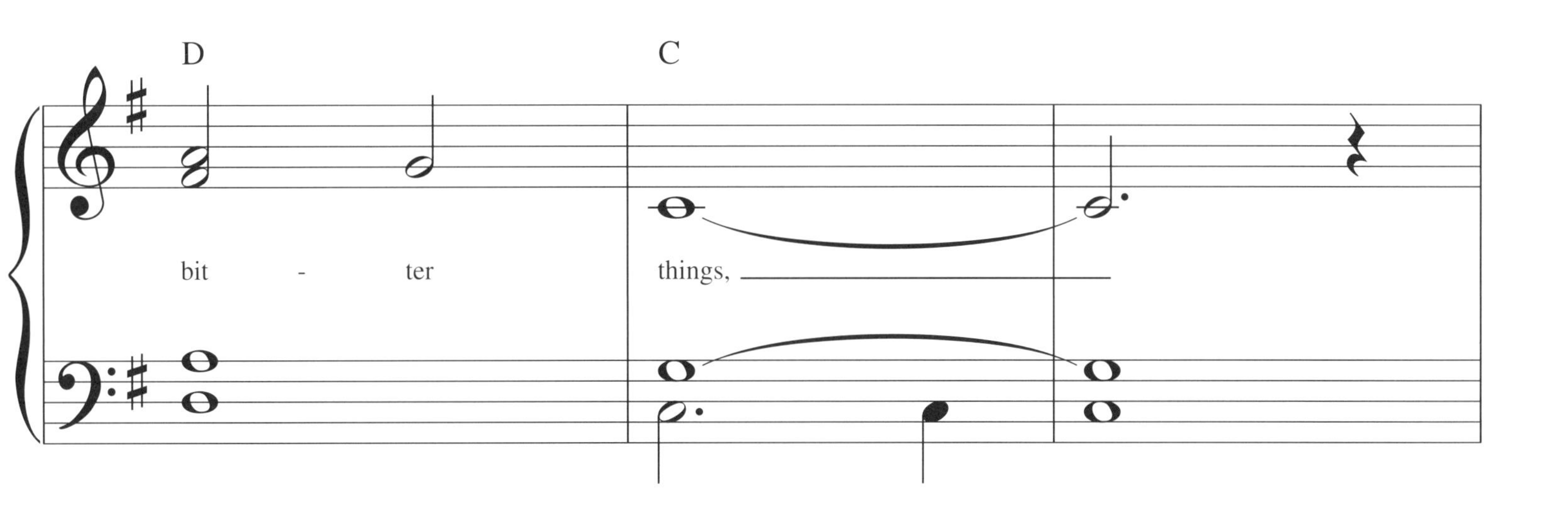
D
C
bit - ter things,

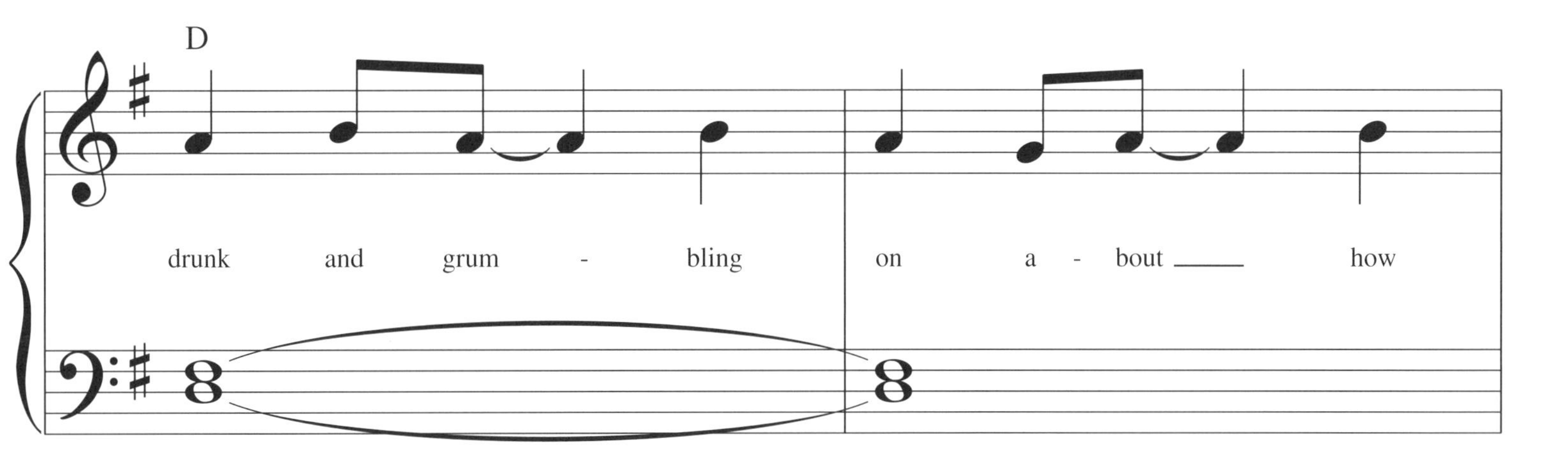
D
drunk and grum - bling on a - bout how

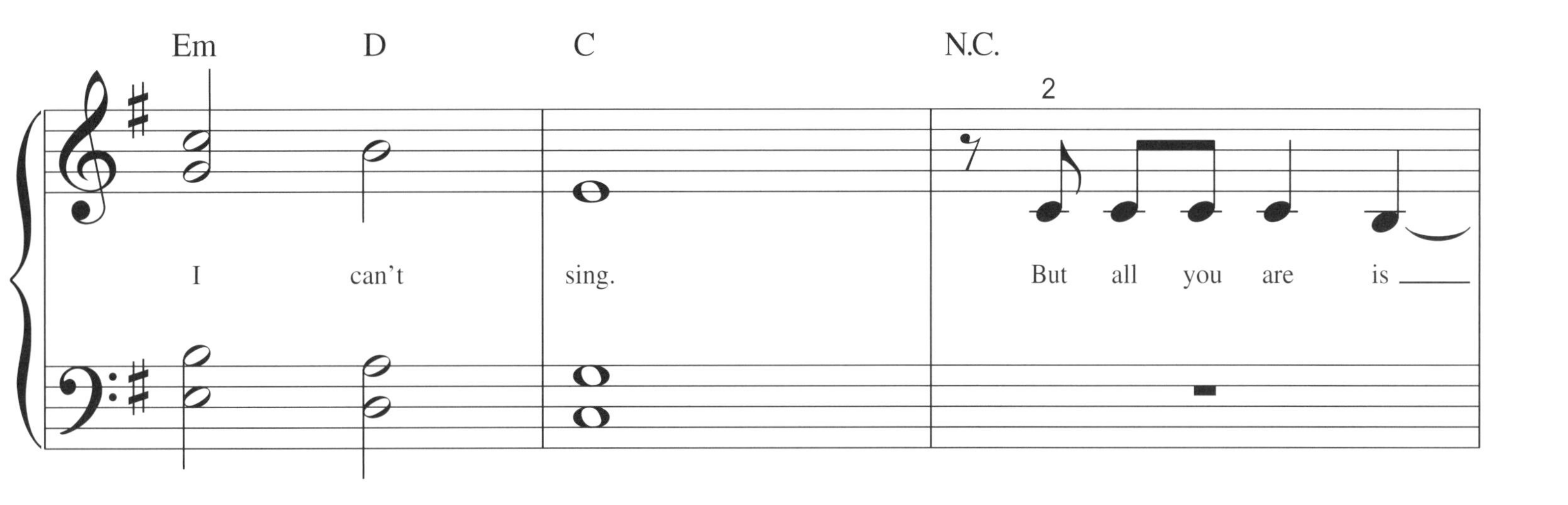
Em
D
C
N.C.
2
I can't sing. But all you are is

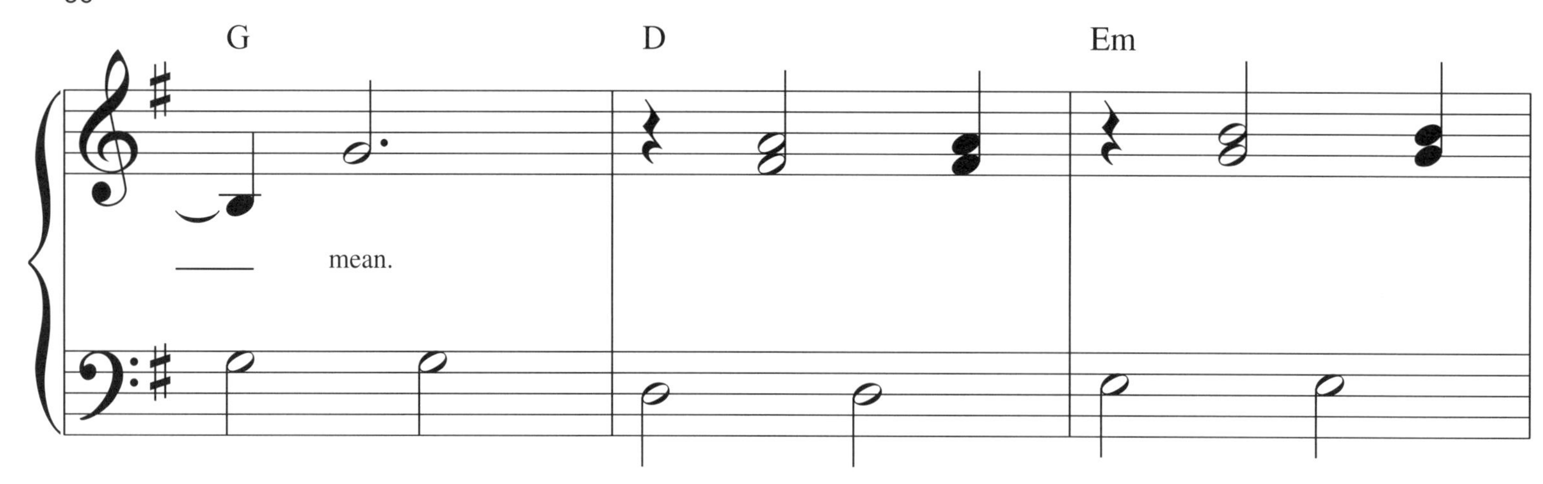
G
D
Em
mean.

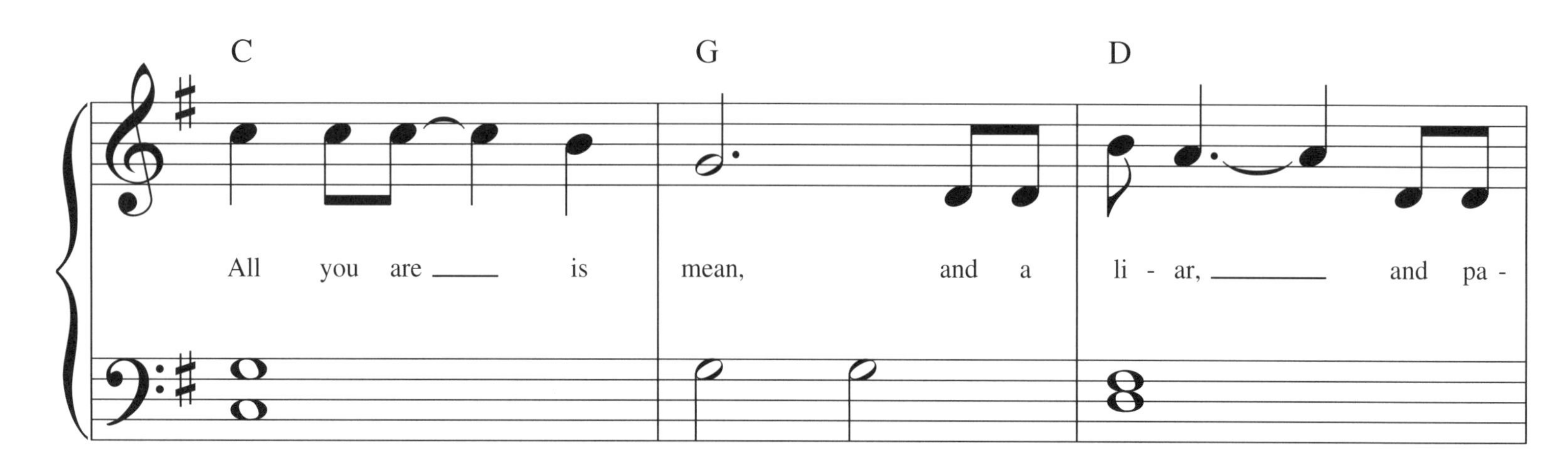
C
G
D
All you are is mean, and a li - ar, and pa -

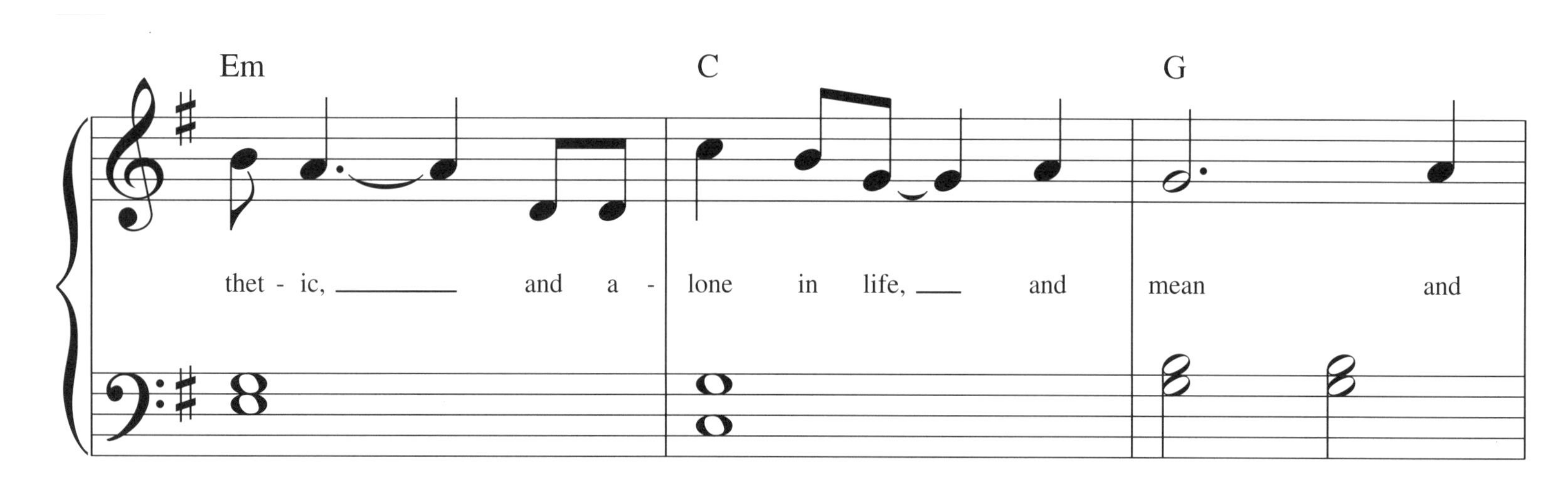
Em
C
G
thet - ic, and a - lone in life, and mean and

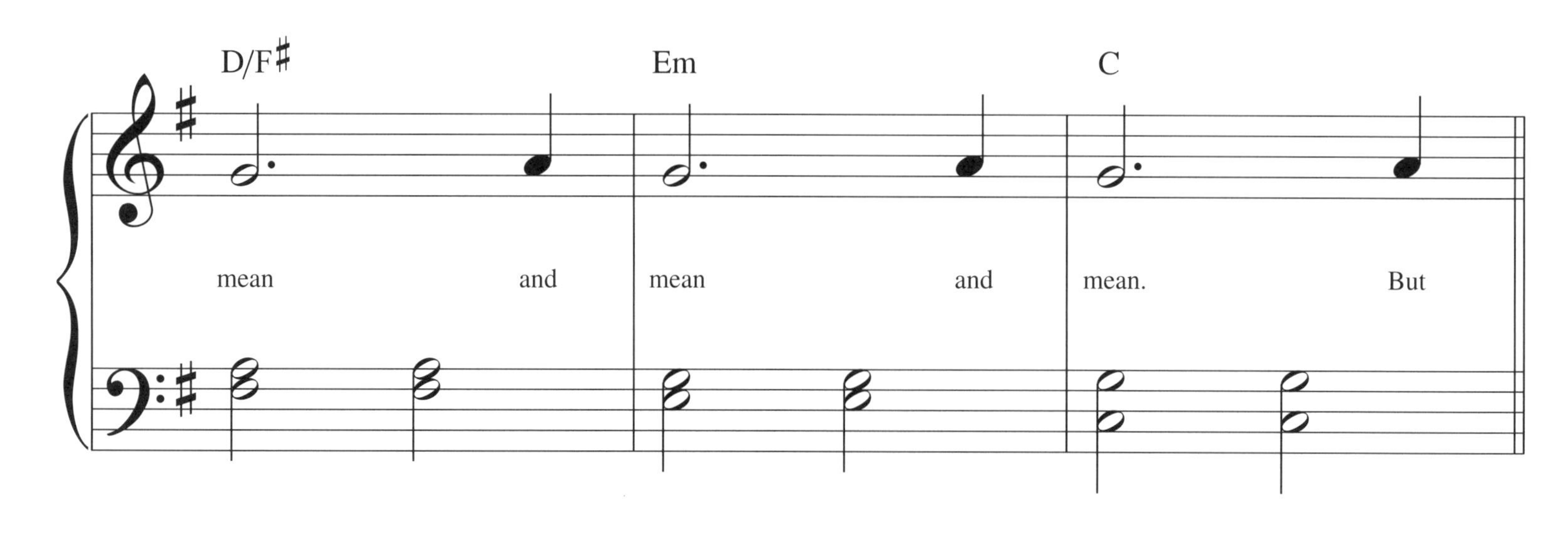
D/F♯
Em
C
mean and mean and mean. But

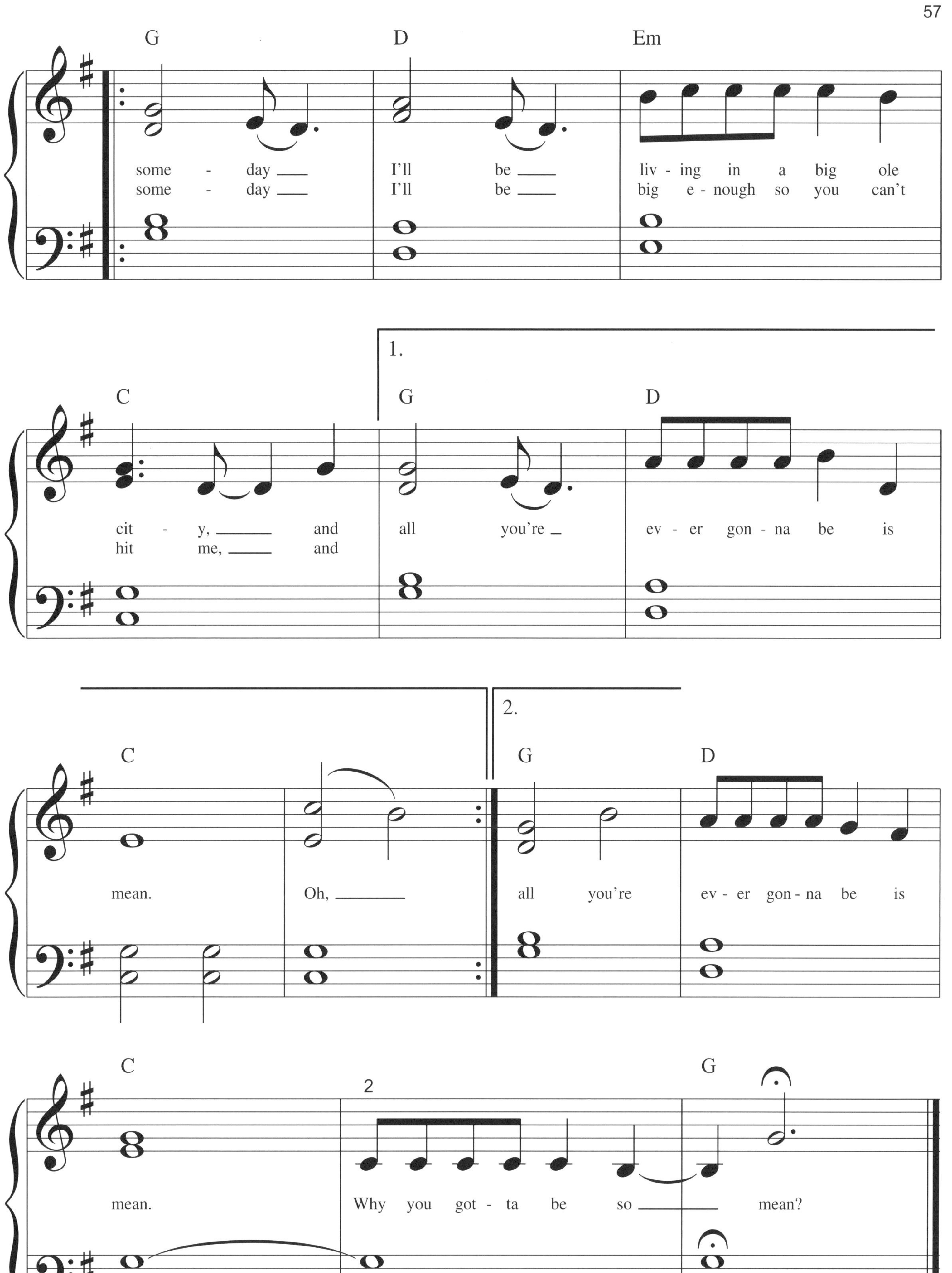
G
D
Em
some - day
I'll
be
liv - ing in a big ole
some - day
I'll
be
big e - nough so you can't
1.
C
G
D
cit - y,
and
all
you're
ev - er gon - na be is
hit
me,
and
2.
C
G
D
mean.
Oh,
all
you're
ev - er gon - na be is
C
2
G
mean.
Why you got - ta be so
mean?

MINE

Words and Music by
TAYLOR SWIFT

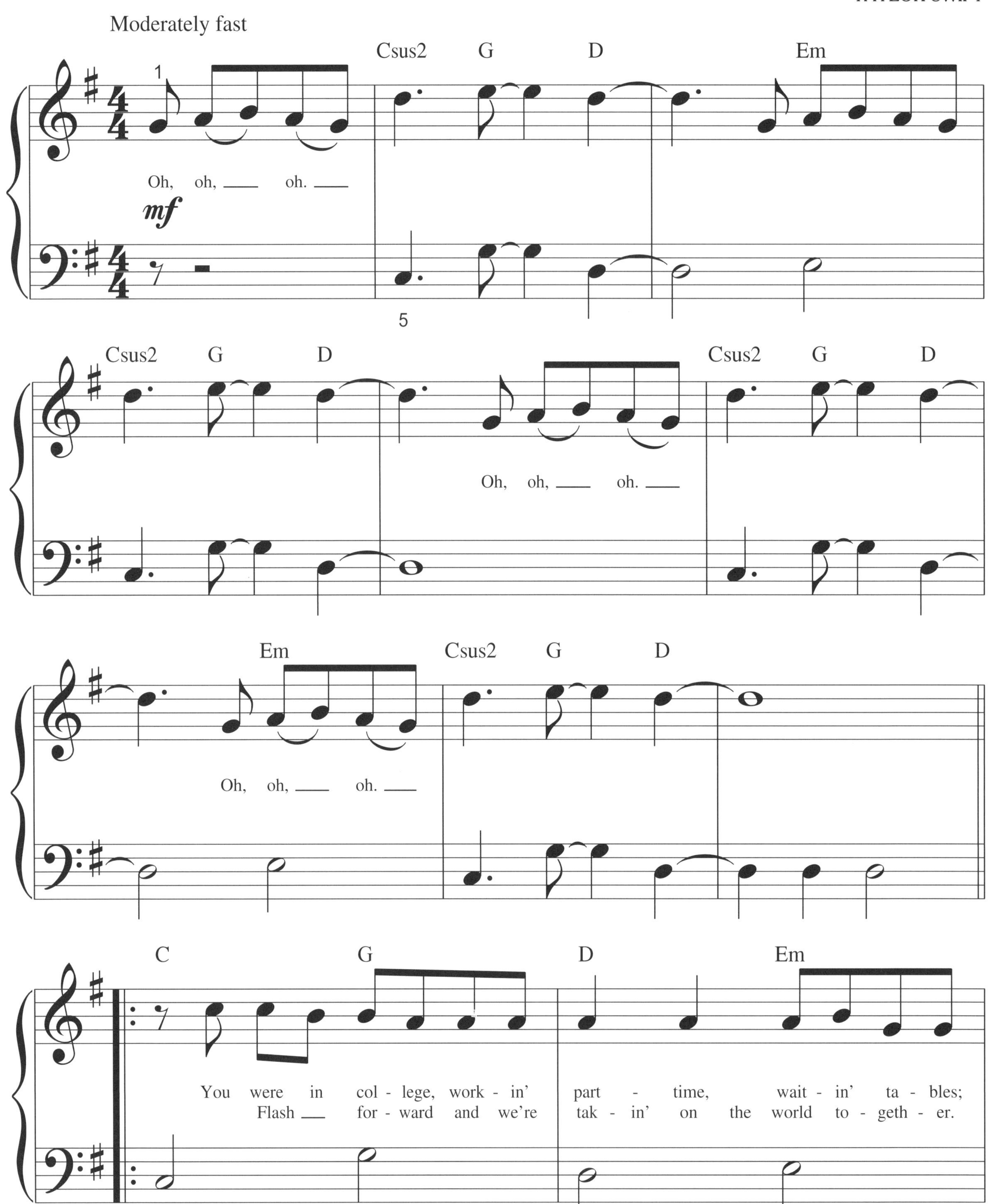

C G D Em C G
2
left a small __ town, nev - er looked back. __ I was a flight __ risk
And there's a drawer __ of my things at your place. You learn my se - crets and you fig-
D Em C G D Em
with a fear of fall - in', won - d'rin' why we'd both - er with love if it nev - er lasts.
ure out why I'm guard - ed. You say we'll nev - er make my par - ents' mis - takes. ___
Csus2 G D Csus2 G D
I say, ___ "Can you be - lieve __ it?"
But we got bills to pay;

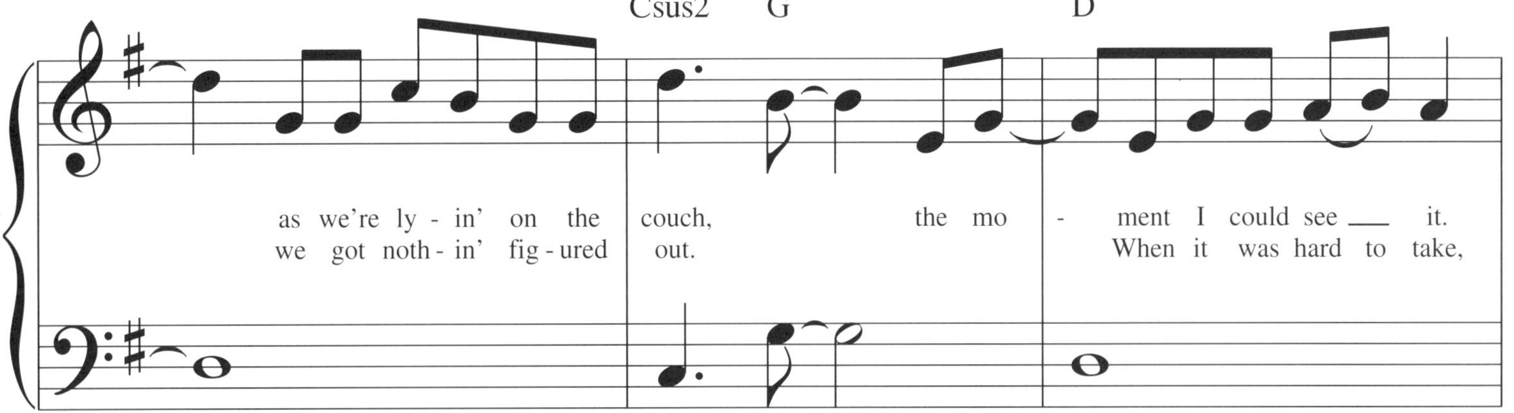
Csus2 G D
as we're ly - in' on the couch, the mo - ment I could see __ it.
we got noth - in' fig - ured out. When it was hard to take,

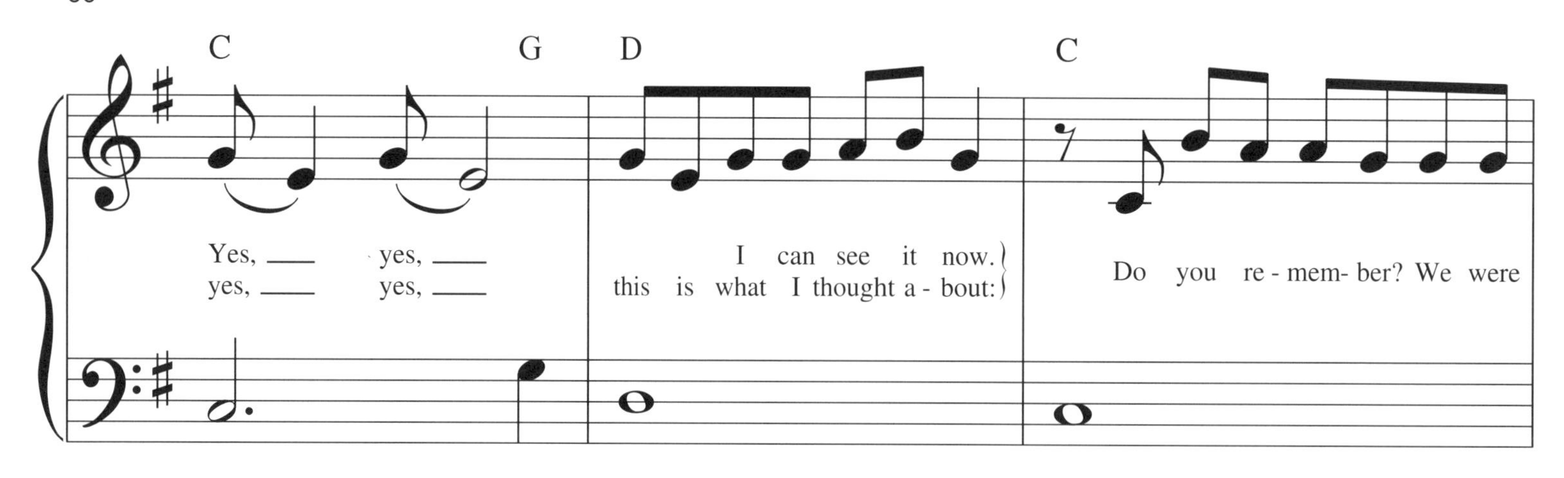
C
G
D
C
Yes, ___ yes, ___
yes, ___ yes, ___
I can see it now.
this is what I thought a - bout:
Do you re - mem- ber? We were

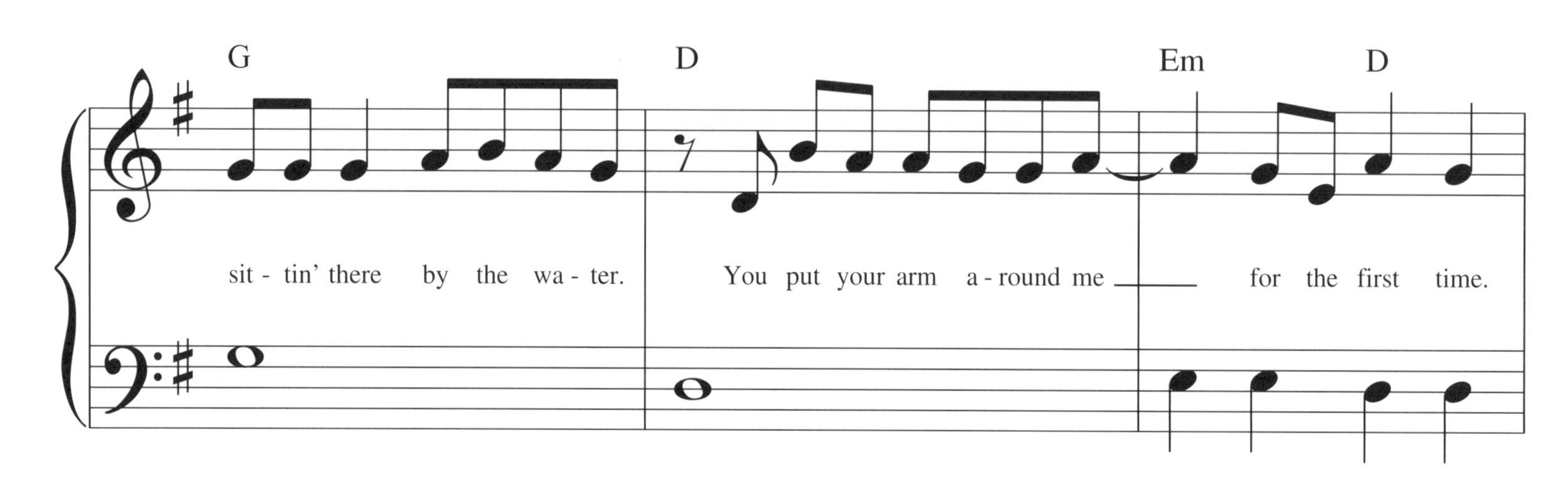
G
D
Em
D
sit - tin' there by the wa - ter.
You put your arm a - round me ___
for the first time.

C
G
D
You made a reb - el of a
care - less man's care - ful daugh- ter.
You are the best thing

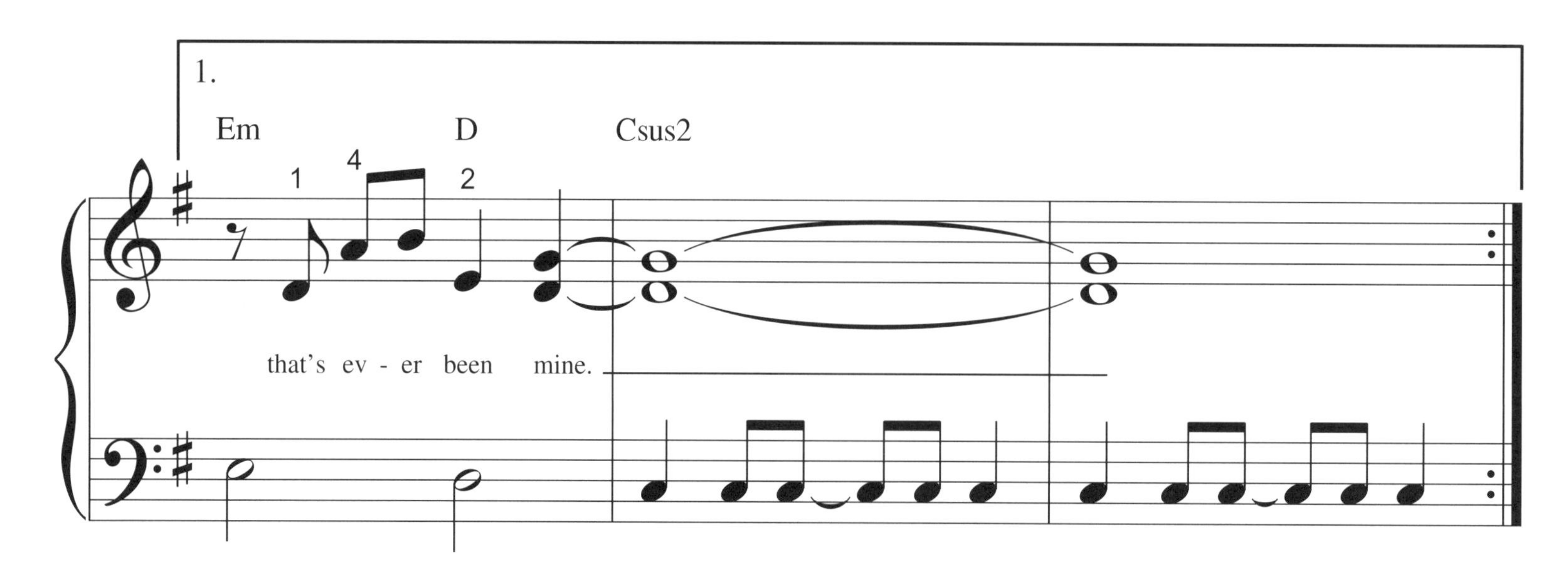
1.
Em
D
Csus2
1
4
2
that's ev - er been mine. ___

2.
Em
D
C
1
4
2
that's ev - er been mine.
Do you re - mem - ber all the
G
D
cit - y lights on the wa - ter?
You saw me start to be - lieve
Em
D
C
for the first time.
You made a reb - el of a
G
D
Em
D
care - less man's care - ful daugh - ter.
You are the best thing
that's ev - er been mine.

Csus2 G D Em Csus2 G D
Oh, oh, oh.

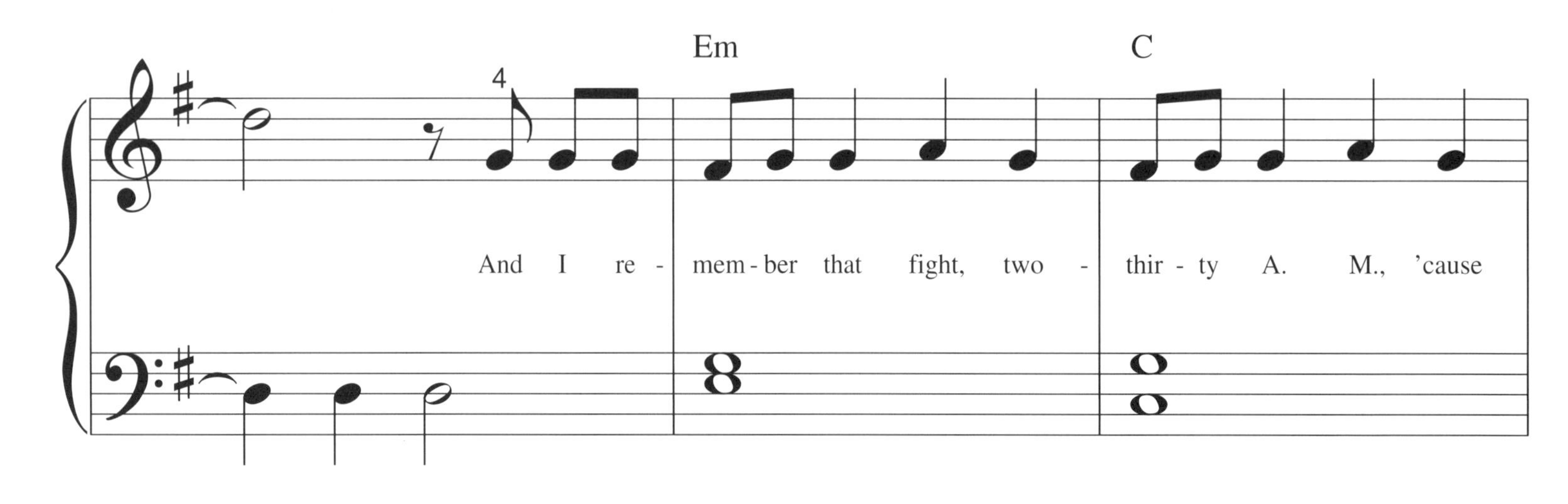
Em C
4
And I re - mem - ber that fight, two - thir - ty A. M., 'cause

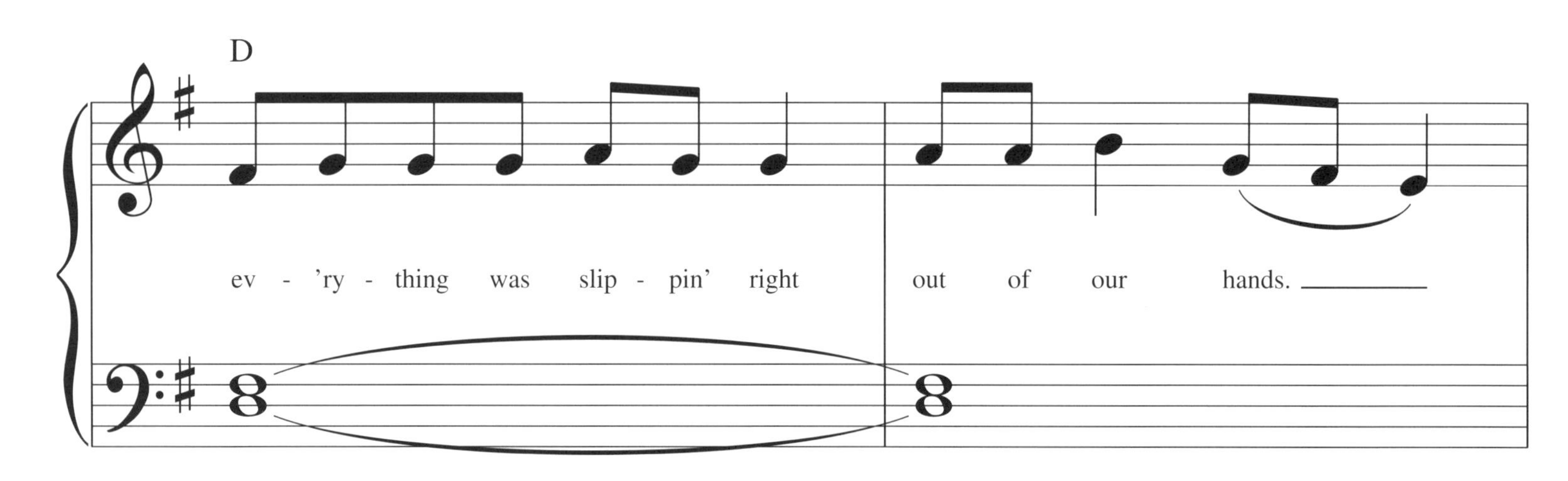
D
ev - 'ry - thing was slip - pin' right out of our hands.

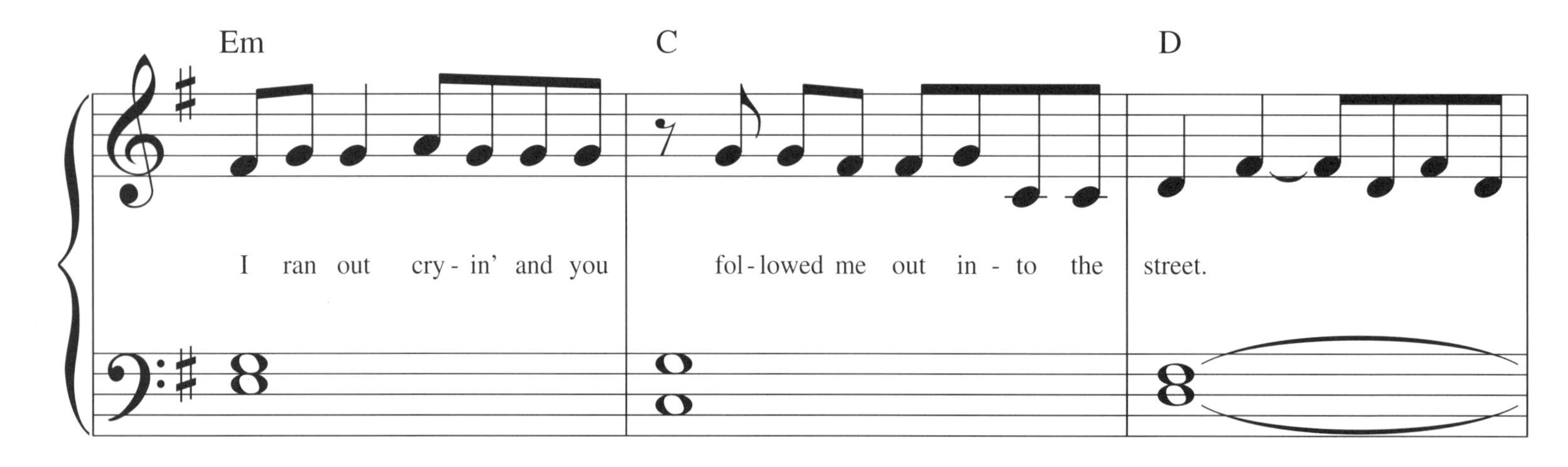
Em C D
I ran out cry - in' and you fol - lowed me out in - to the street.

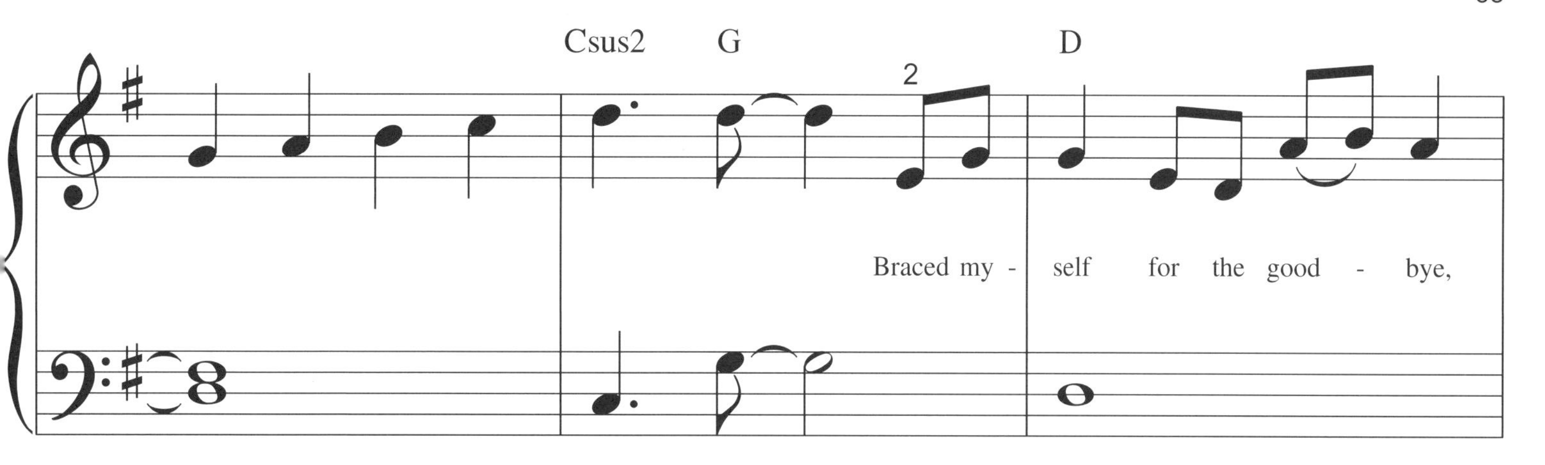
Csus2
G
D
2
Braced my - self for the good - bye,

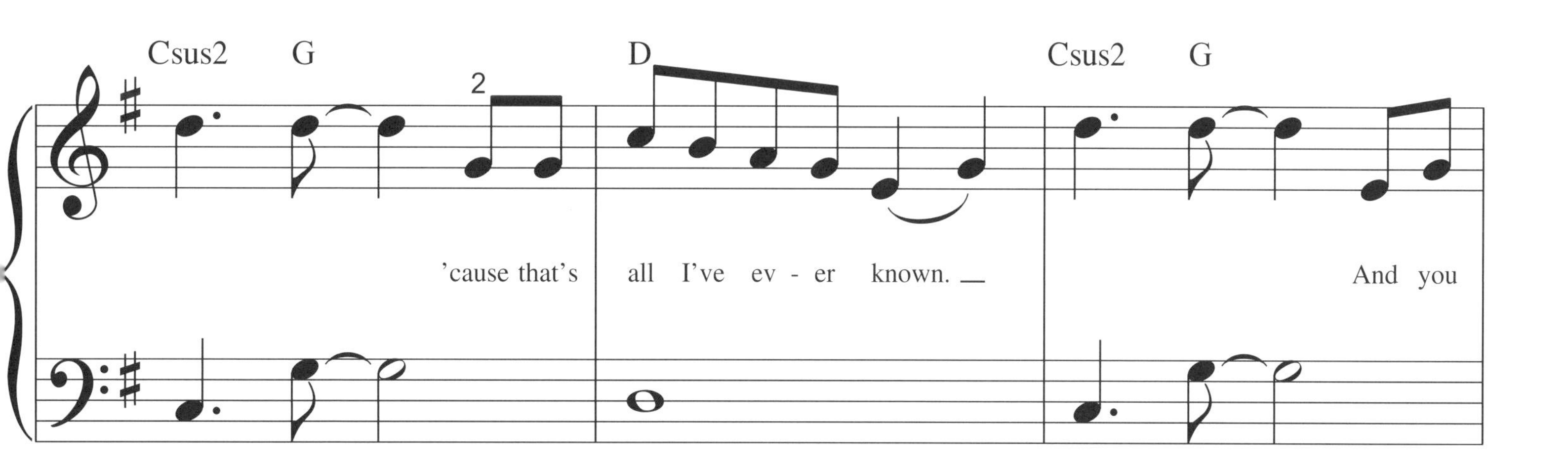
Csus2
G
D
Csus2
G
2
'cause that's all I've ev - er known. And you

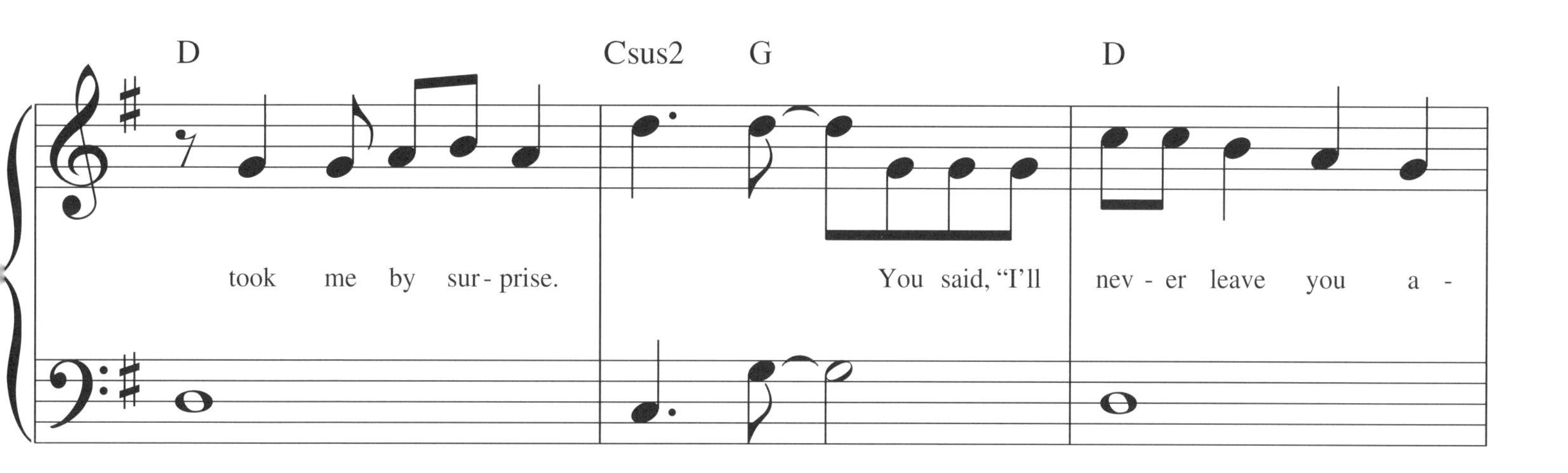
D
Csus2
G
D
took me by sur - prise. You said, "I'll nev - er leave you a -

C
lone." You said, "I re - mem - ber how we

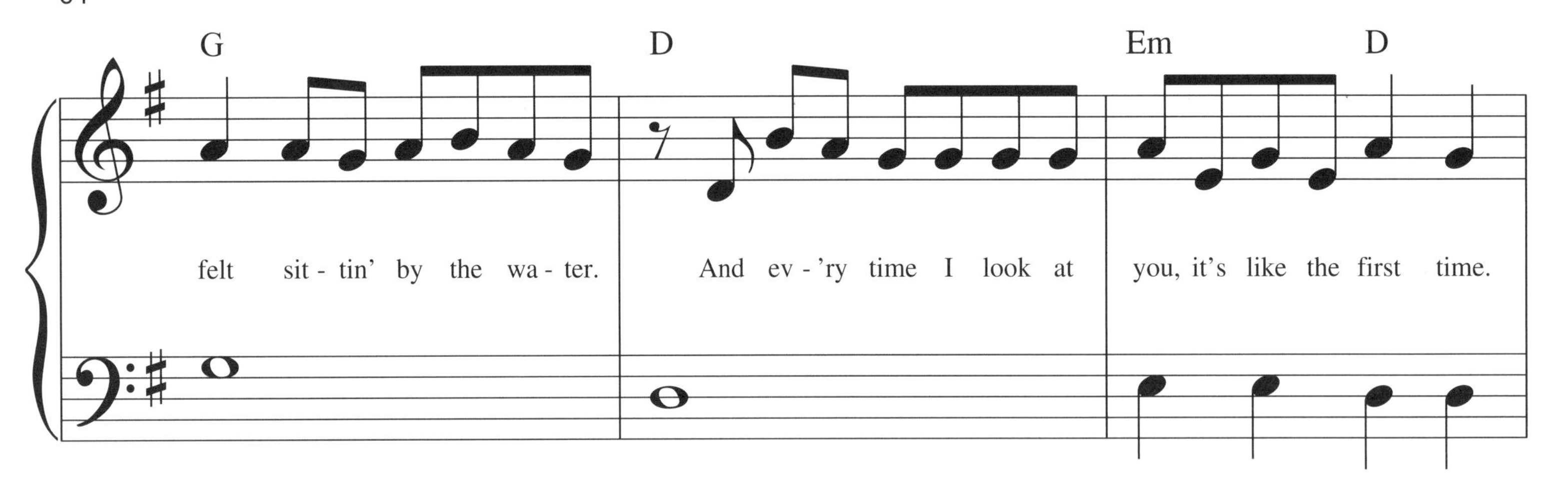
G
D
Em
D
felt sit - tin' by the wa - ter.
And ev - 'ry time I look at
you, it's like the first time.

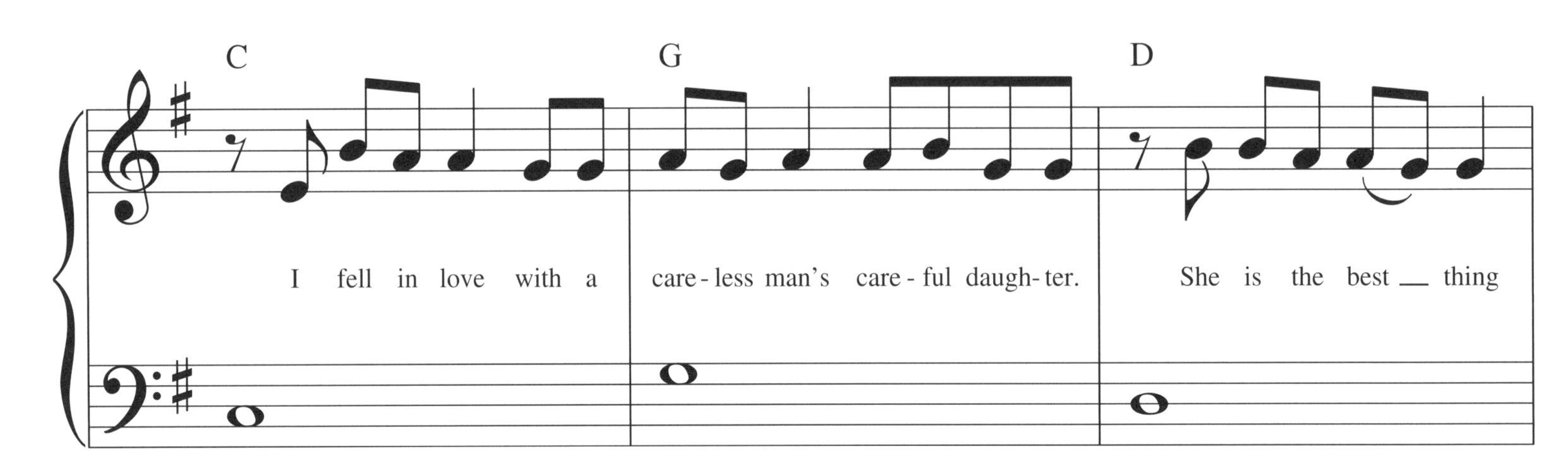
C
G
D
I fell in love with a
care - less man's care - ful daugh - ter.
She is the best thing

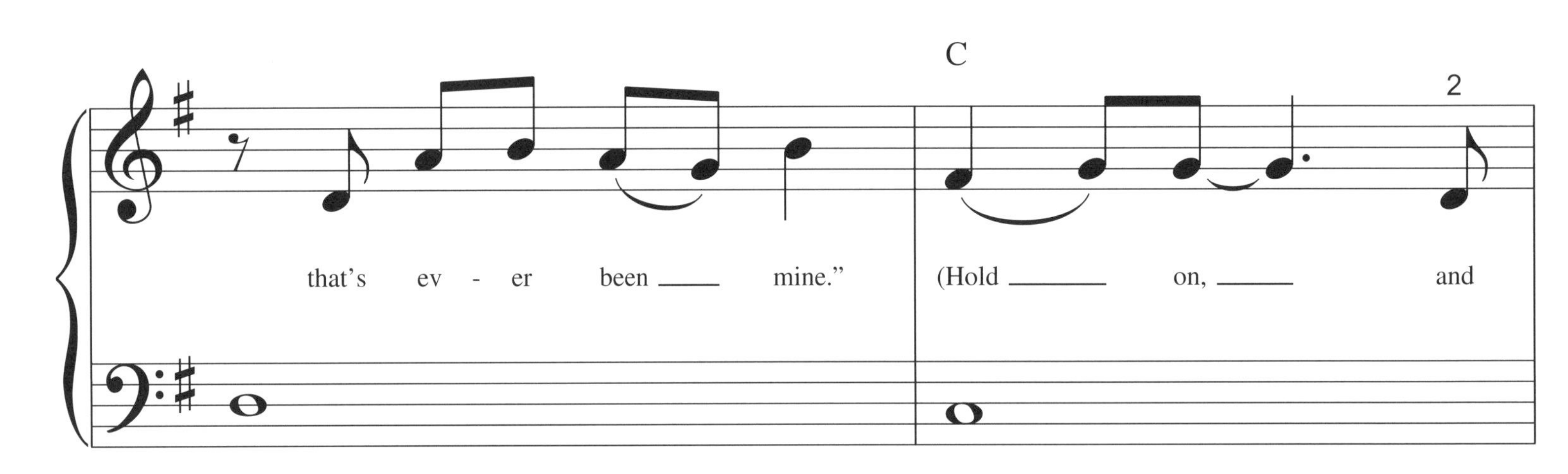
C
2
that's ev - er been mine."
(Hold on, and

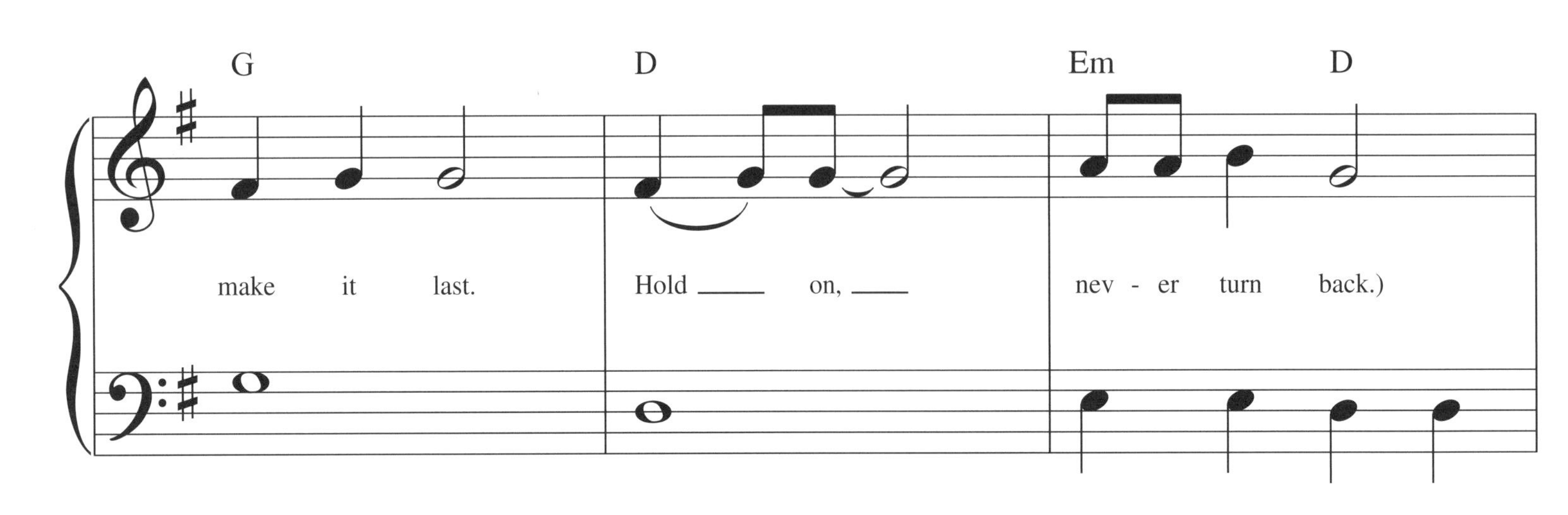
G
D
Em
D
make it last.
Hold on,
nev - er turn back.)

Csus2
G
D
You made a reb - el of a
care - less man's care - ful daugh - ter.
You are the best thing

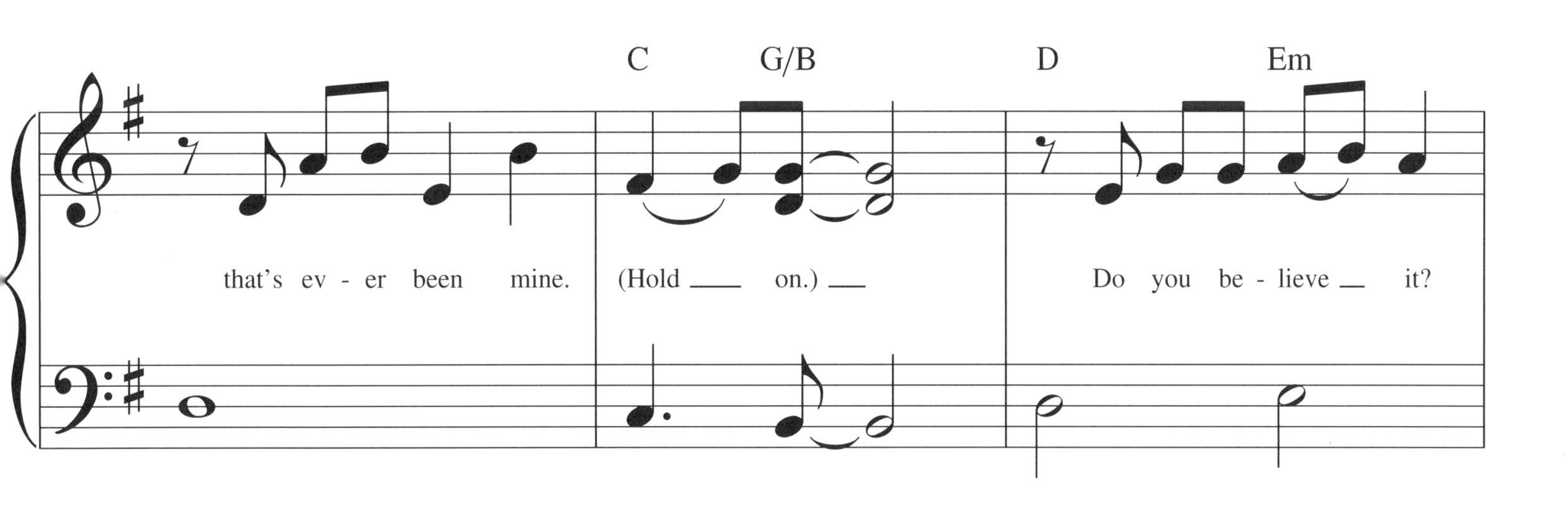
C
G/B
D
Em
that's ev - er been mine.
(Hold on.)
Do you be - lieve it?

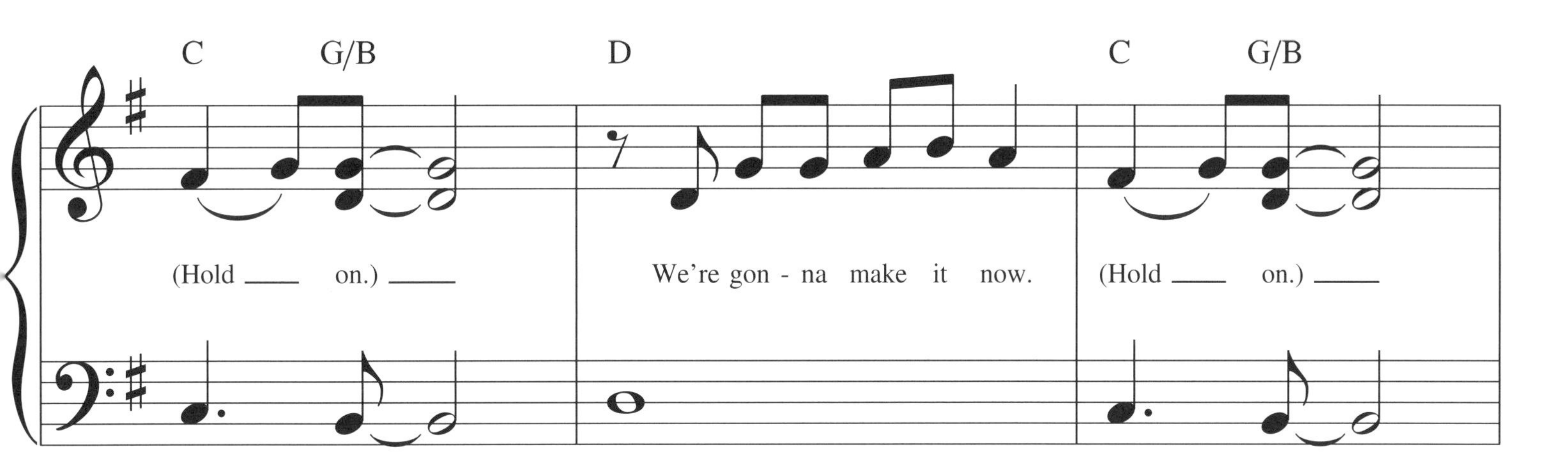
C
G/B
D
C
G/B
(Hold on.)
We're gon - na make it now.
(Hold on.)

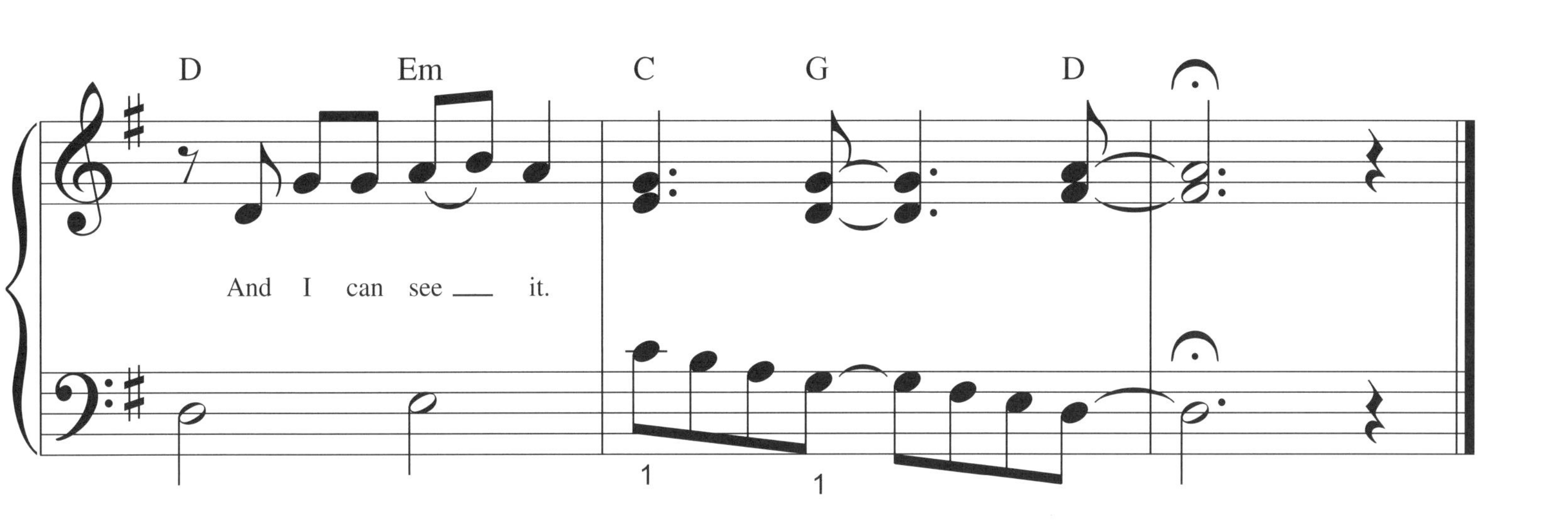
D
Em
C
G
D
And I can see it.
1
1

RED

Words and Music by
TAYLOR SWIFT

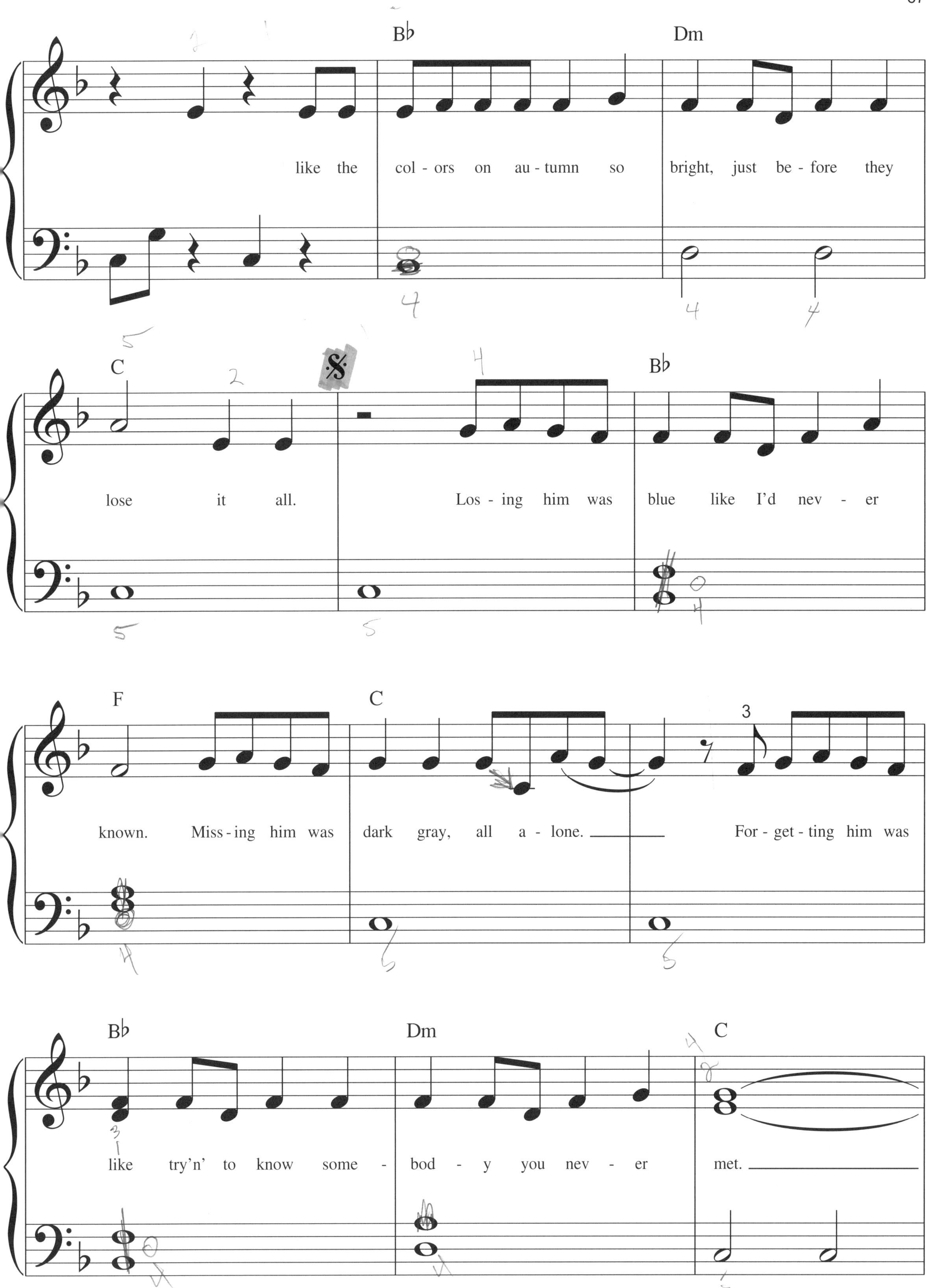
B♭
Dm
like the col - ors on au - tumn so bright, just be - fore they
C
B♭
lose it all. Los - ing him was blue like I'd nev - er
F
C
3
known. Miss - ing him was dark gray, all a - lone. For - get - ting him was
B♭
Dm
C
like try'n' to know some - bod - y you nev - er met.

To Coda
B♭
Dm
C
Dm
C
B♭
Dm
C
But lov - ing him was red.
Lov - ing him was red.
Touch-ing him was like
re - al - iz - ing all you ev - er want-ed was right there in front of you.

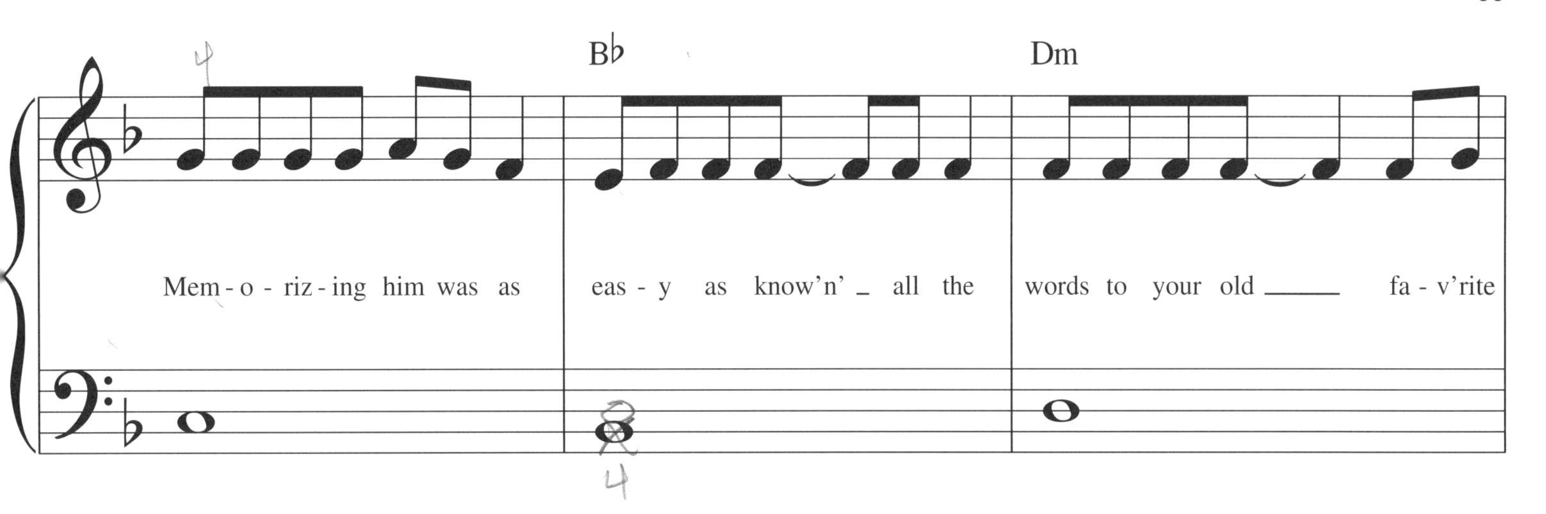
B♭
Dm
Mem - o - riz - ing him was as
eas - y as know'n' all the
words to your old fa - v'rite

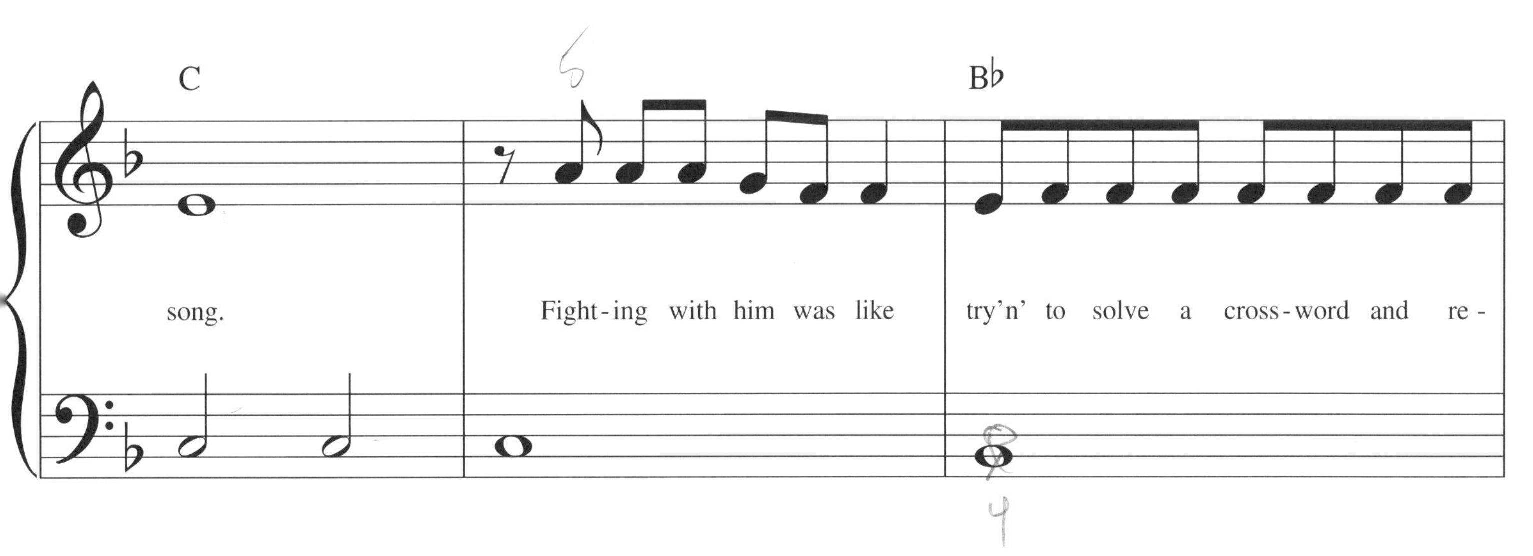
C
B♭
song.
Fight - ing with him was like
try'n' to solve a cross - word and re -

Dm
C
al - iz - in' there's no right
an - swer.
Re - gret - ting him was like

B♭
Dm
C
D.S. al Coda
wish - ing you nev - er found
out that love could be
that strong.

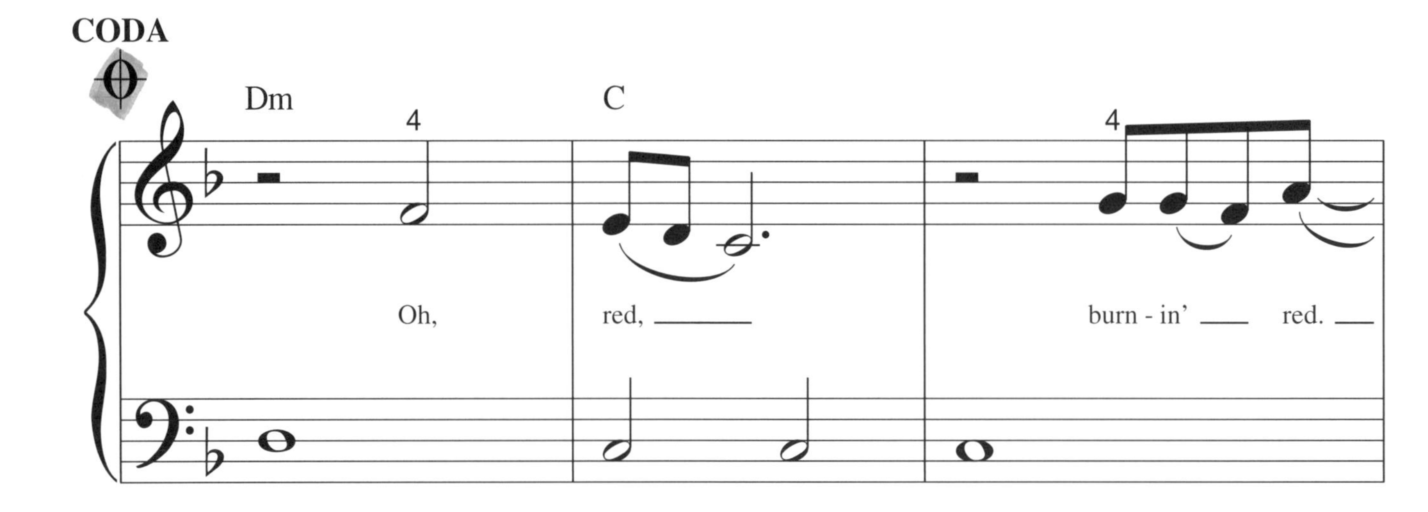
CODA
Dm
C
4
4
Oh, red, burn - in' red.

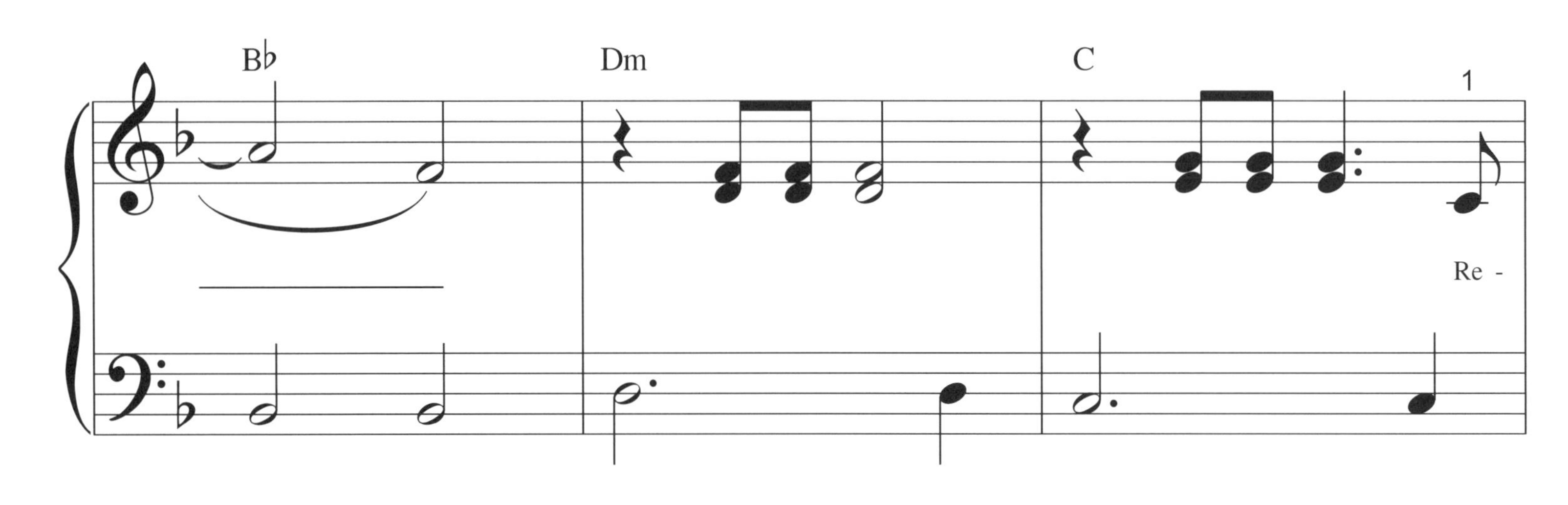
B♭
Dm
C
1
Re -

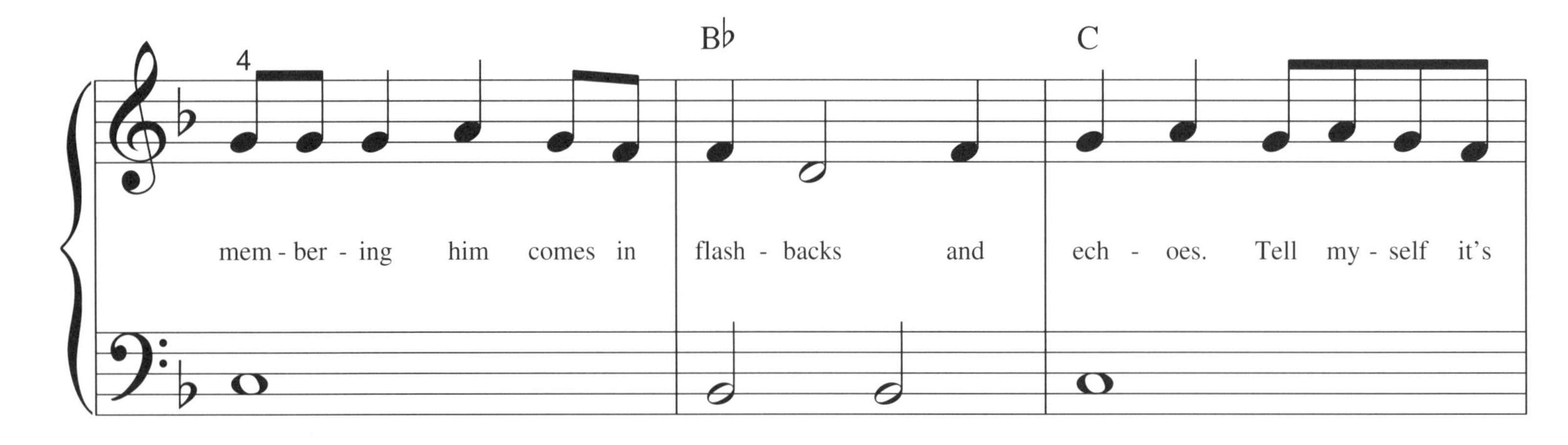
4
B♭
C
mem - ber - ing him comes in flash - backs and ech - oes. Tell my - self it's

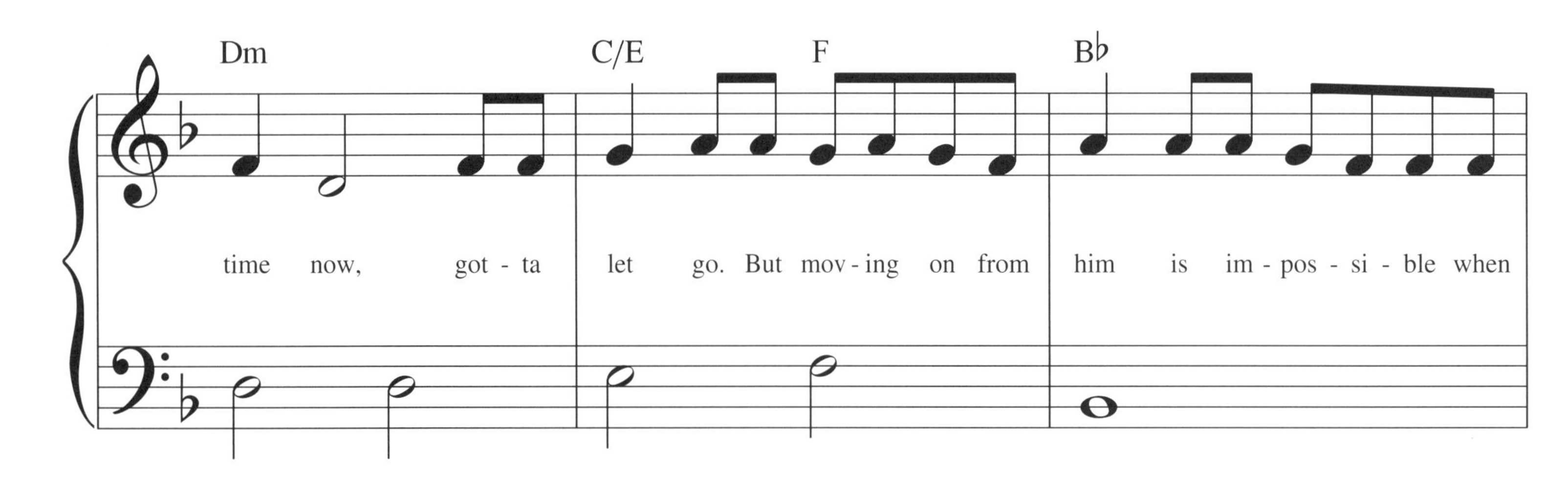
Dm
C/E
F
B♭
time now, got - ta let go. But mov - ing on from him is im - pos - si - ble when

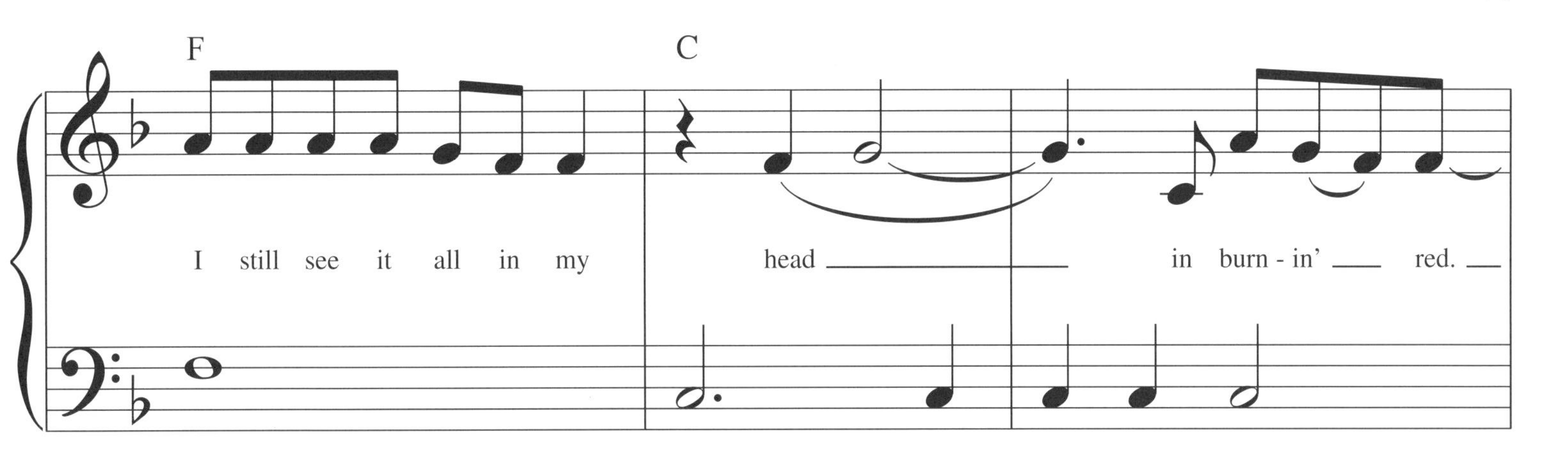
F
C
I still see it all in my
head
in burn - in' red.

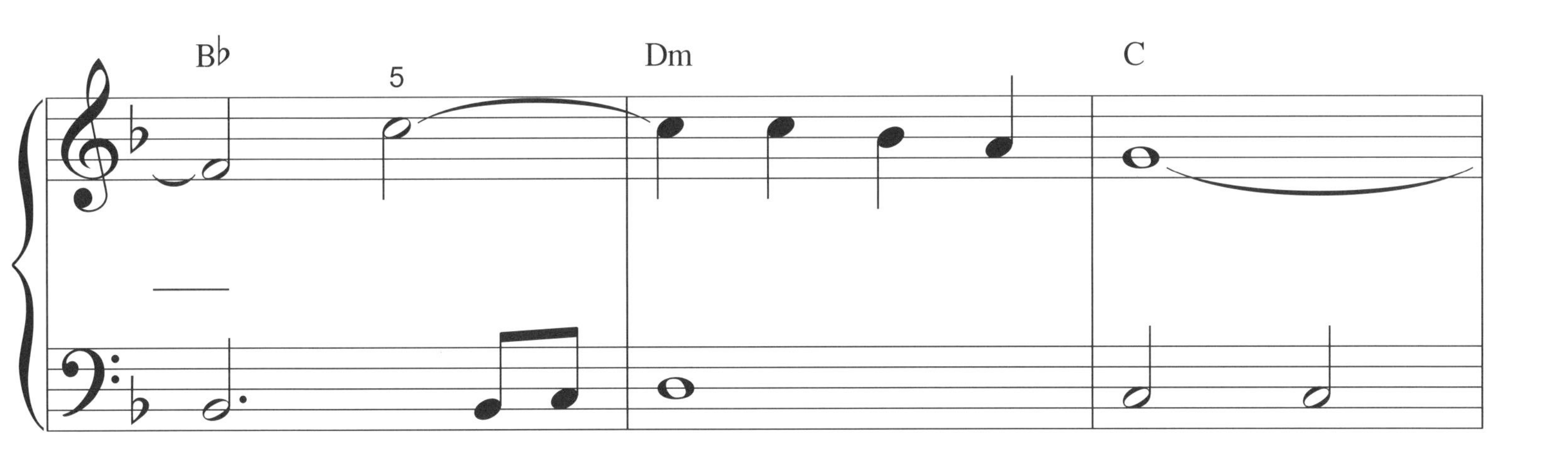
B♭
5
Dm
C

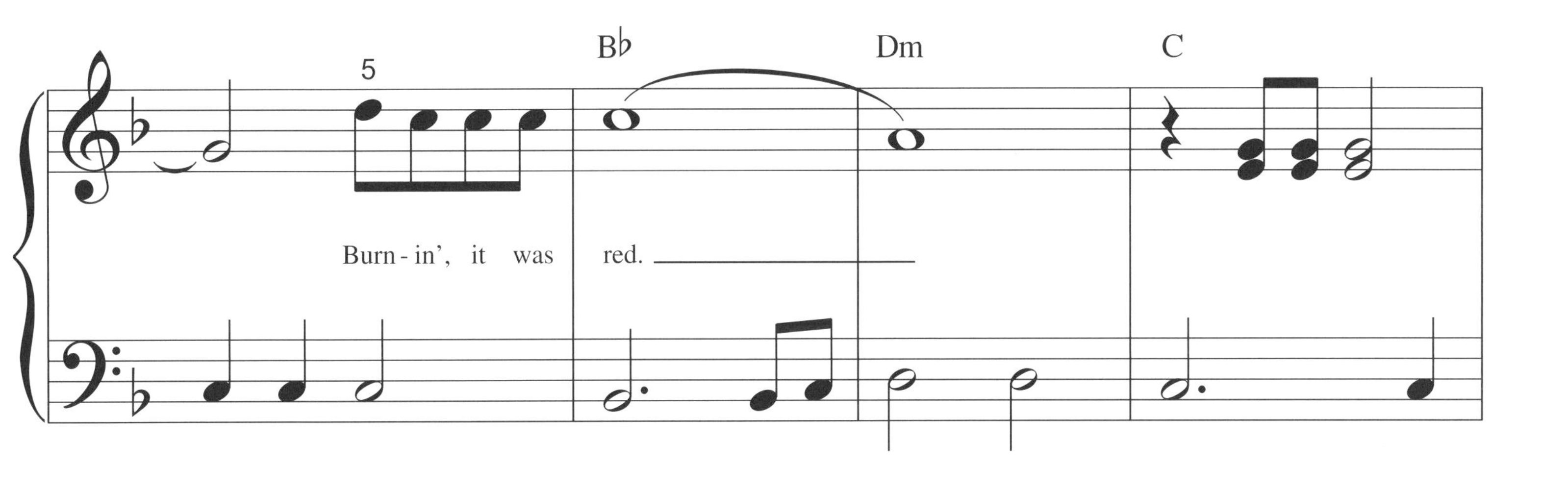
5
B♭
Dm
C
Burn - in', it was
red.

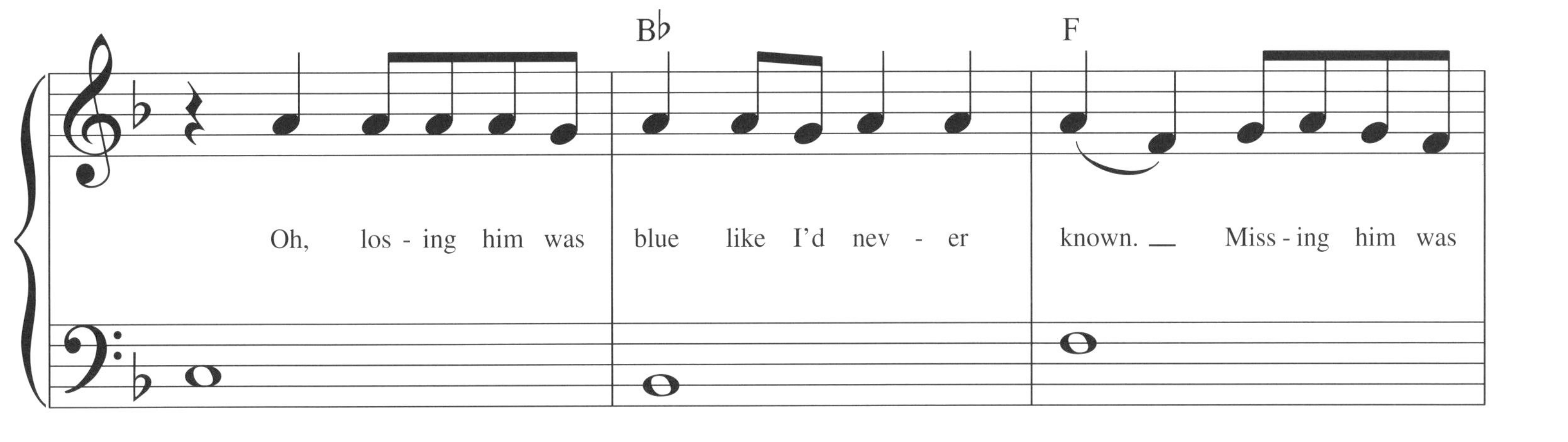
B♭
F
Oh, los - ing him was
blue like I'd nev - er
known. Miss - ing him was

C
B♭
dark gray, all a - lone.
For - get - ting him was
like try'n' to know some -

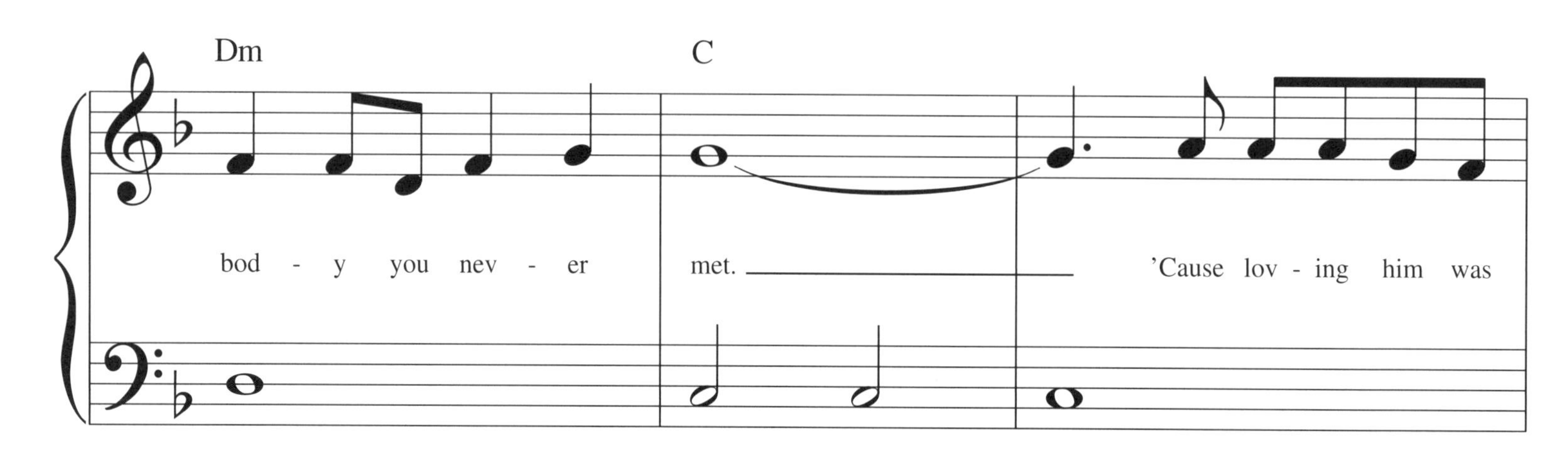
Dm
C
bod - y you nev - er
met.
'Cause lov - ing him was

B♭
Dm
C
2
red,
yeah,
yeah,
red.

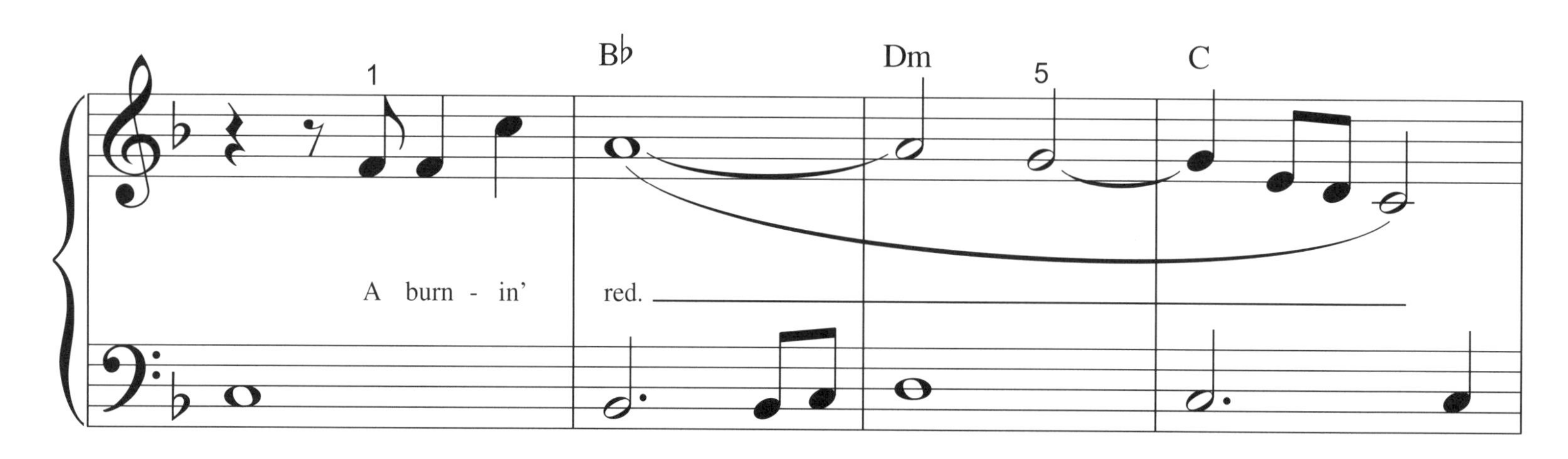
1
B♭
Dm
5
C
A burn - in'
red.

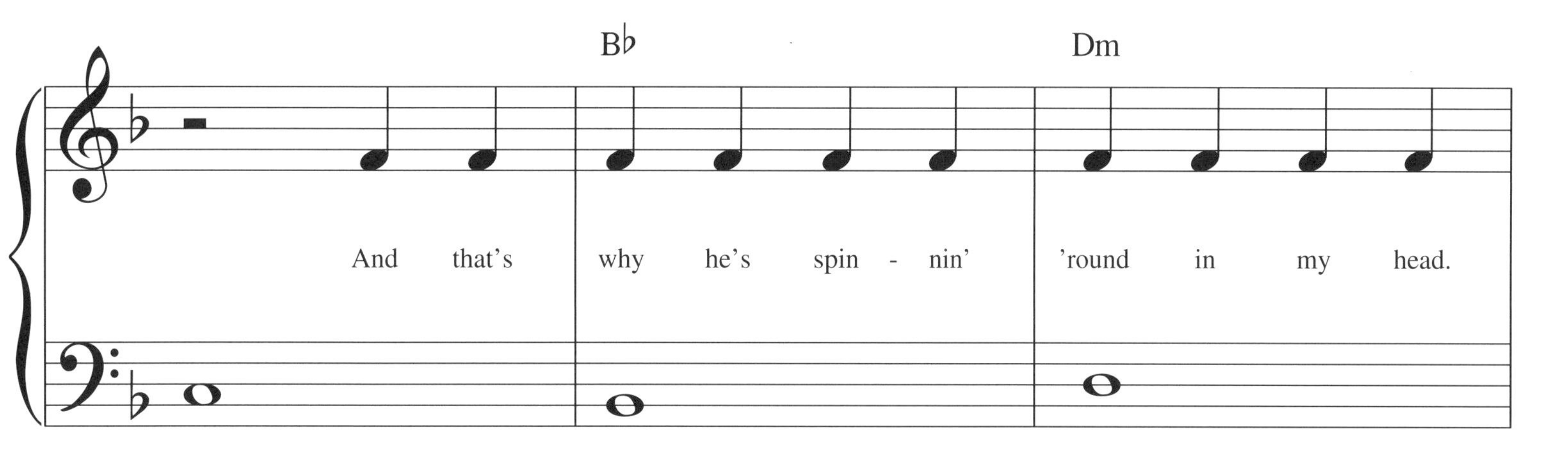

B♭
Dm
And that's why he's spin - nin' 'round in my head.

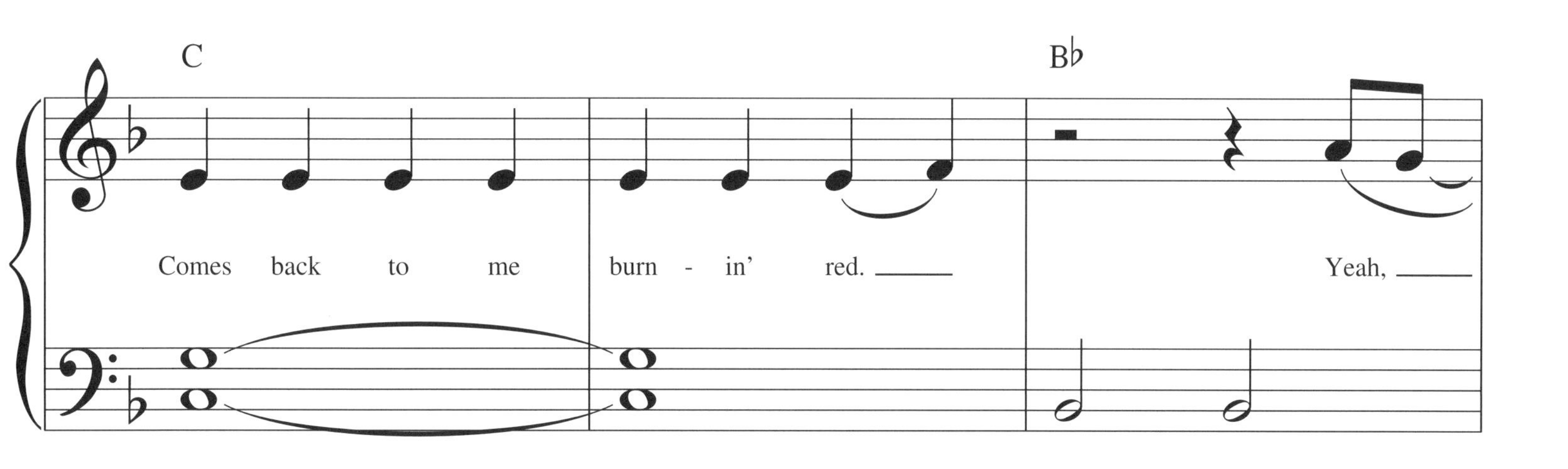

C
B♭
Comes back to me burn - in' red.
Yeah,

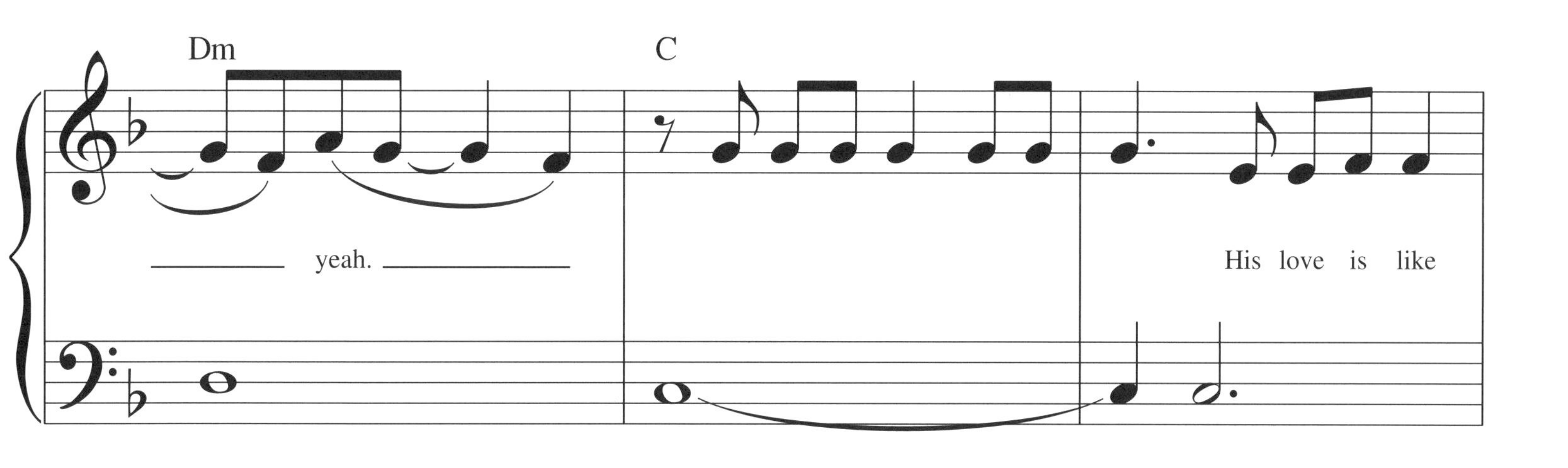

Dm
C
yeah.
His love is like

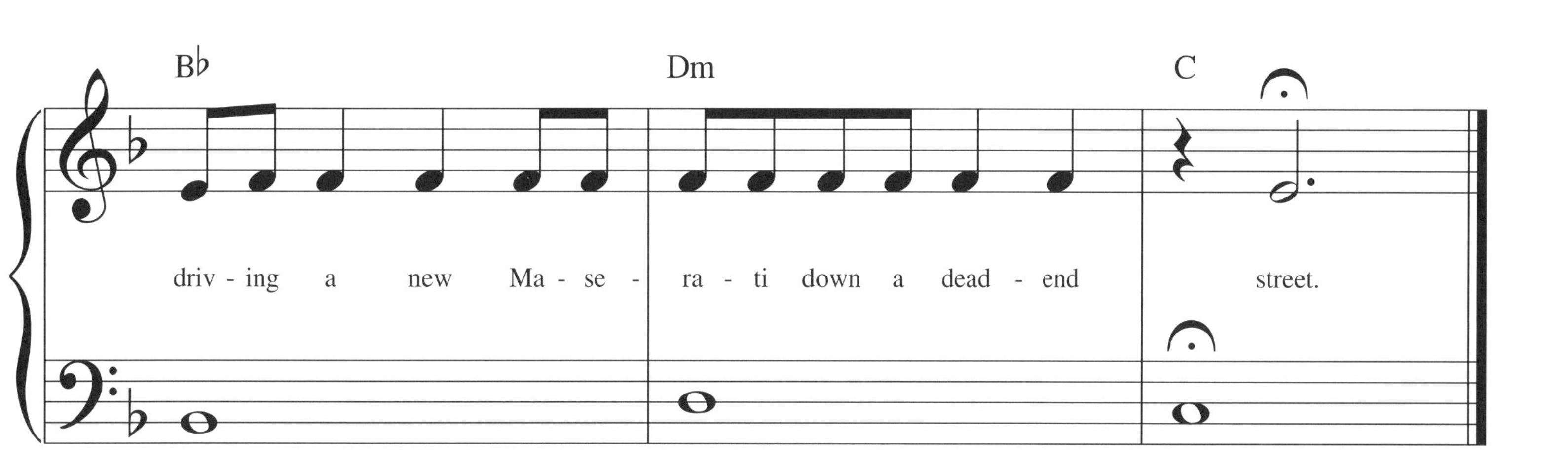

B♭
Dm
C
driv - ing a new Ma - se - ra - ti down a dead - end street.

STARLIGHT

Words and Music by
TAYLOR SWIFT

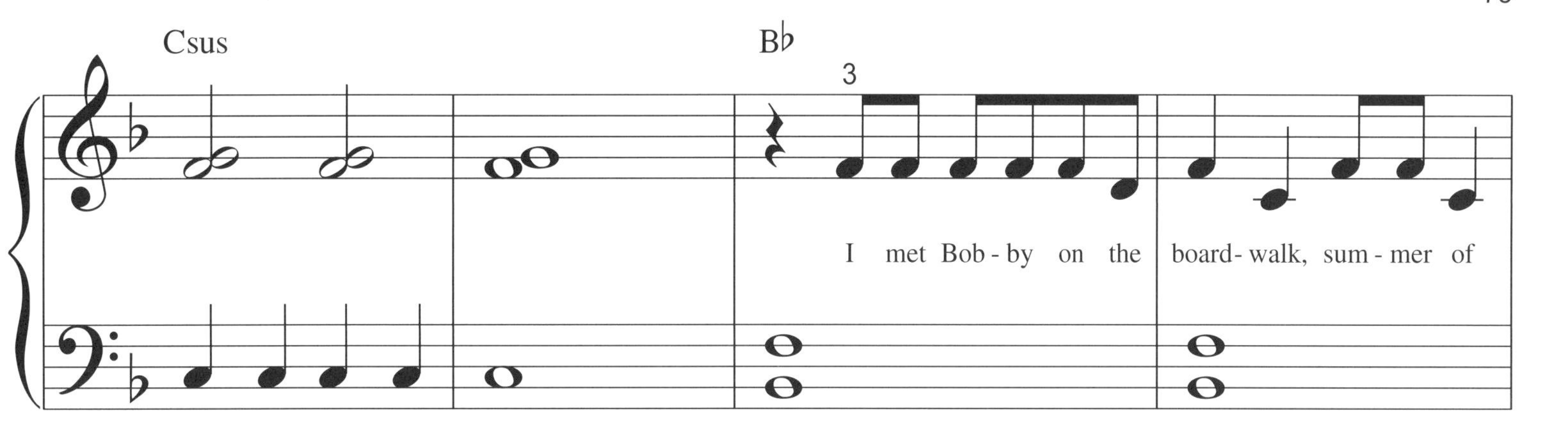
Csus
B♭
3
I met Bob - by on the board- walk, sum - mer of

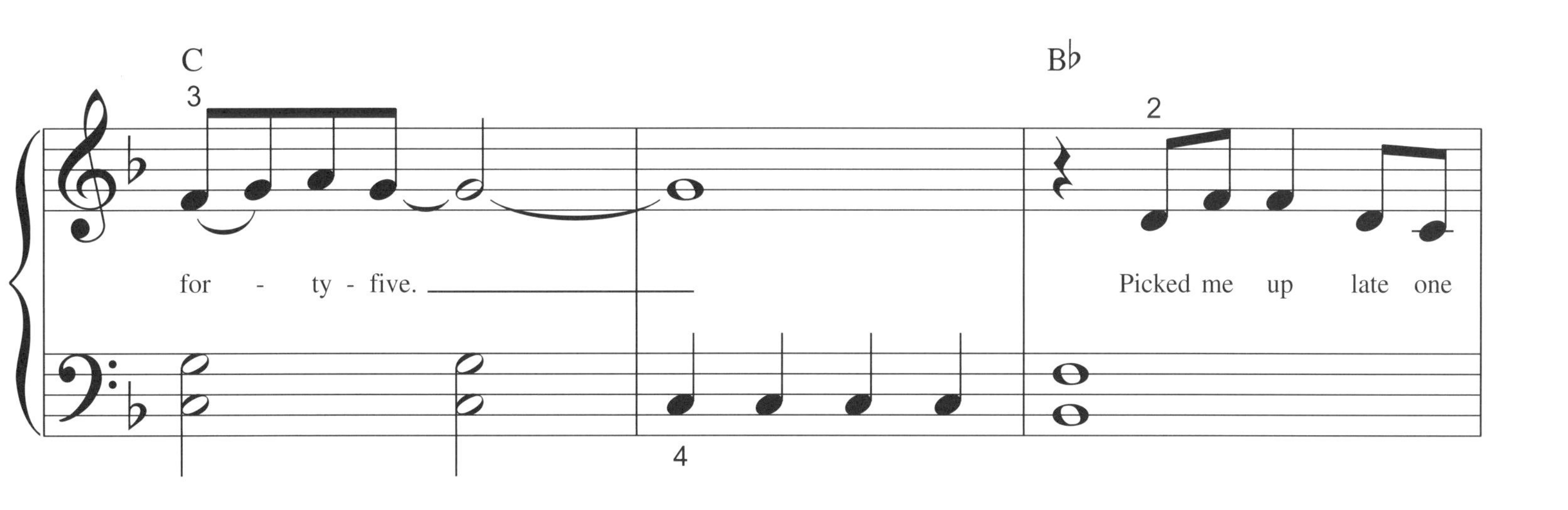
C
B♭
3
2
for - ty - five.
Picked me up late one
4

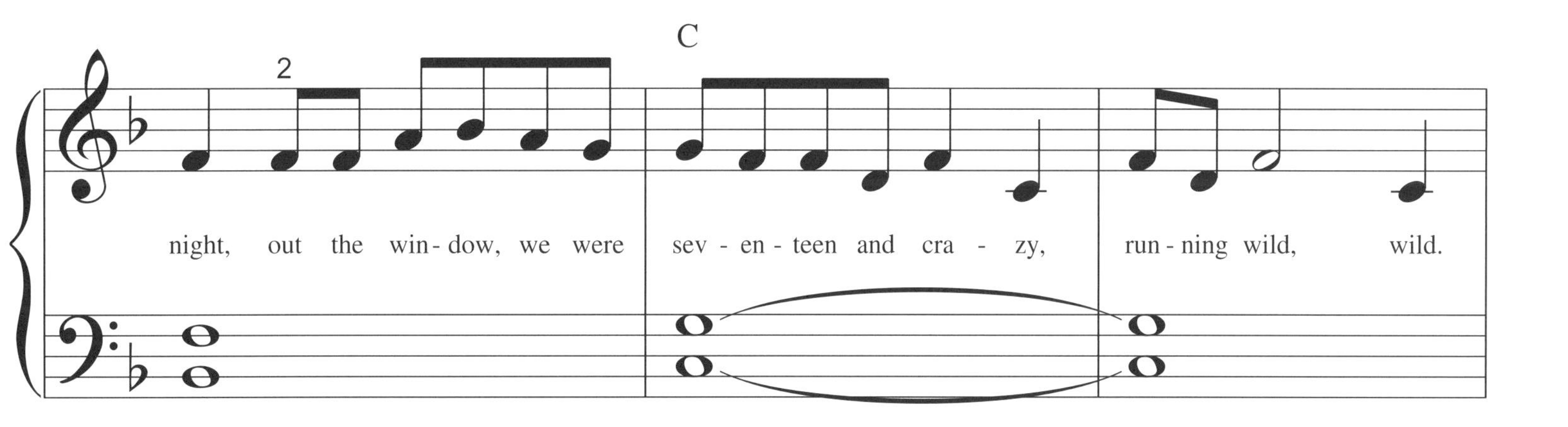
C
2
night, out the win - dow, we were sev - en - teen and cra - zy, run - ning wild, wild.

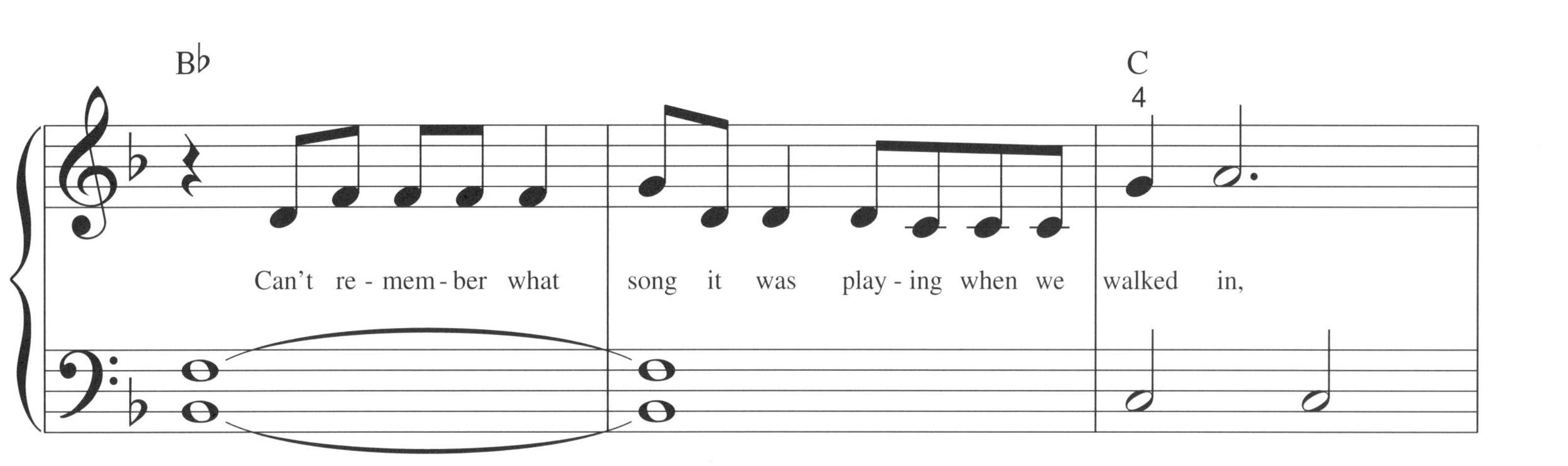
B♭
C
4
Can't re - mem - ber what song it was play - ing when we walked in,

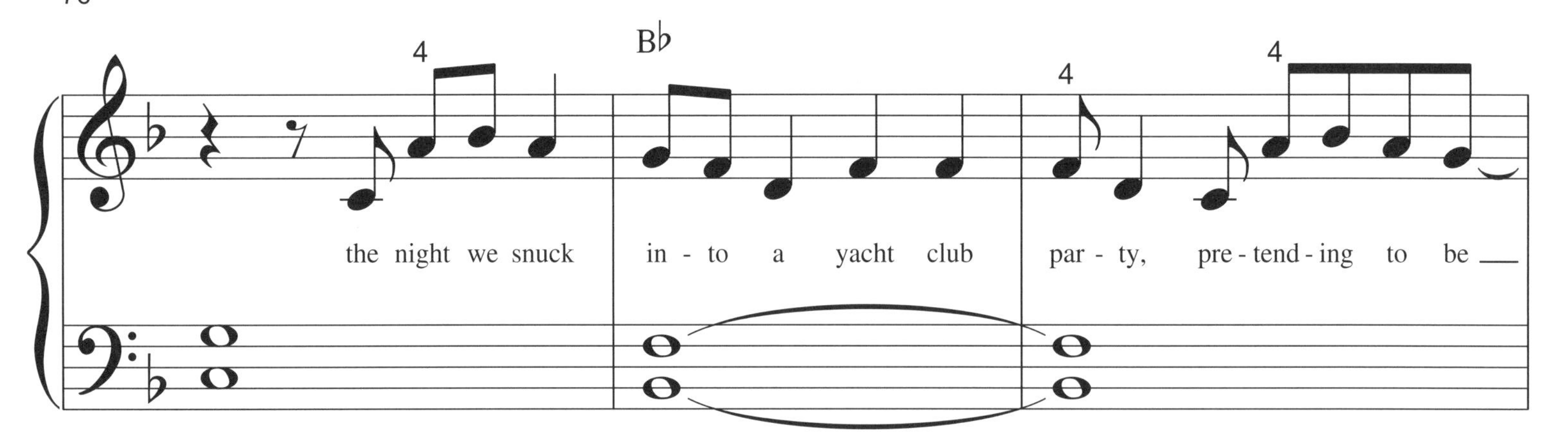
4
B♭
4
4
the night we snuck in - to a yacht club par - ty, pre - tend - ing to be

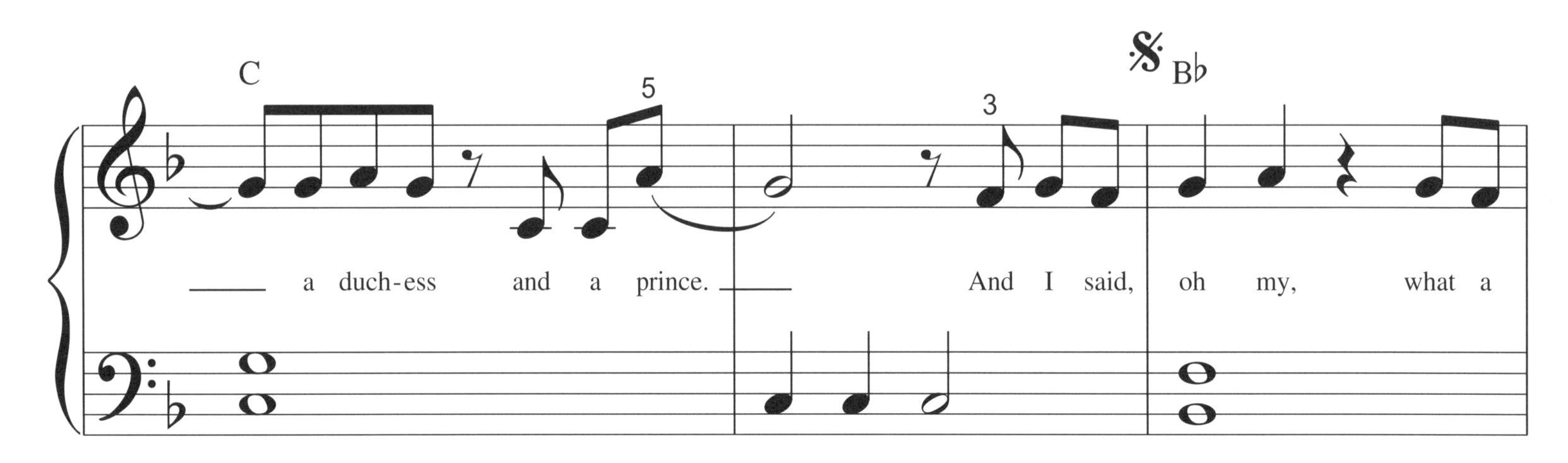
C
5
3
B♭
a duch-ess and a prince. And I said, oh my, what a

C
F
Dm
mar - ve - lous tune. It was the best night. Nev - er would for - get how he moved. The

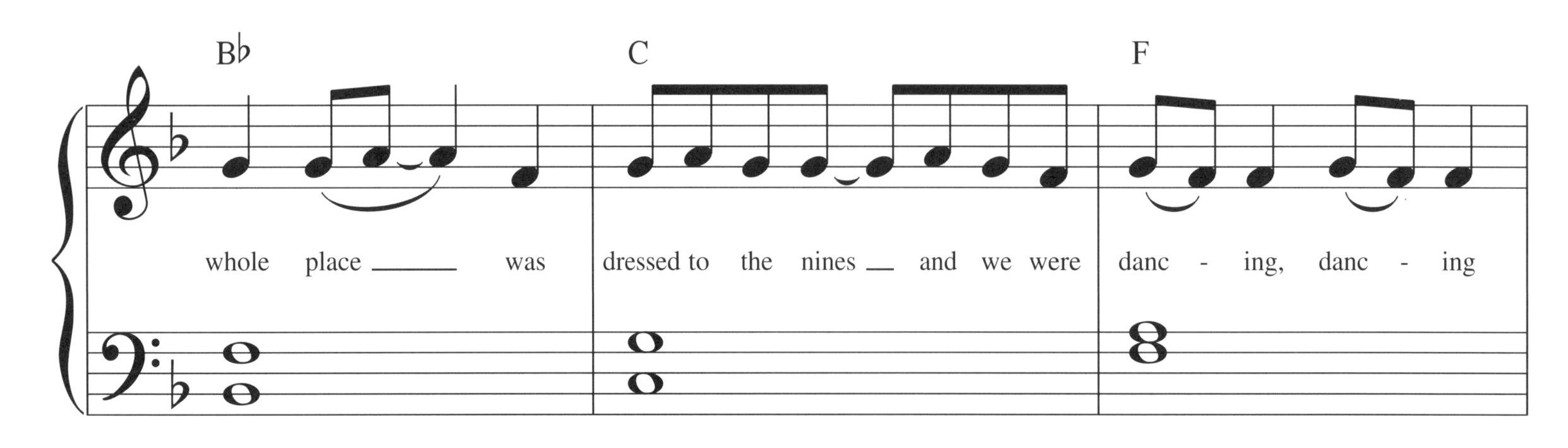
B♭
C
F
whole place was dressed to the nines and we were danc - ing, danc - ing

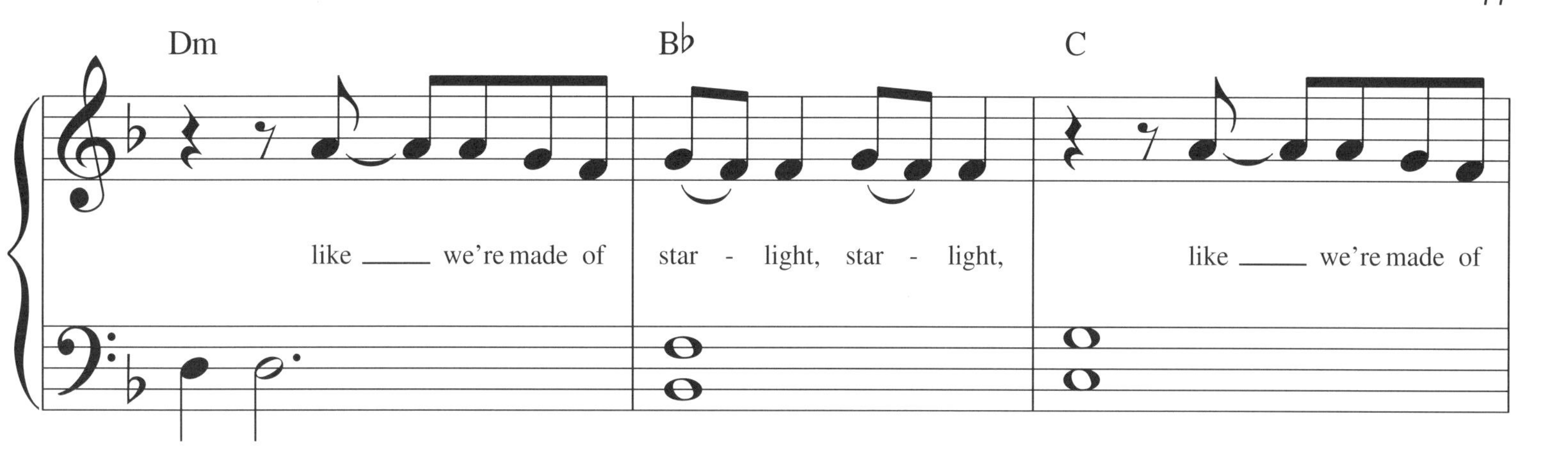
Dm
B♭
C
like we're made of
star - light, star - light,
like we're made of

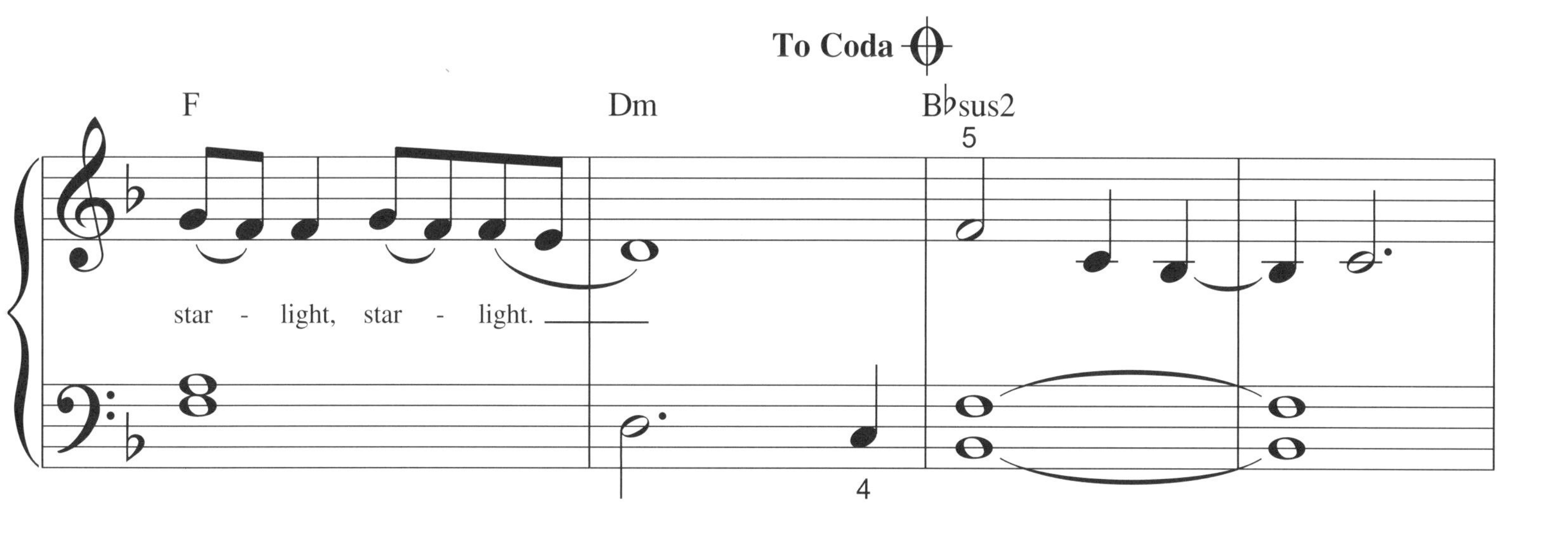
To Coda
F
Dm
B♭sus2
star - light, star - light.

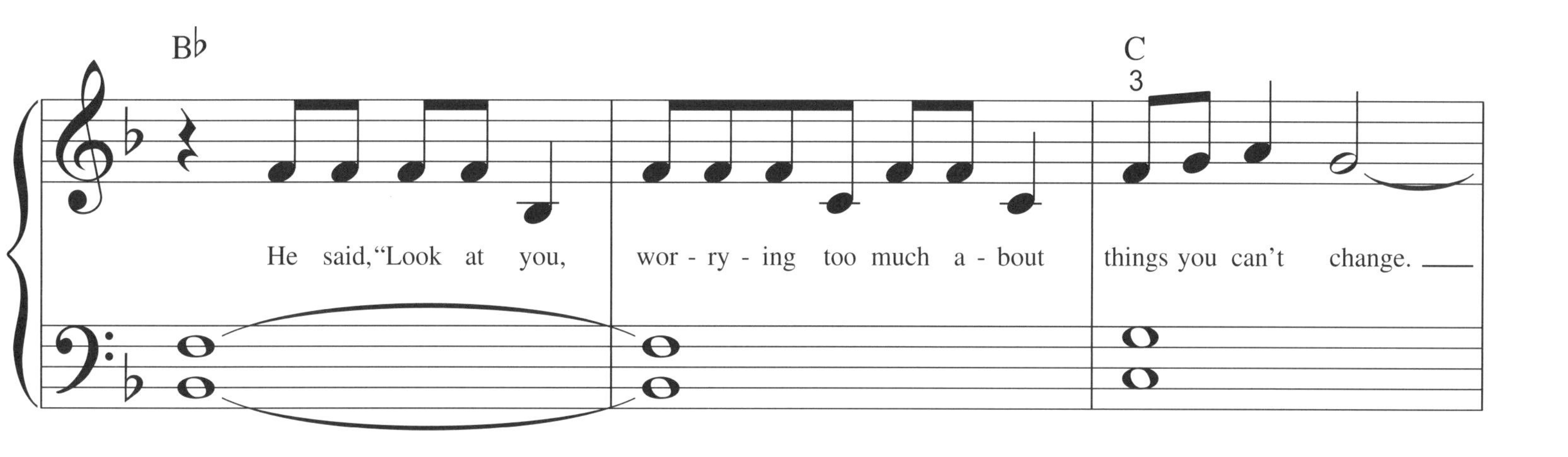
B♭
C
He said, "Look at you,
wor - ry - ing too much a - bout
things you can't change.

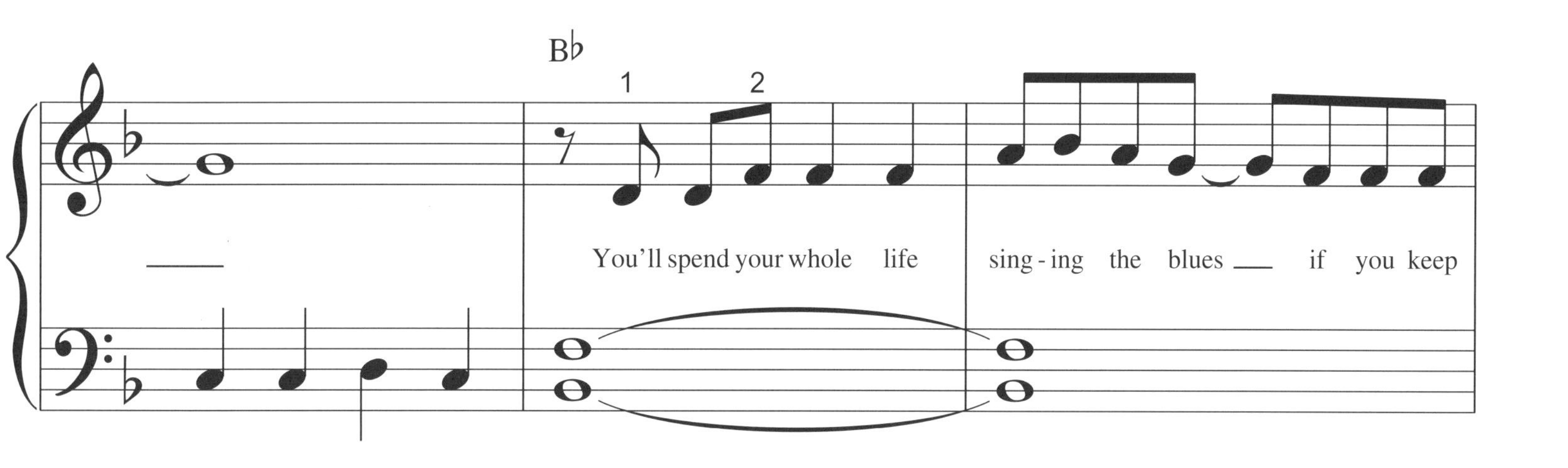
B♭
You'll spend your whole life
sing - ing the blues if you keep

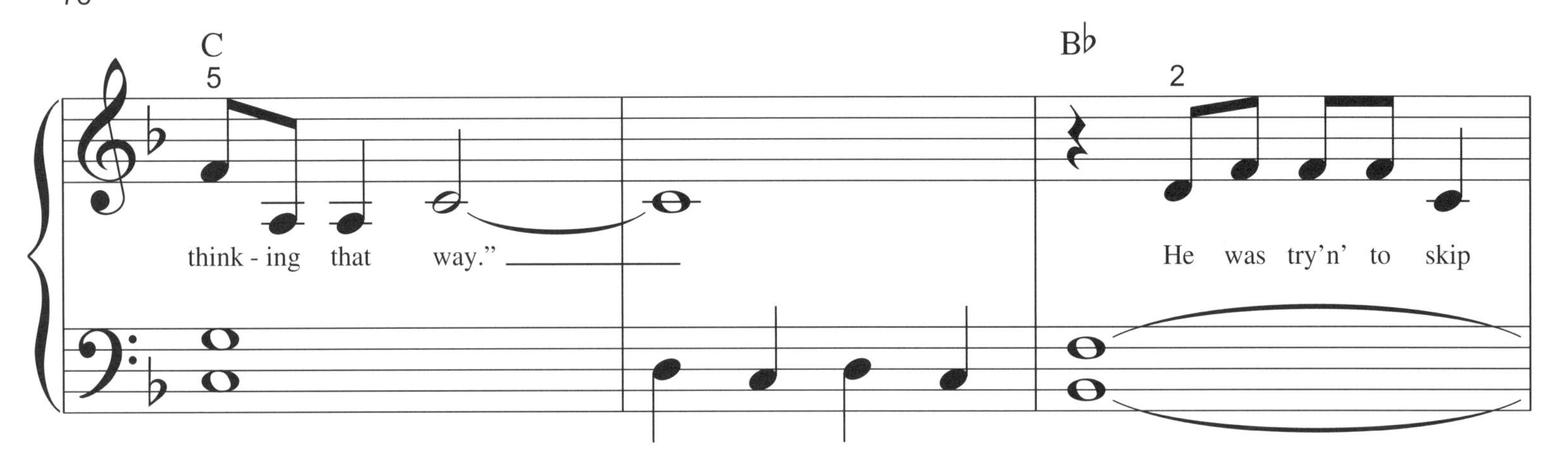
C
5
think - ing that way."
B♭
2
He was try'n' to skip

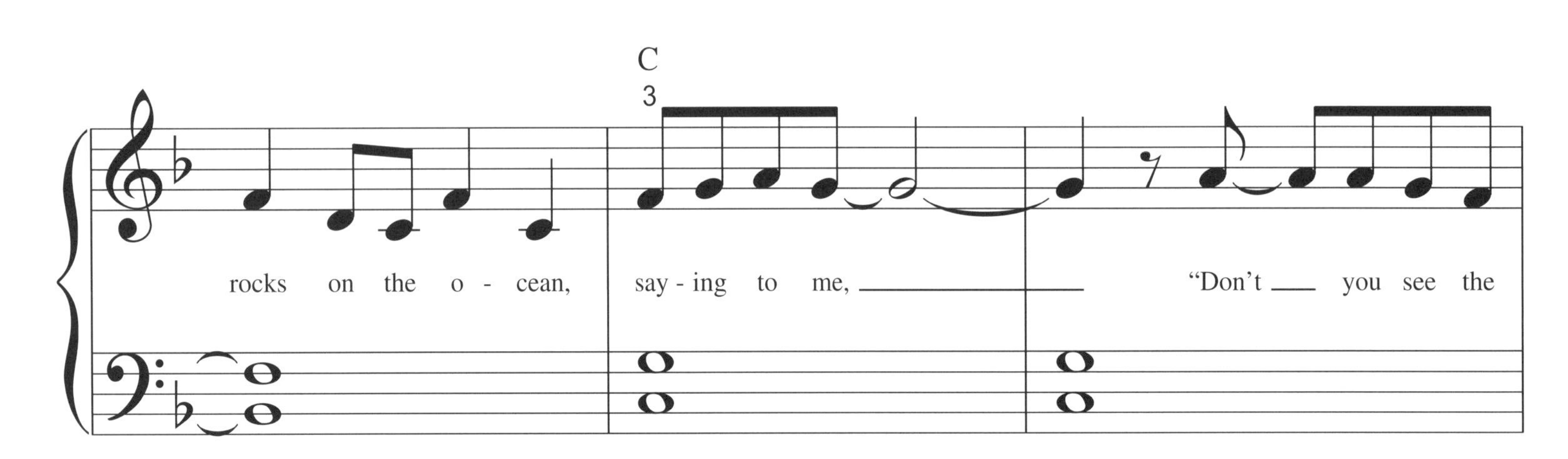
rocks on the o - cean,
C
3
say - ing to me,
"Don't you see the

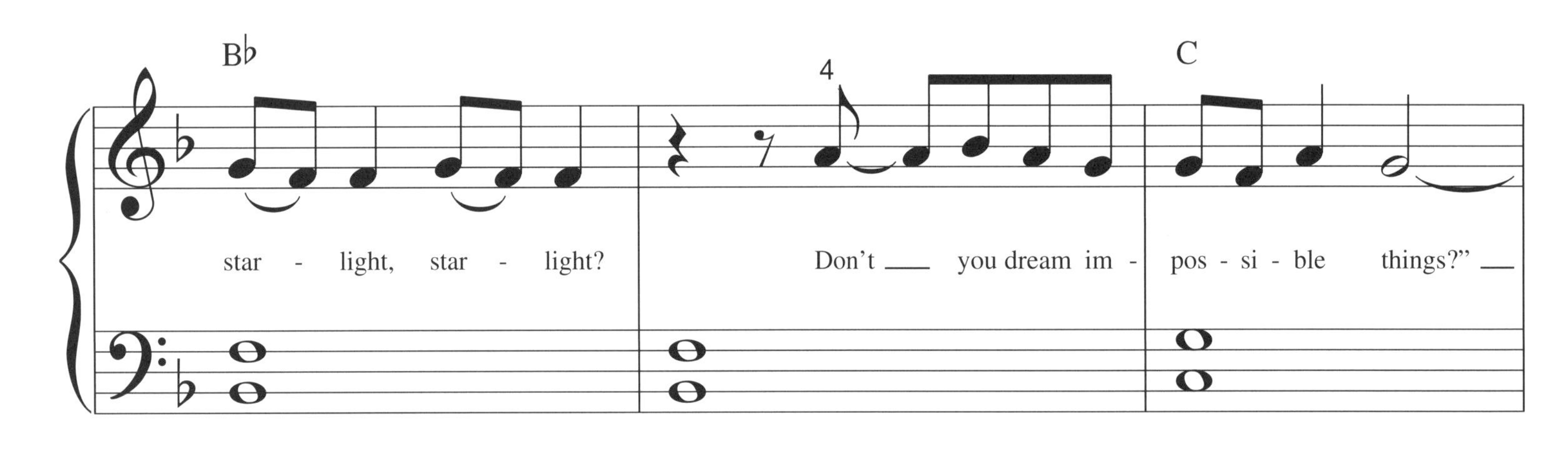
B♭
star - light, star - light?
4
Don't you dream im -
C
pos - si - ble things?"

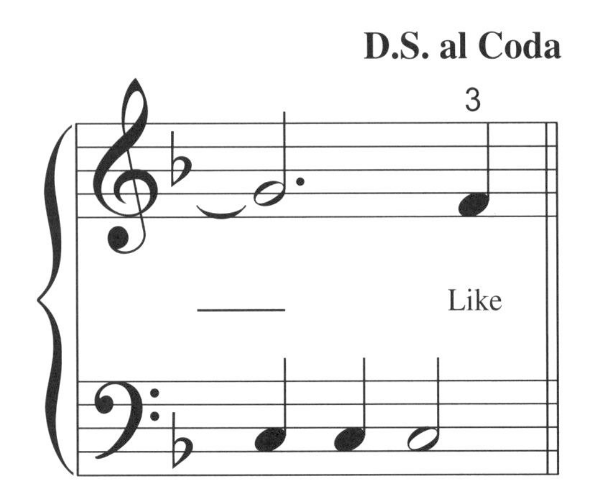
D.S. al Coda
3
Like

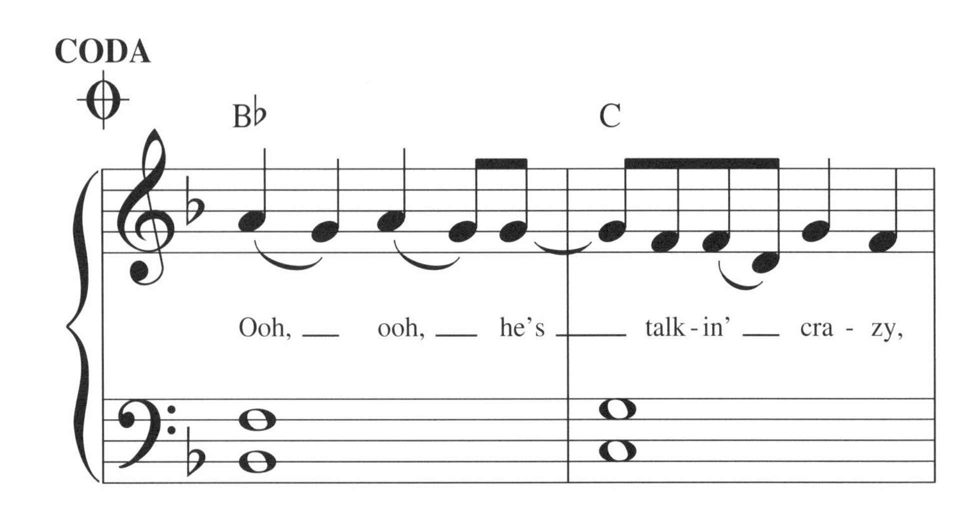
CODA
B♭
C
Ooh, ooh, he's talk - in' cra - zy,

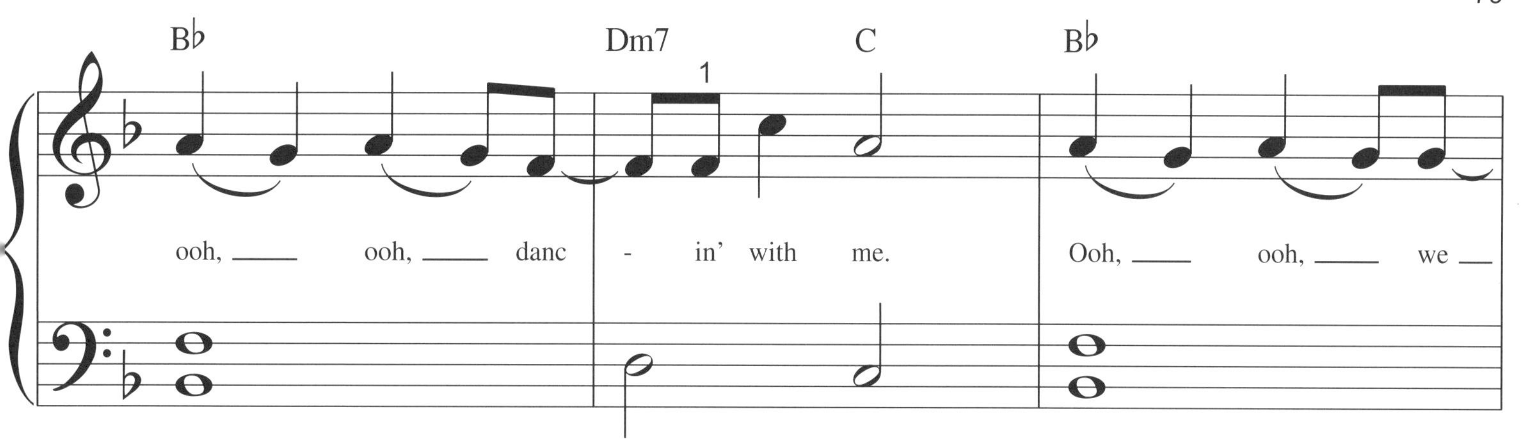
B♭
Dm7
C
B♭
1
ooh, ooh, danc - in' with me.
Ooh, ooh, we

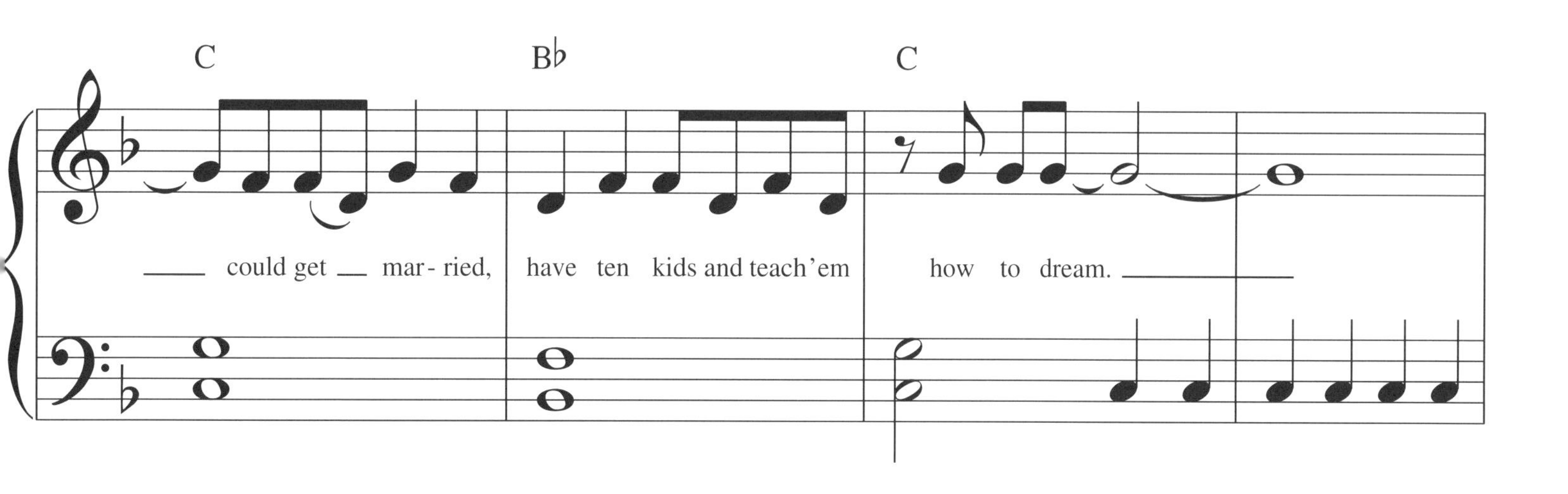
C
B♭
C
could get mar - ried,
have ten kids and teach 'em
how to dream.

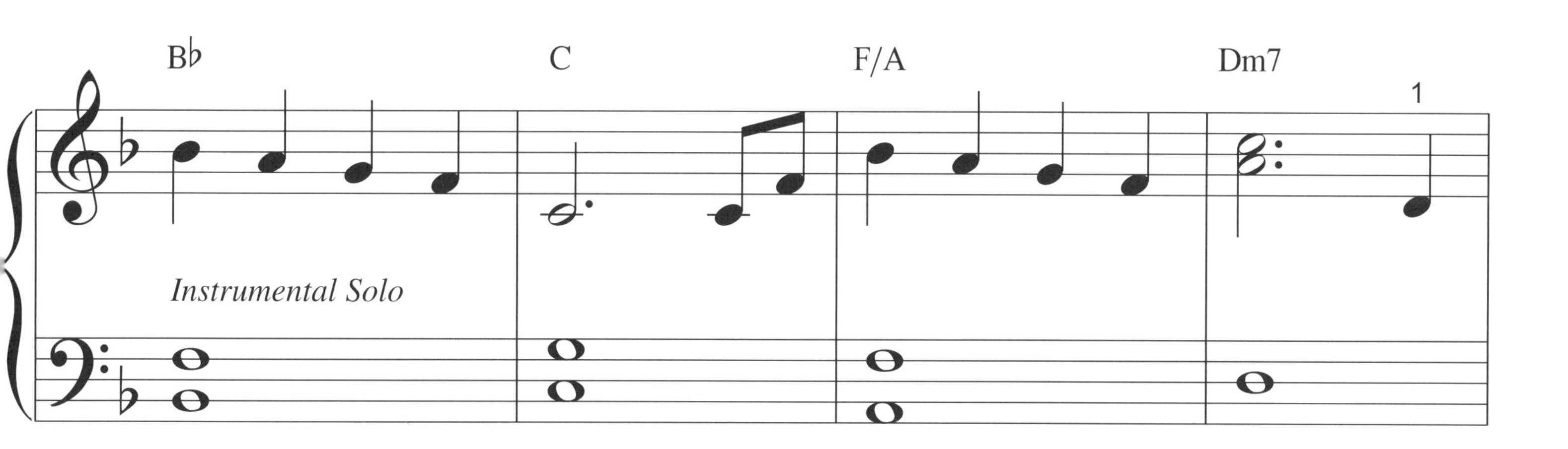
B♭
C
F/A
Dm7
1
Instrumental Solo

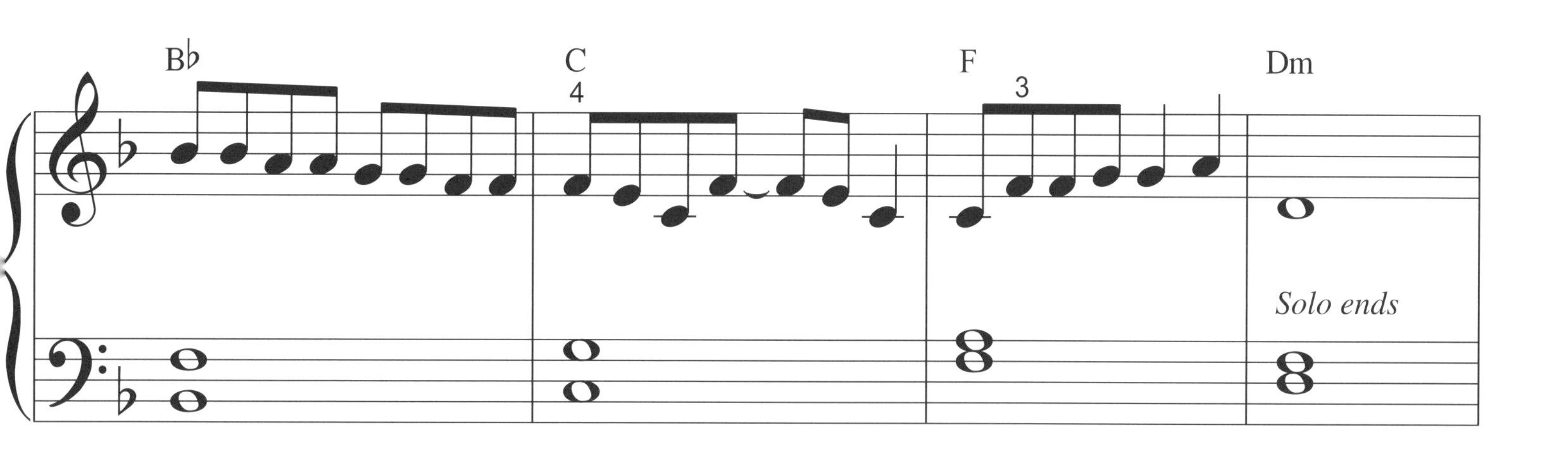
B♭
C
F
Dm
4
3
Solo ends

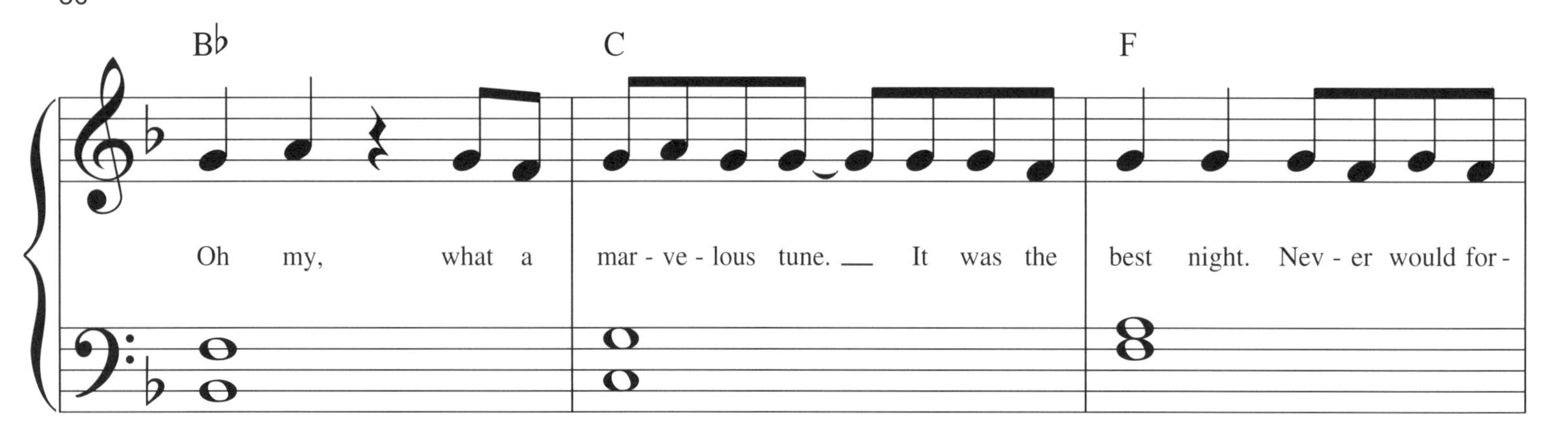
B♭
C
F
Oh my, what a mar - ve - lous tune. It was the best night. Nev - er would for -

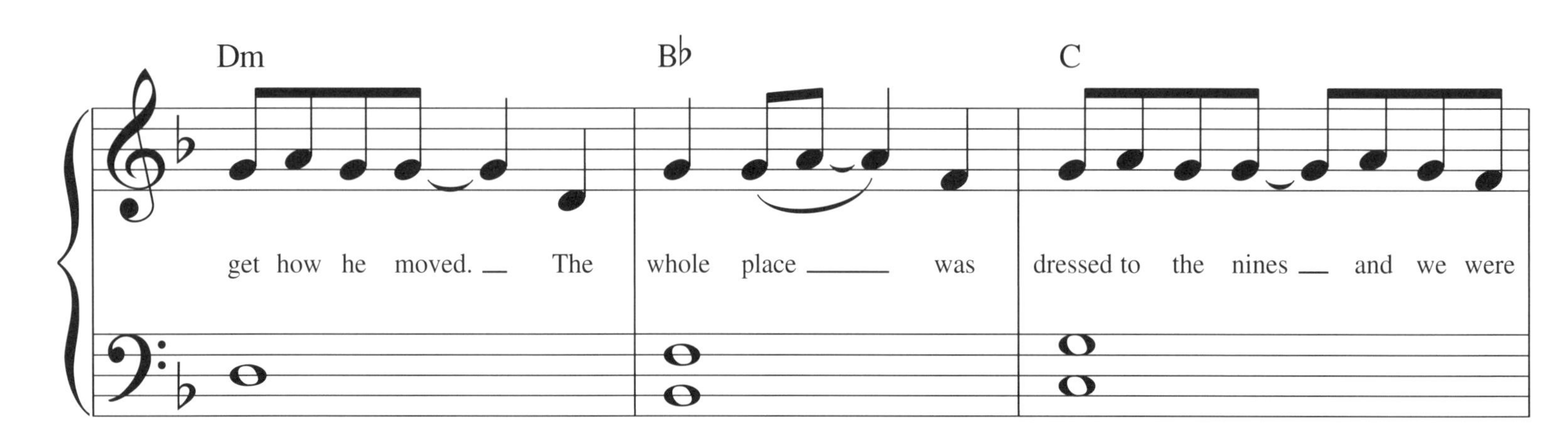
Dm
B♭
C
get how he moved. The whole place was dressed to the nines and we were

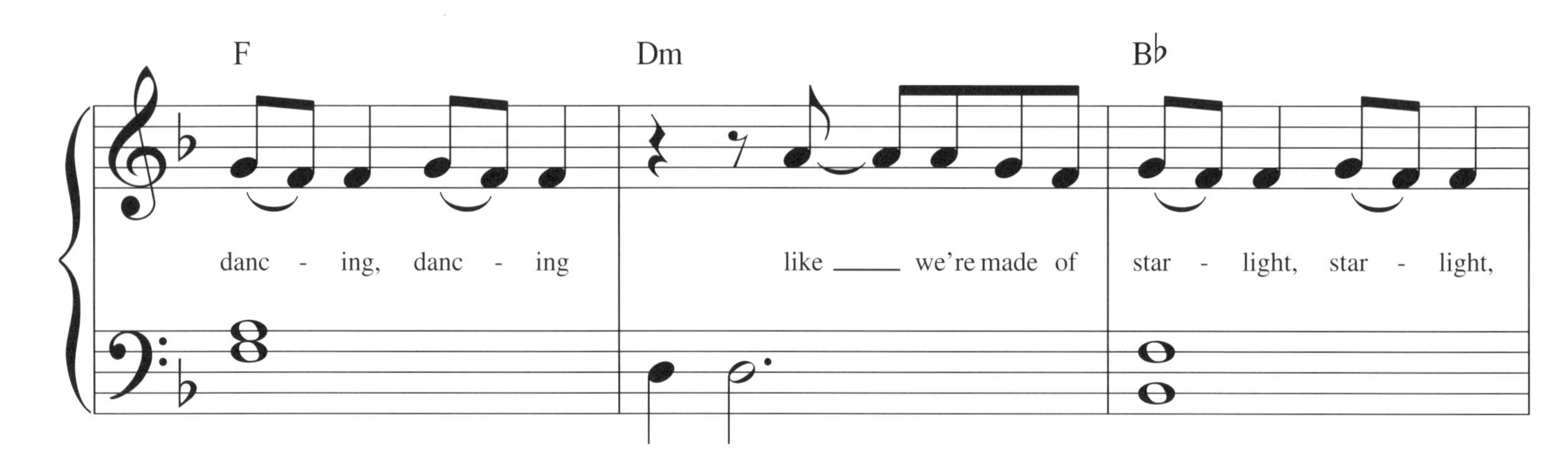
F
Dm
B♭
danc - ing, danc - ing like we're made of star - light, star - light,

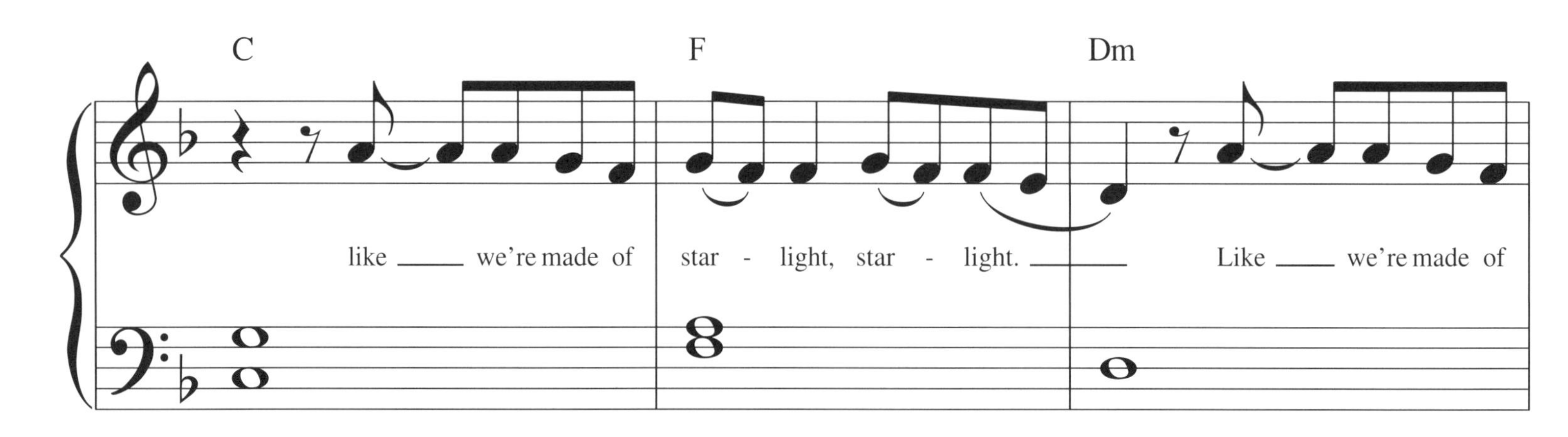
C
F
Dm
like we're made of star - light, star - light. Like we're made of

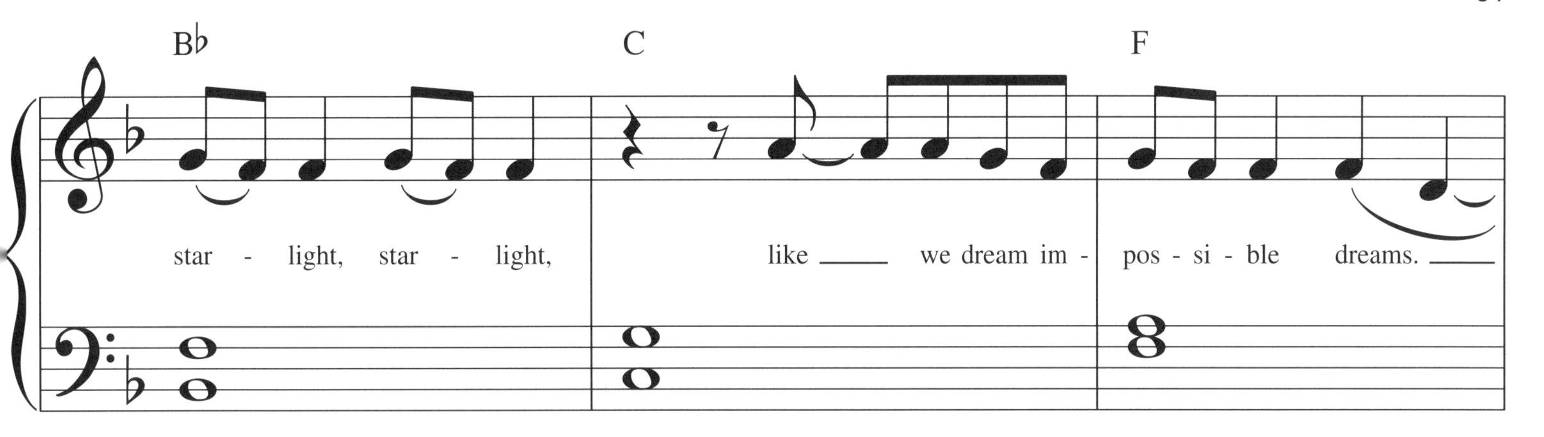
B♭
C
F
star - light, star - light,
like we dream im -
pos - si - ble dreams.

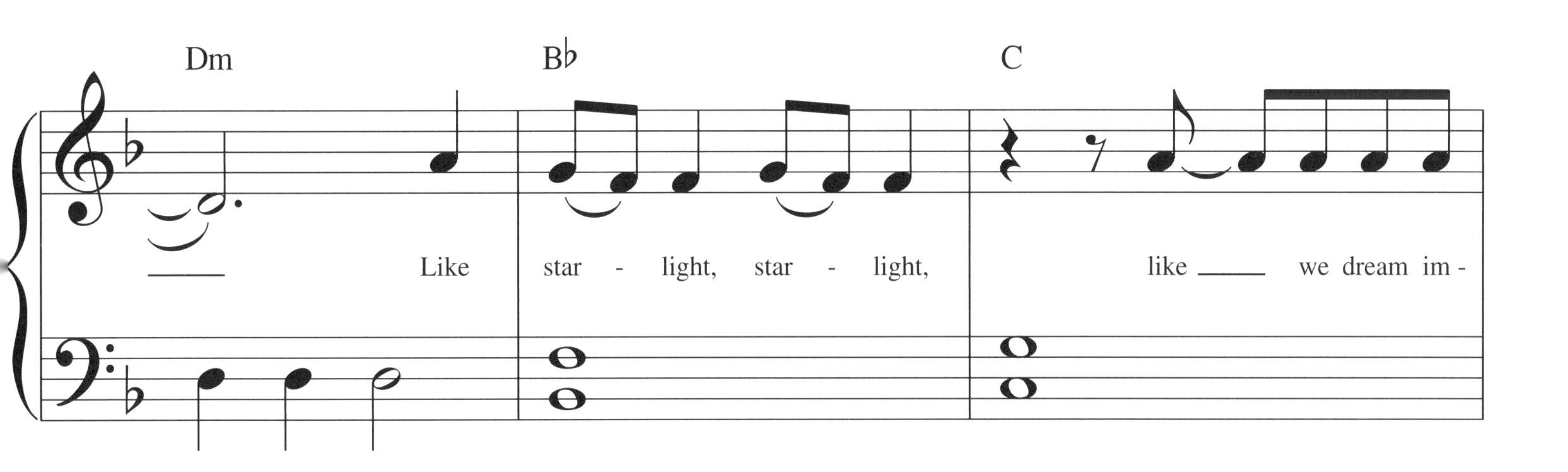
Dm
B♭
C
Like
star - light, star - light,
like we dream im -

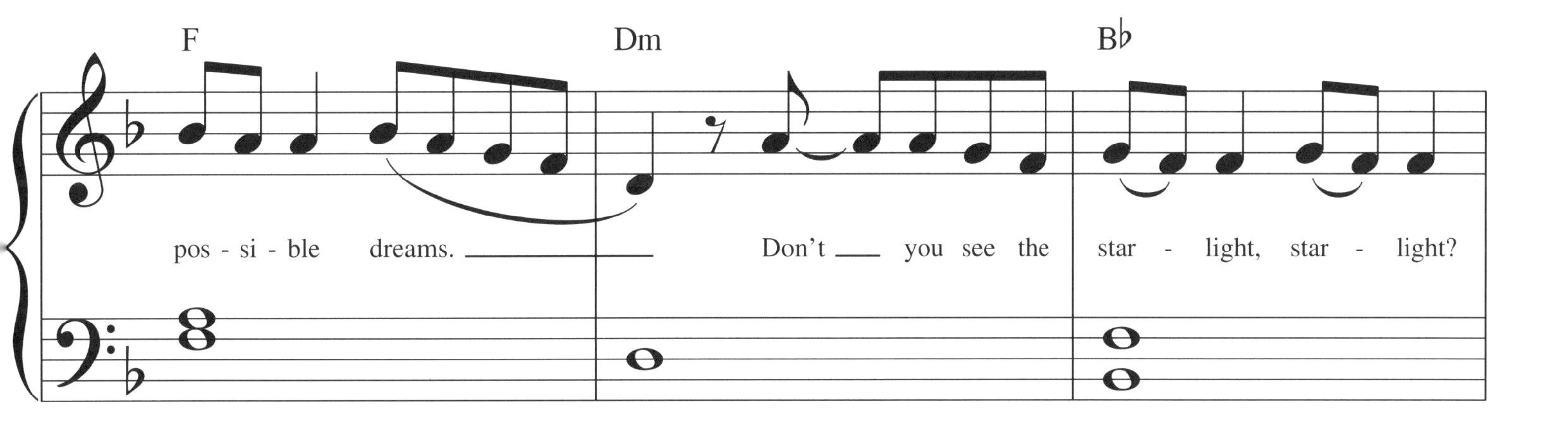
F
Dm
B♭
pos - si - ble dreams.
Don't you see the
star - light, star - light?

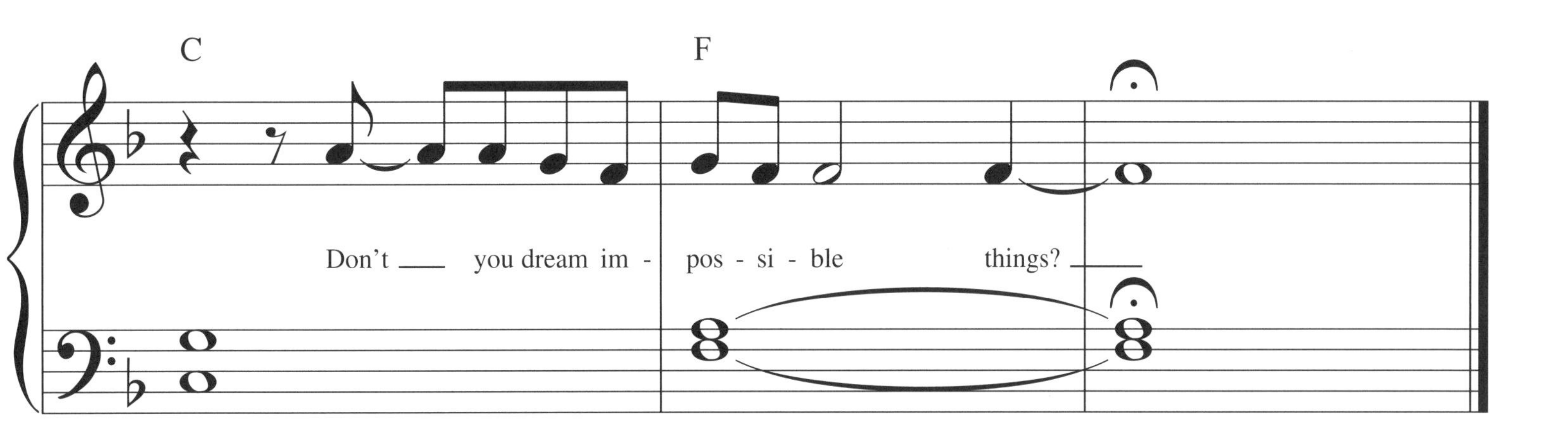
C
F
Don't you dream im -
pos - si - ble things?

STAY STAY STAY

Words and Music by
TAYLOR SWIFT

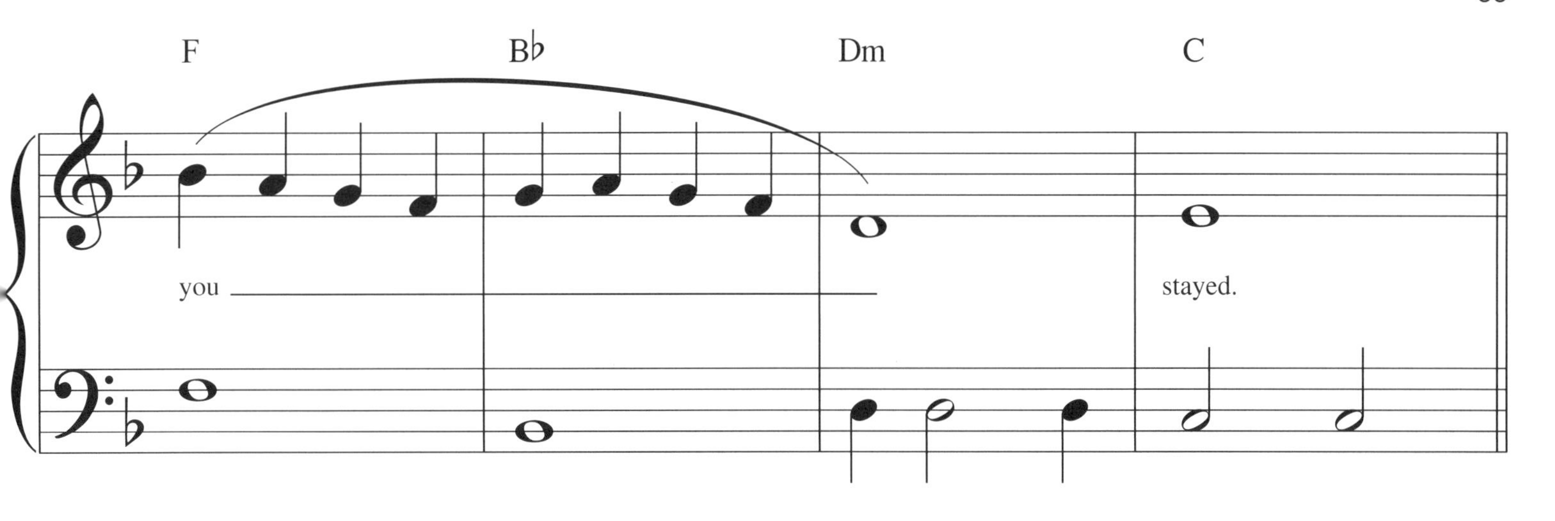
F
B♭
Dm
C
you
stayed.

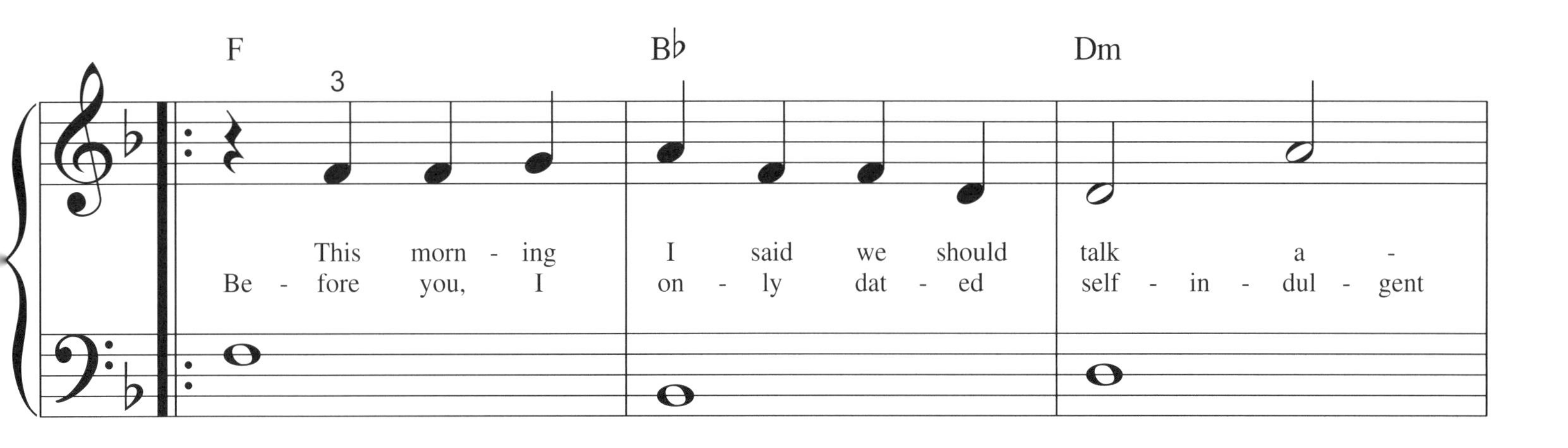
F
B♭
Dm
3
This morn - ing I said we should talk a -
Be - fore you, I on - ly dat - ed self - in - dul - gent

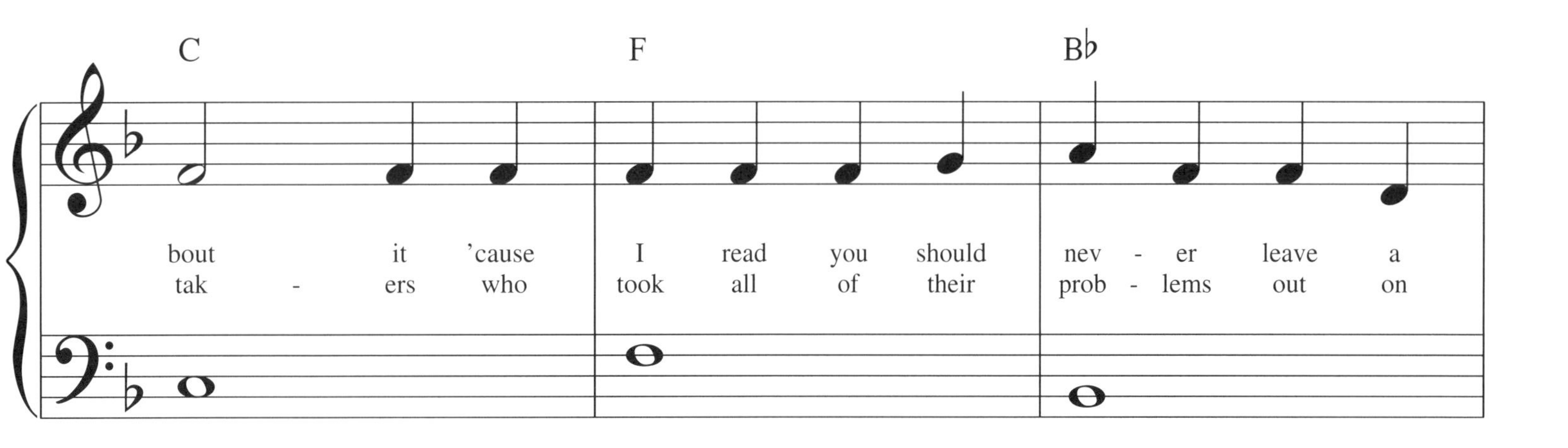
C
F
B♭
bout it 'cause I read you should nev - er leave a
tak - ers who took all of their prob - lems out on

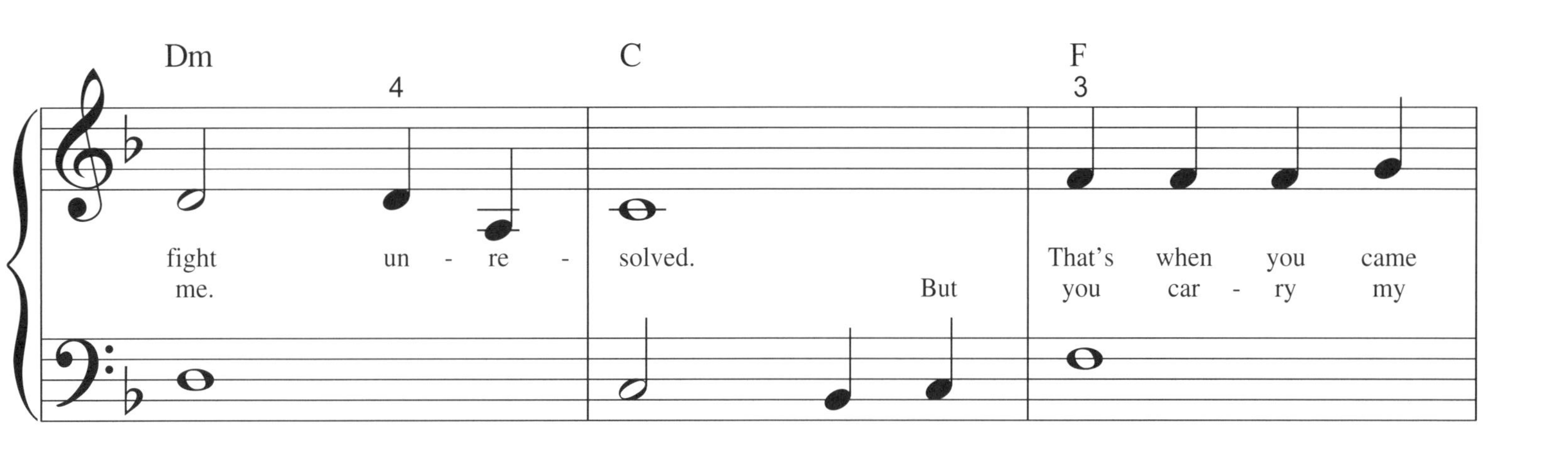
Dm
C
F
4
3
fight un - re - solved. That's when you came
me. But you car - ry my

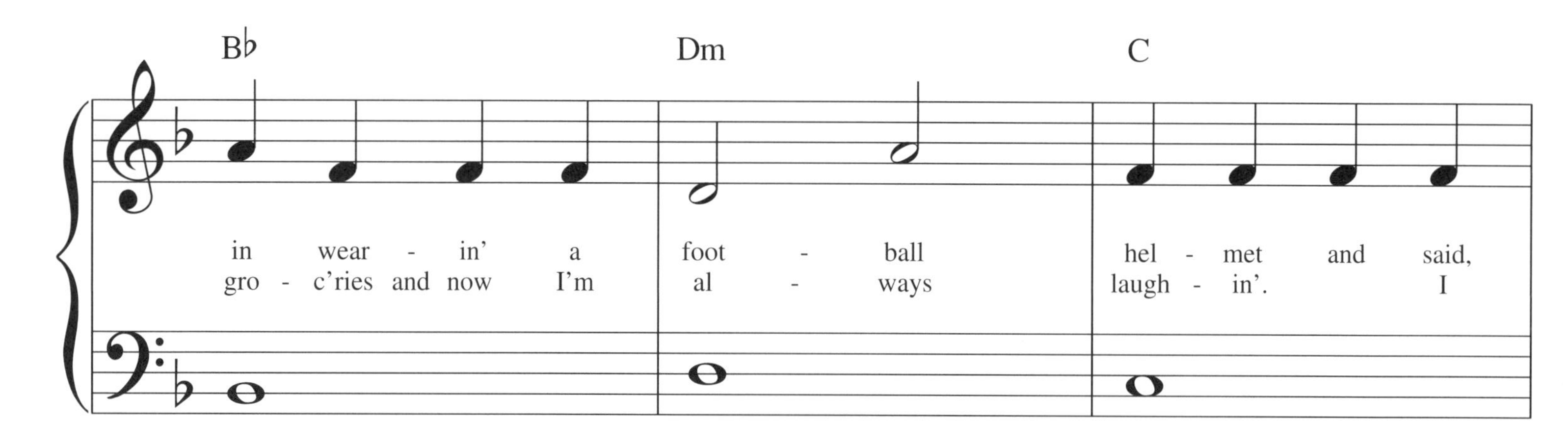
B♭
Dm
C
in wear - in' a foot - ball hel - met and said,
gro - c'ries and now I'm al - ways laugh - in'. I

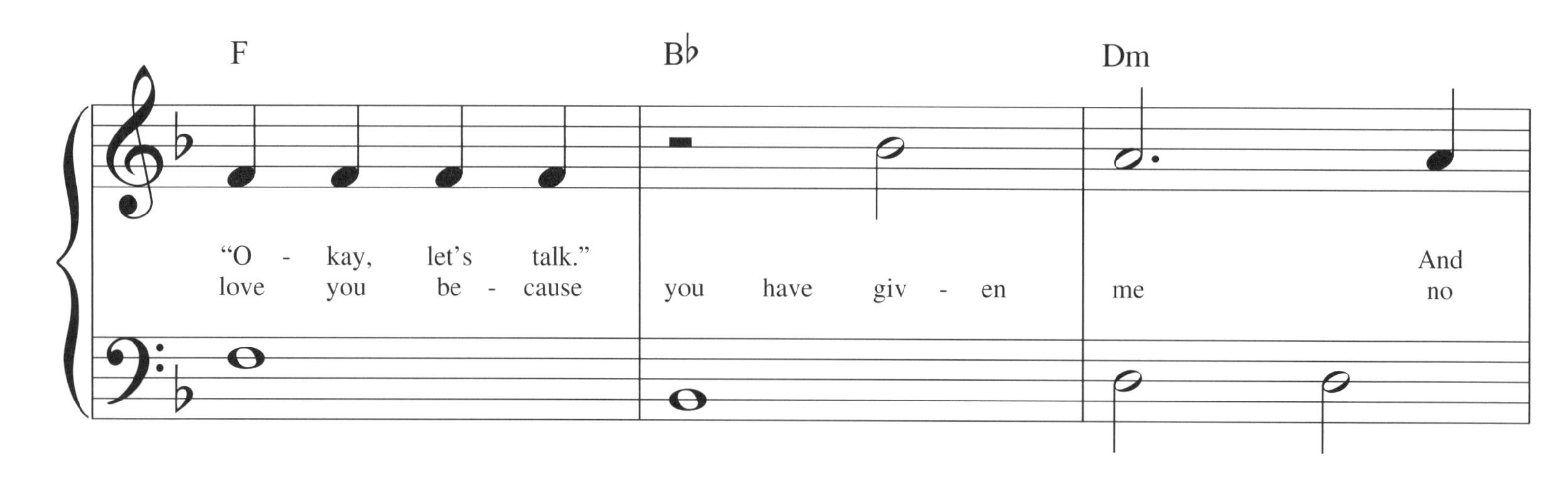
F
B♭
Dm
"O - kay, let's talk." And
love you be - cause you have giv - en me no

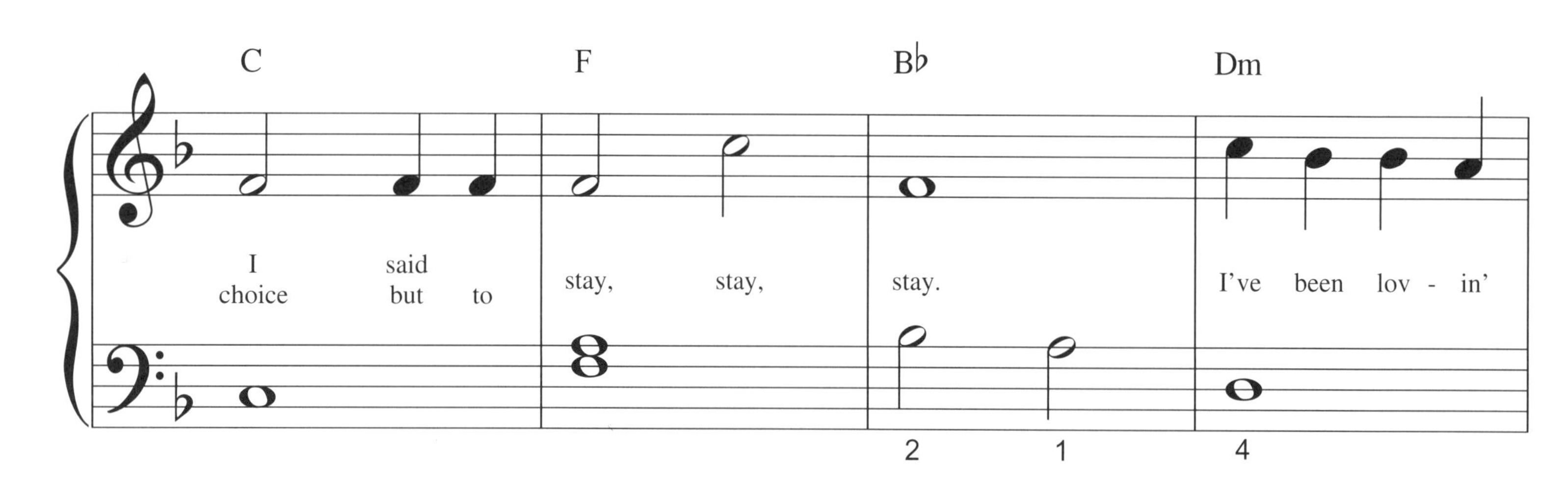
C
F
B♭
Dm
I said
choice but to stay, stay, stay. I've been lov - in'
2 1 4

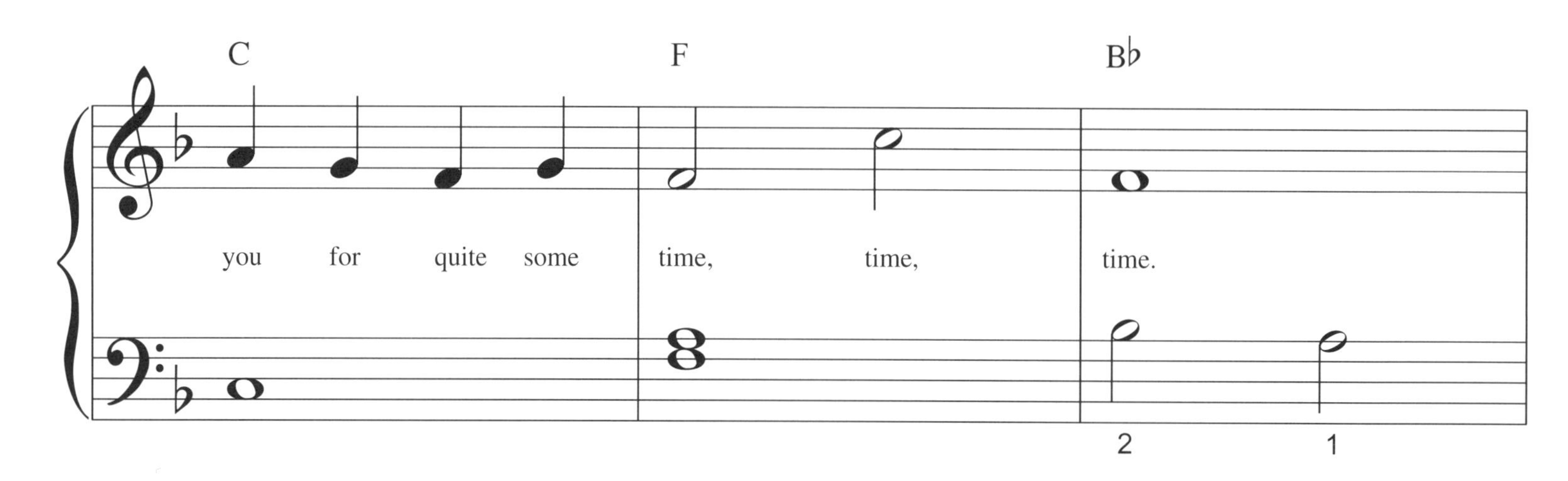
C
F
B♭
you for quite some time, time, time.
2 1

Dm
C
F
You think that it's fun - ny when I'm mad, mad,
4
B♭
Dm
C
mad. But I think that it's best if we both
2 1
F
1.
B♭
Dm
C
stay.
2.
B♭
3
1
Dm
C
F
stay, stay, stay.

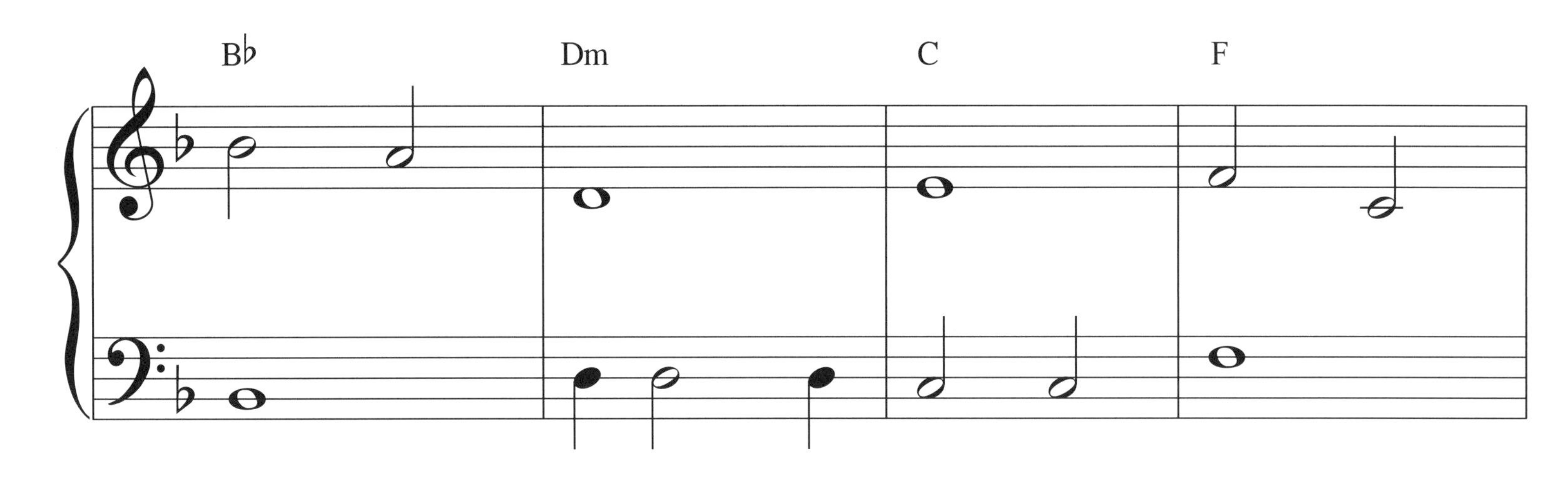
B♭
Dm
C
F

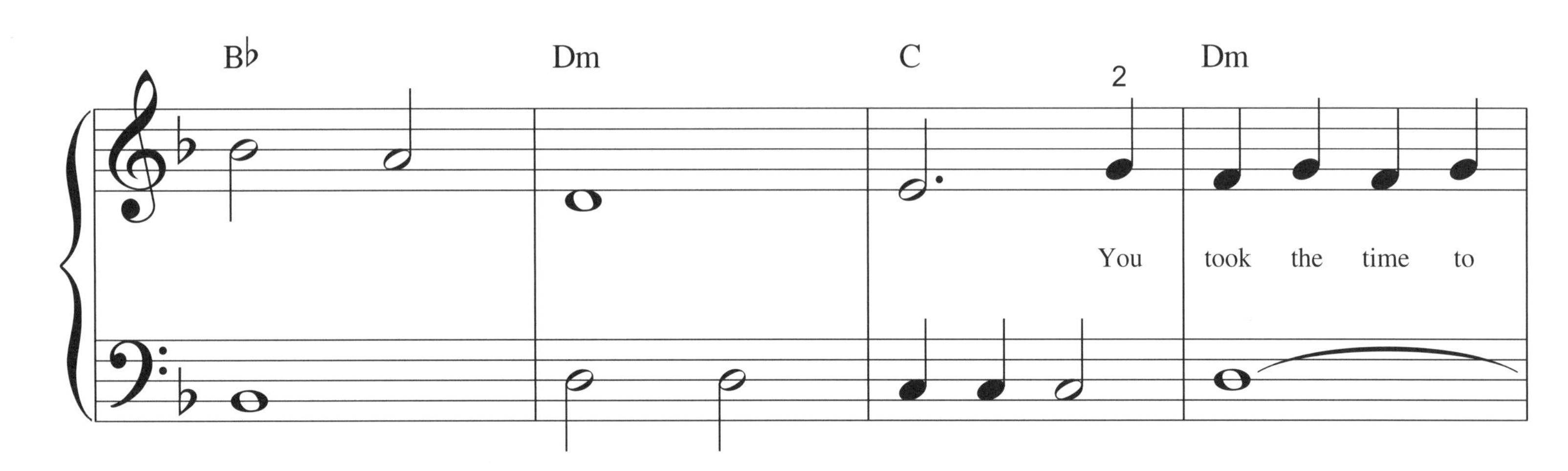
B♭
Dm
C
Dm
2
You took the time to

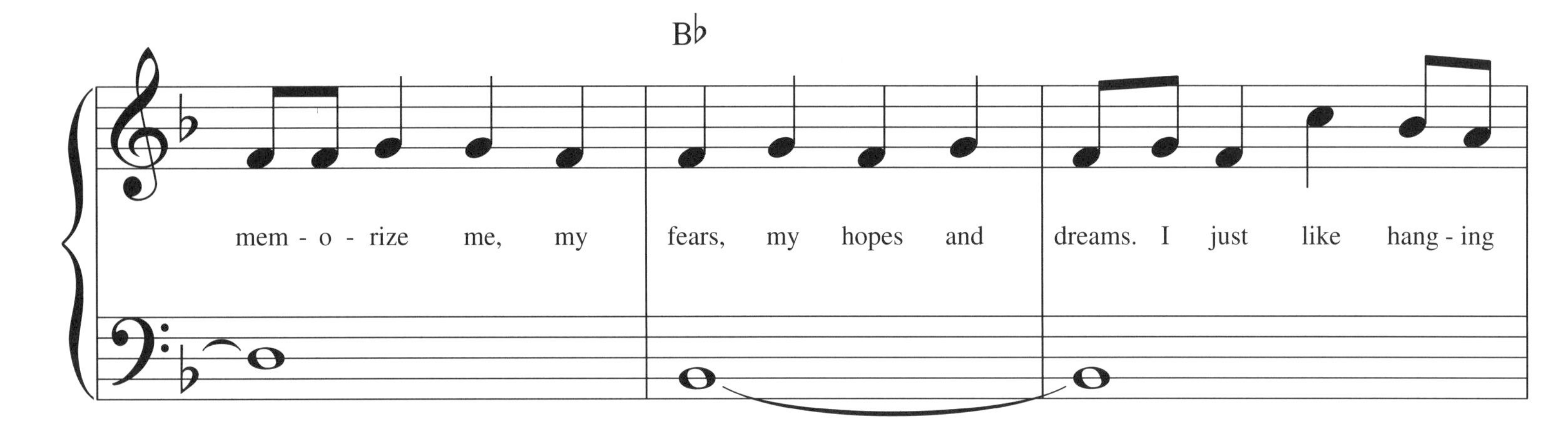
B♭
mem - o - rize me, my fears, my hopes and dreams. I just like hang - ing

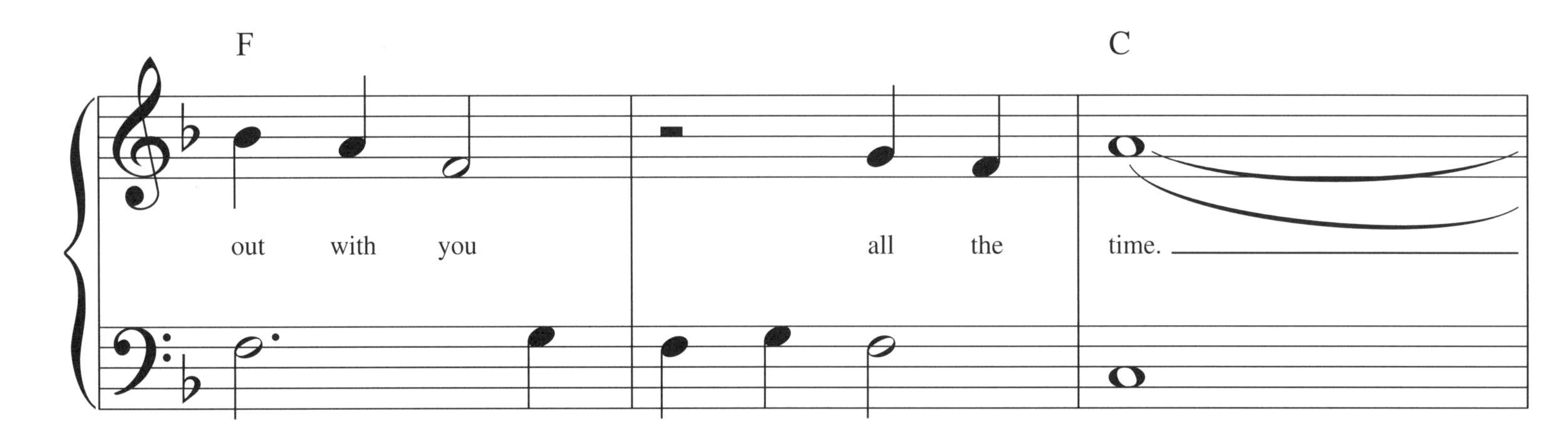
F
C
out with you all the time.

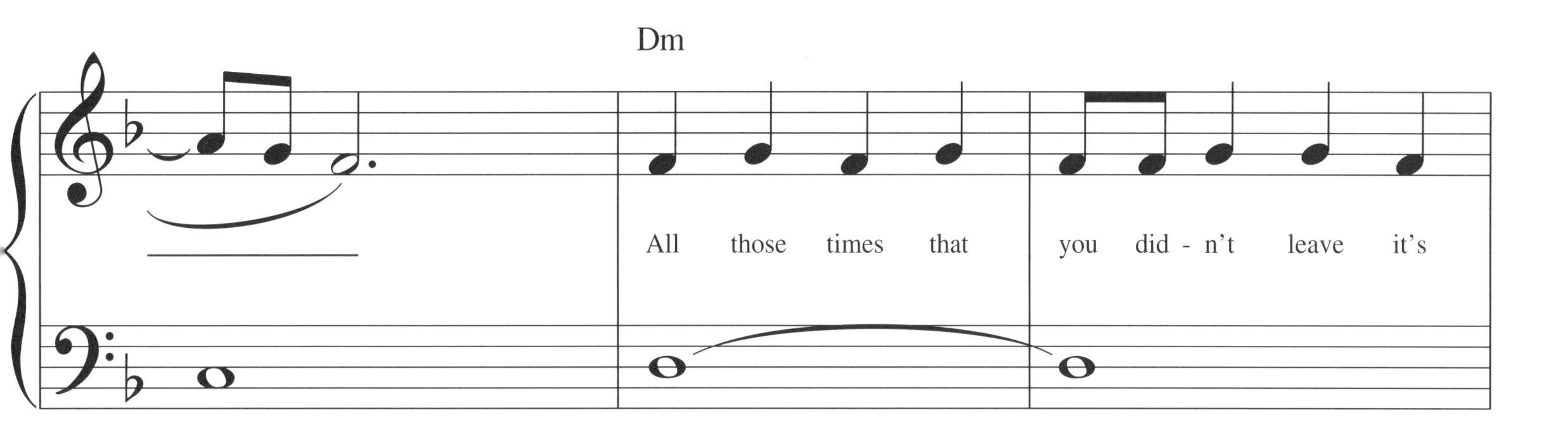
Dm
All those times that you did - n't leave it's

B♭
F
been oc - cur - ring to me I'd like to hang out with you

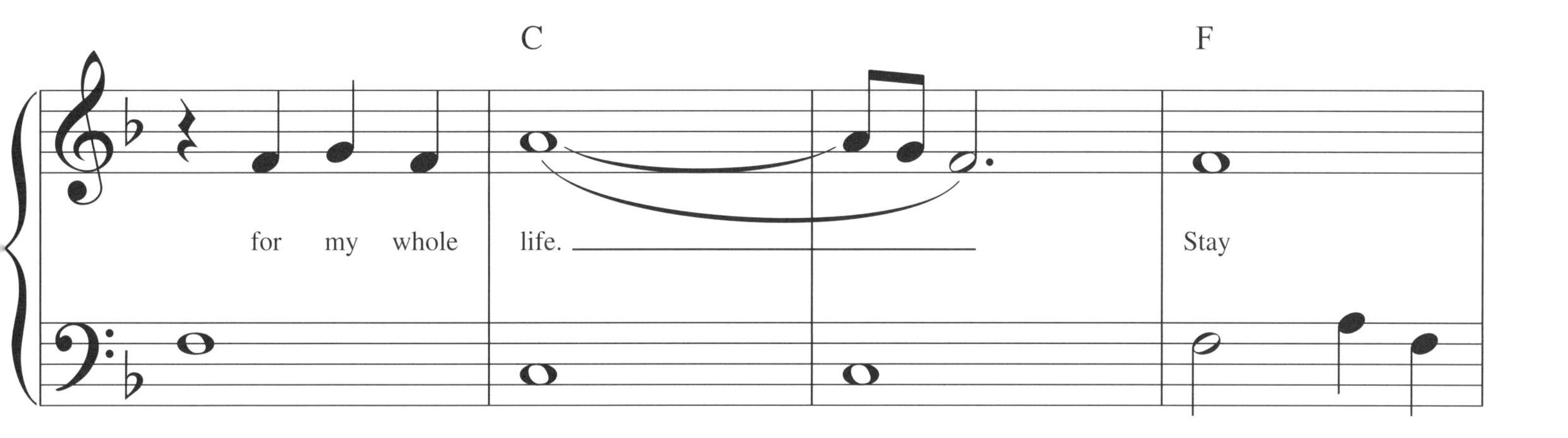
C
F
for my whole life. Stay

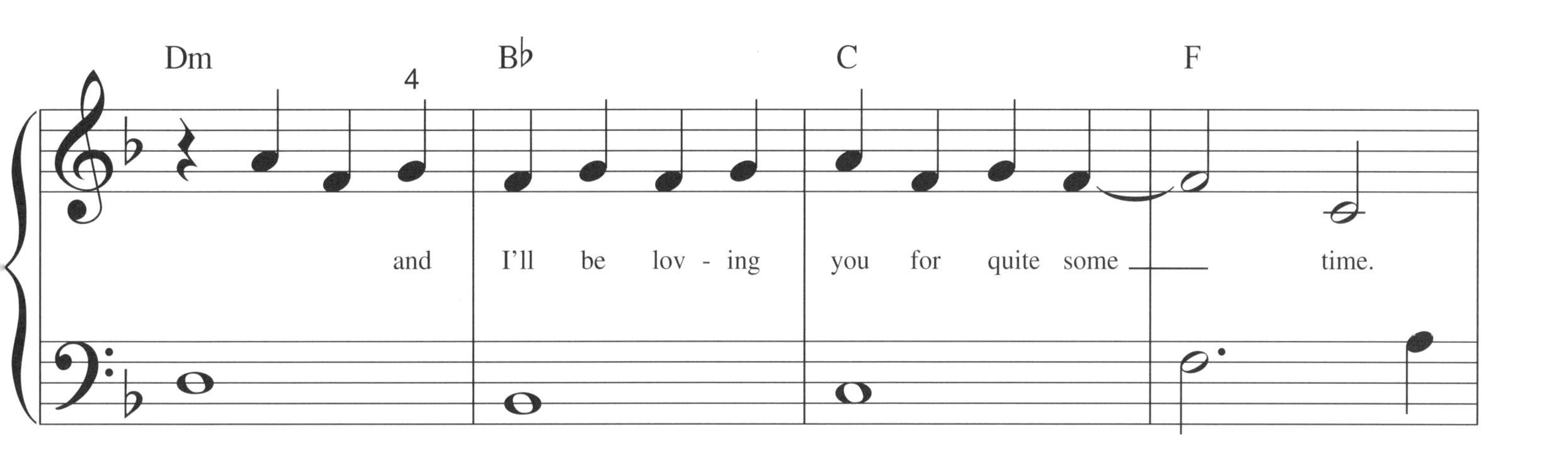
Dm
4
B♭
C
F
and I'll be lov - ing you for quite some time.

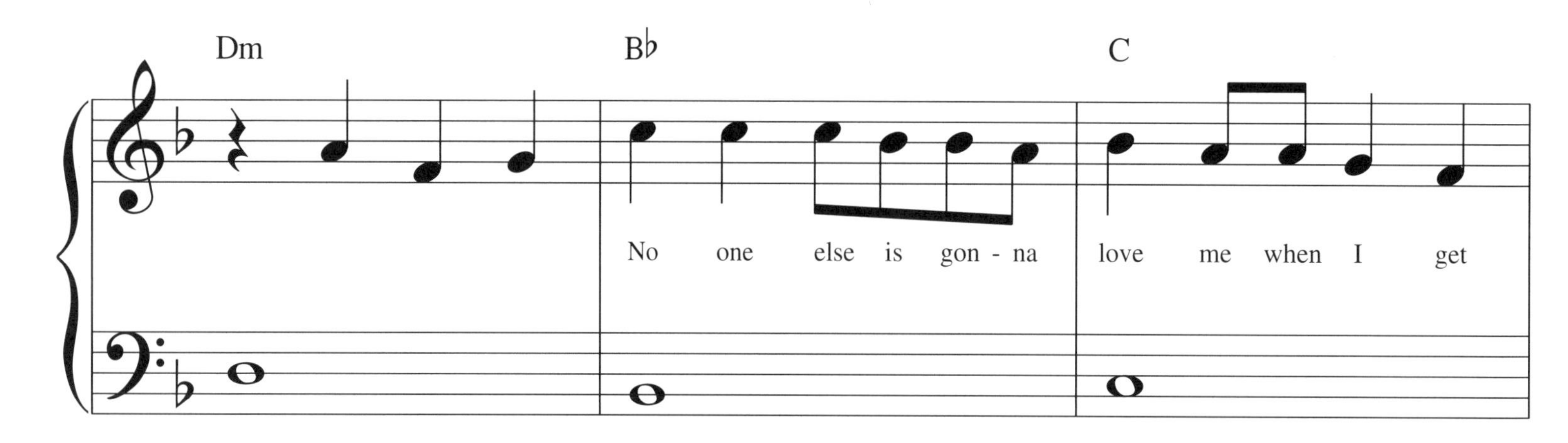
Dm
B♭
C
No one else is gon - na
love me when I get

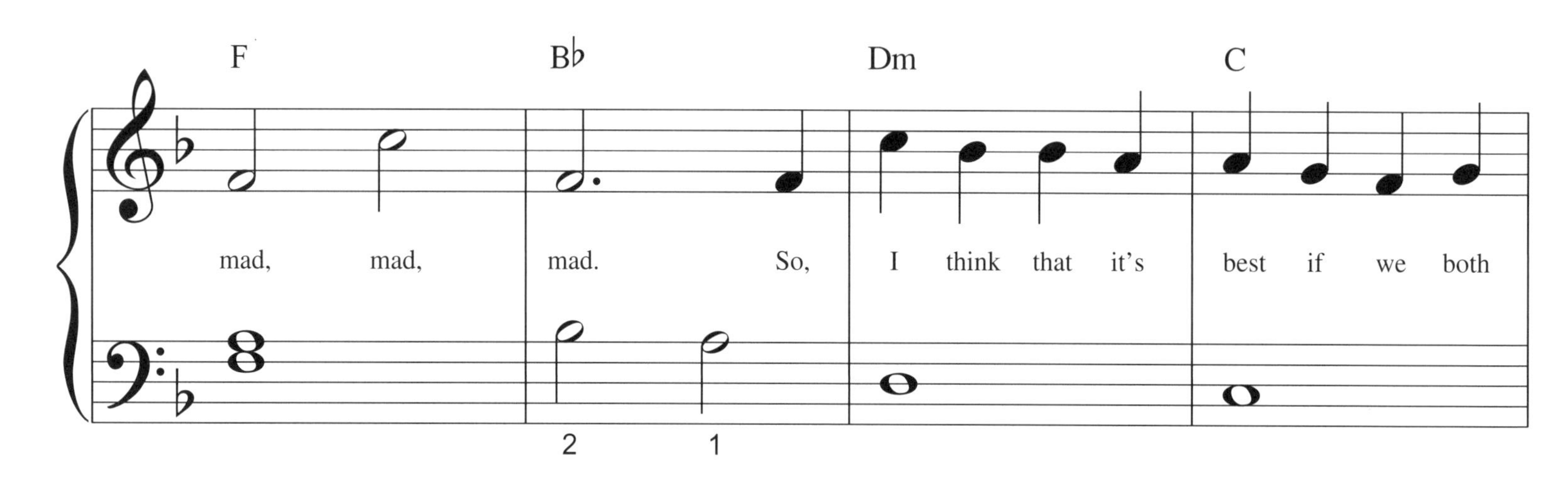
F
B♭
Dm
C
mad, mad,
mad. So,
I think that it's
best if we both
2 1

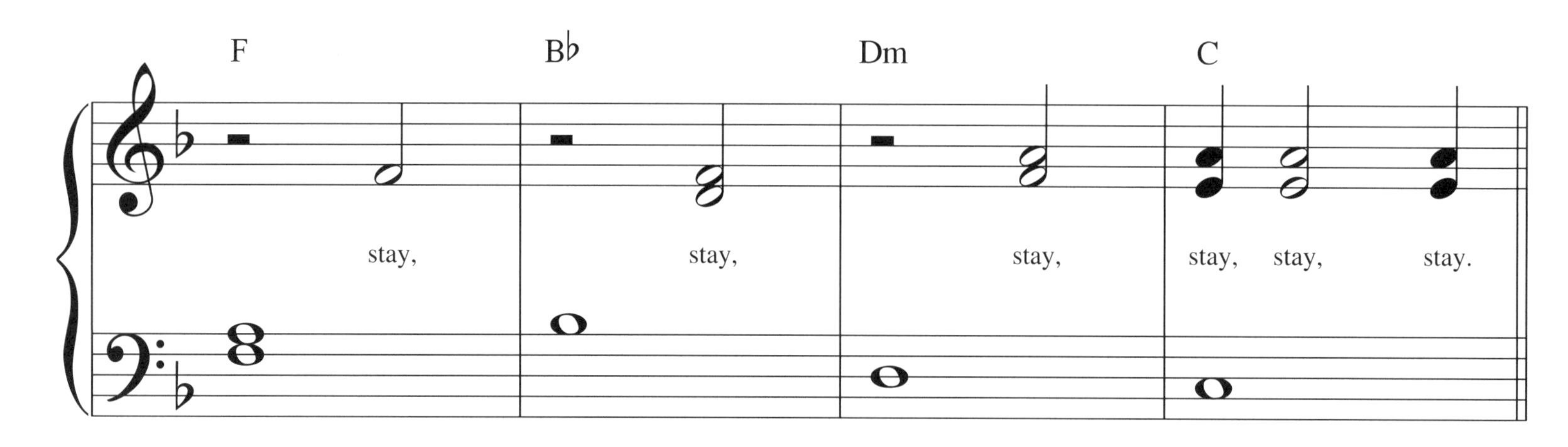
F
B♭
Dm
C
stay,
stay,
stay,
stay, stay, stay.

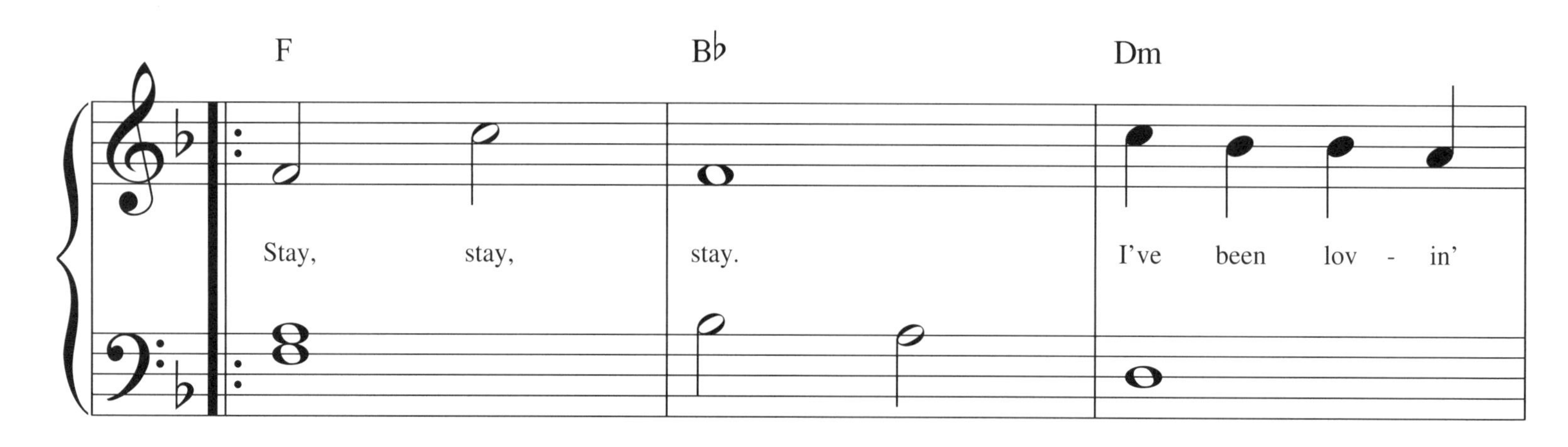
F
B♭
Dm
Stay, stay,
stay.
I've been lov - in'

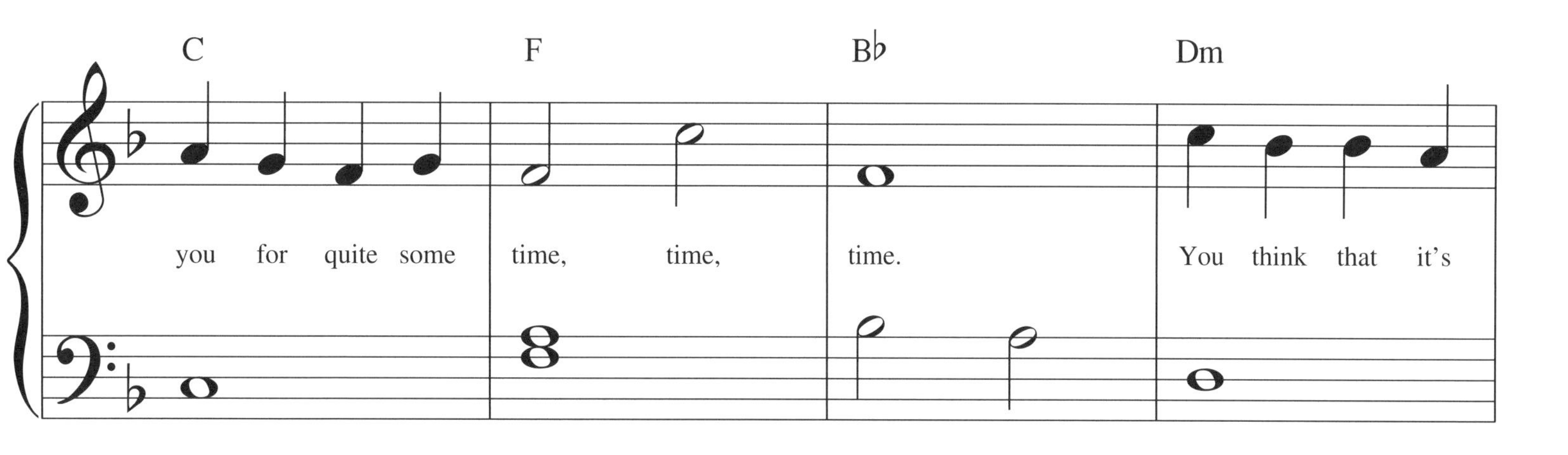
C
F
B♭
Dm
you for quite some time, time, time. You think that it's

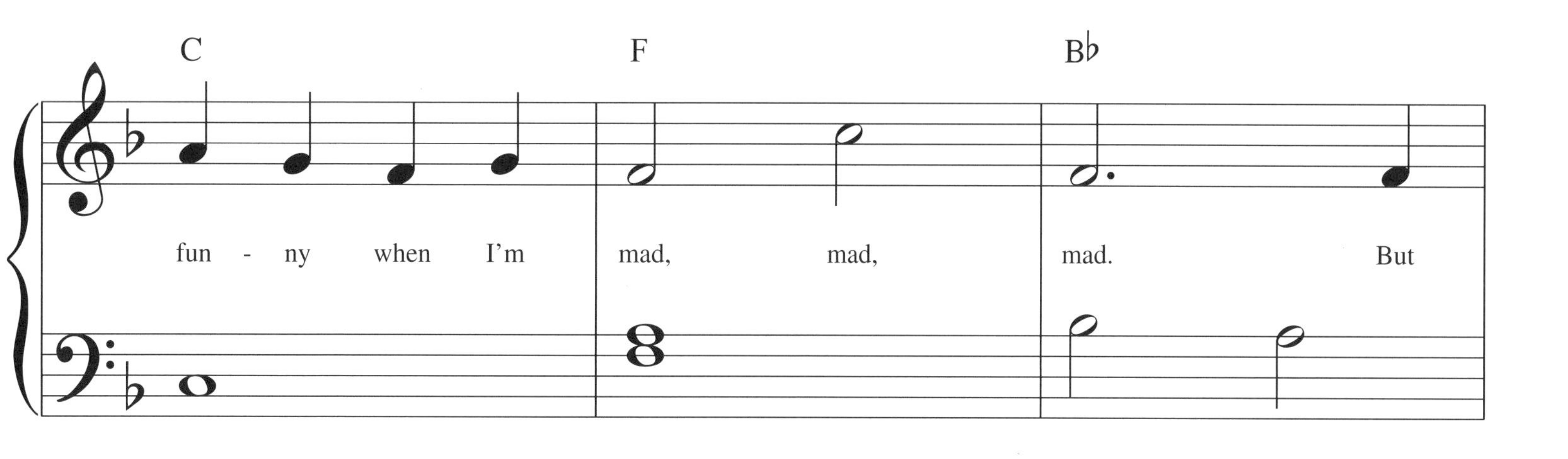
C
F
B♭
fun - ny when I'm mad, mad, mad. But

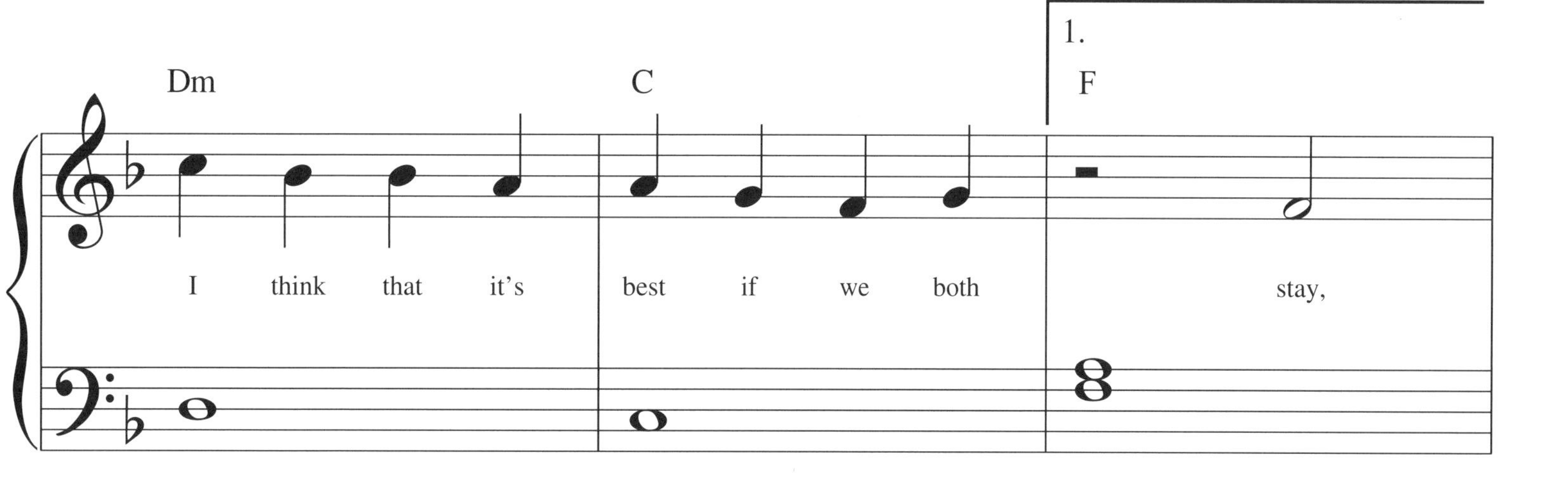
Dm
C
1.
F
I think that it's best if we both stay,

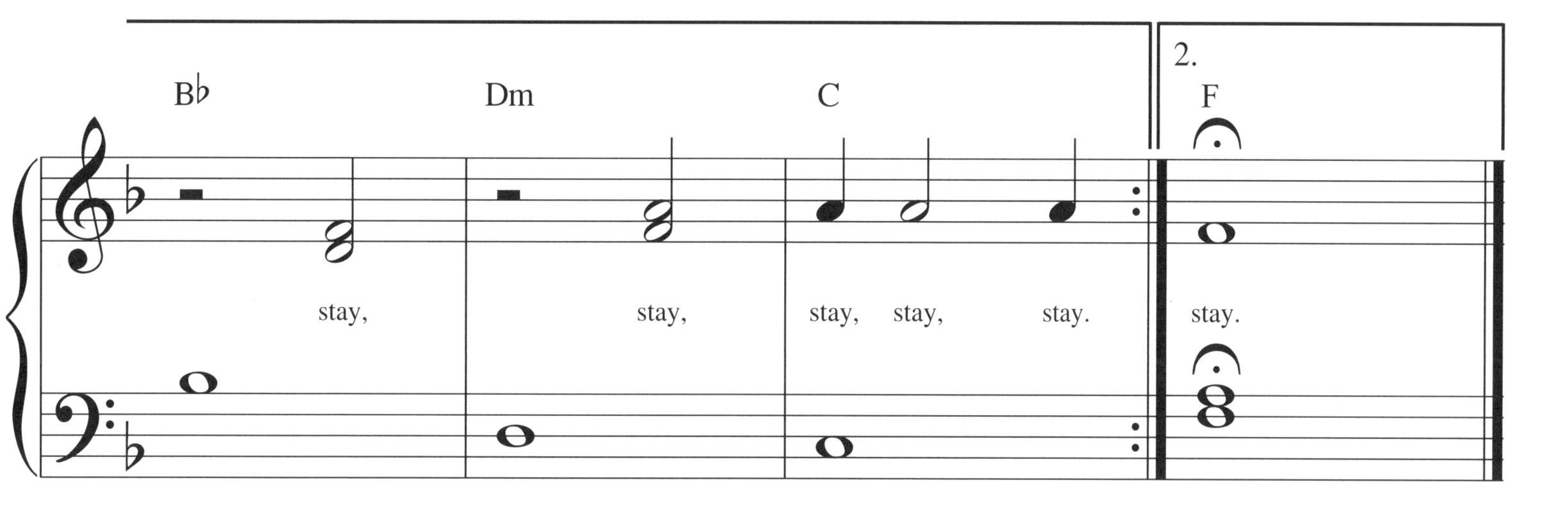
B♭
Dm
C
2.
F
stay, stay, stay, stay, stay. stay.

WE ARE NEVER EVER GETTING BACK TOGETHER

Words and Music by TAYLOR SWIFT,
SHELLBACK and MAX MARTIN

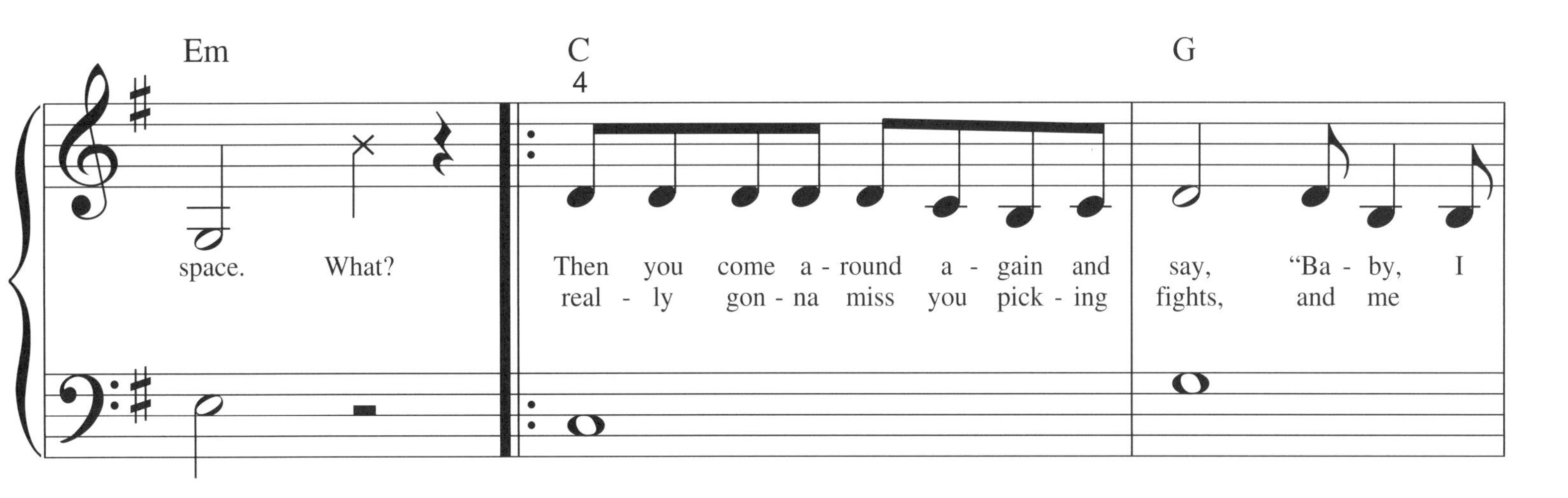
Em
C
4
G
space. What?
Then you come a - round a - gain and say, "Ba - by, I
real - ly gon - na miss you pick - ing fights, and me

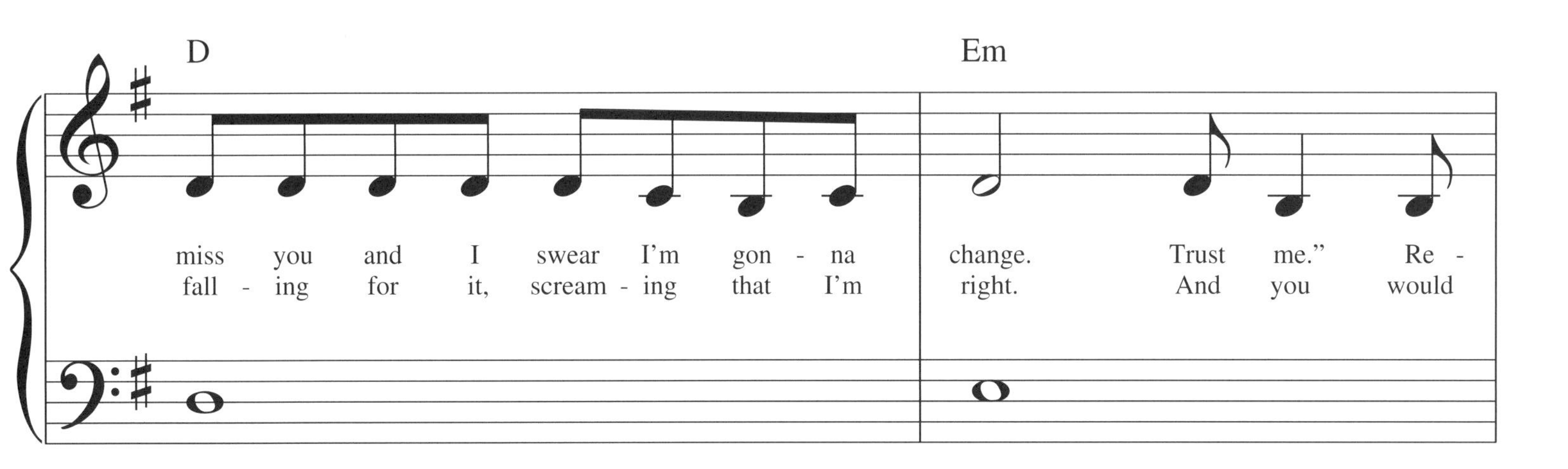
D
Em
miss you and I swear I'm gon - na change. Trust me." Re -
fall - ing for it, scream - ing that I'm right. And you would

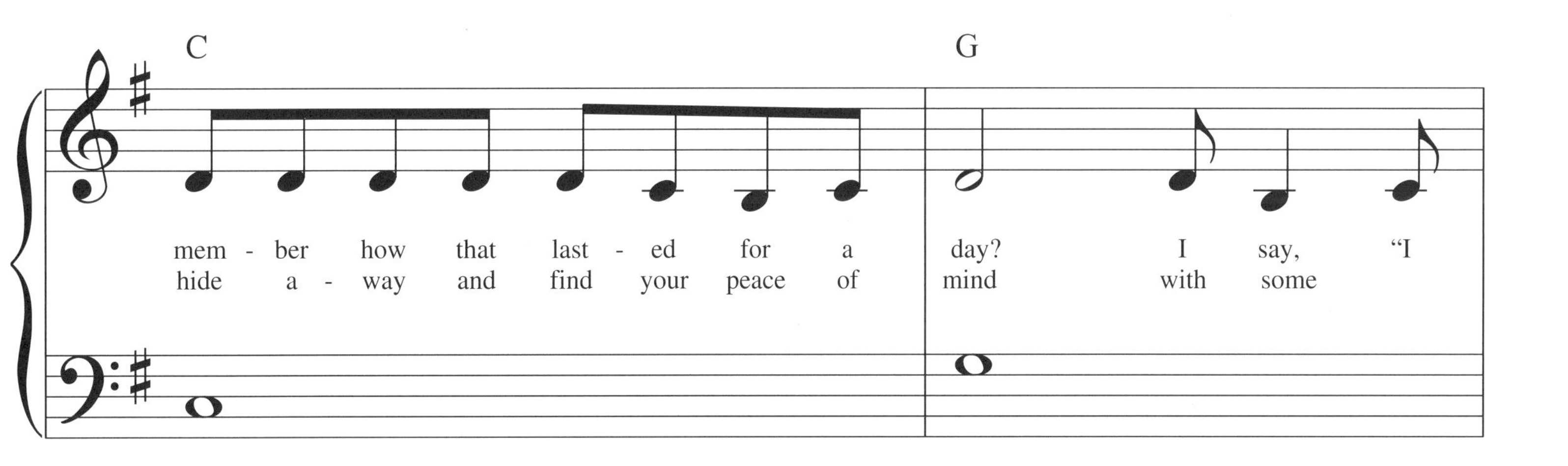
C
G
mem - ber how that last - ed for a day? I say, "I
hide a - way and find your peace of mind with some

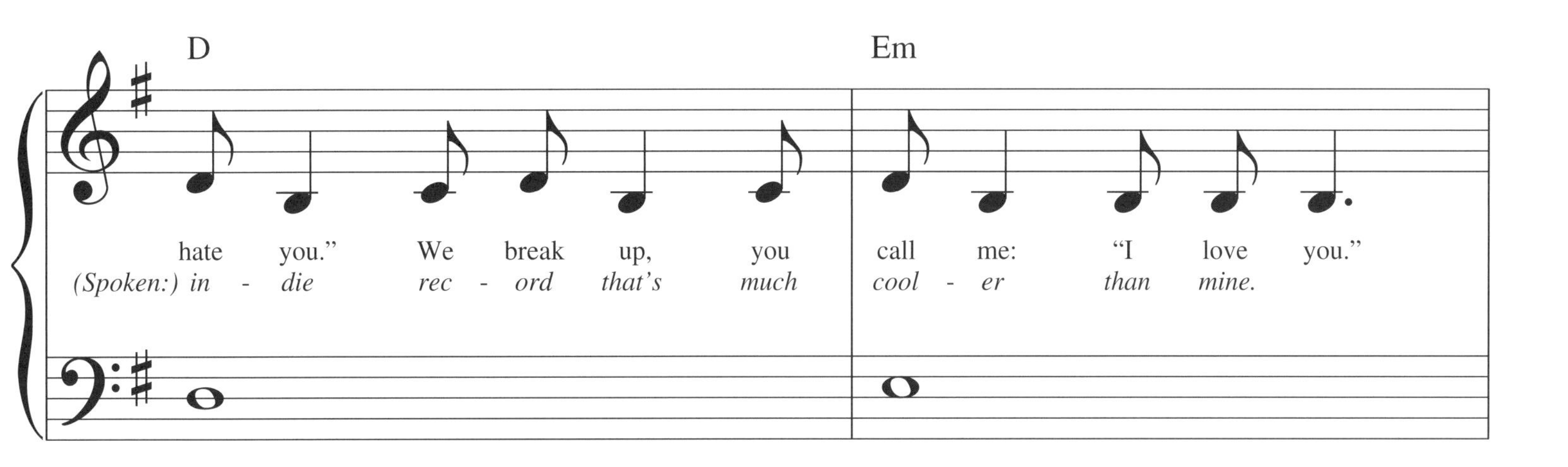
D
Em
hate you." We break up, you call me: "I love you."
(Spoken:) in - die rec - ord that's much cool - er than mine.

C G D
Ooh, ooh, ooh, ooh, we called it off a - gain
Ooh, ooh, ooh, ooh, you called me up a - gain

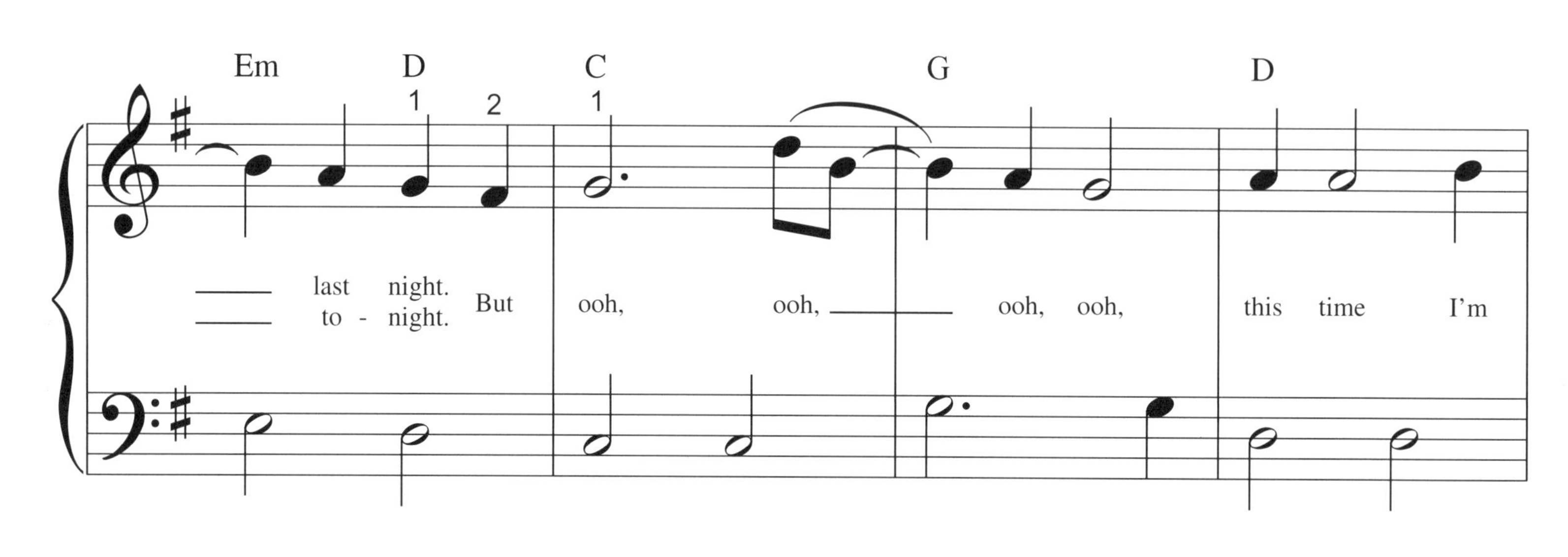
Em D C G D
last night. But ooh, ooh, ooh, ooh, this time I'm
to - night.

Em C G
tell - ing you, I'm tell - ing you, we are nev - er ev - er, ev - er

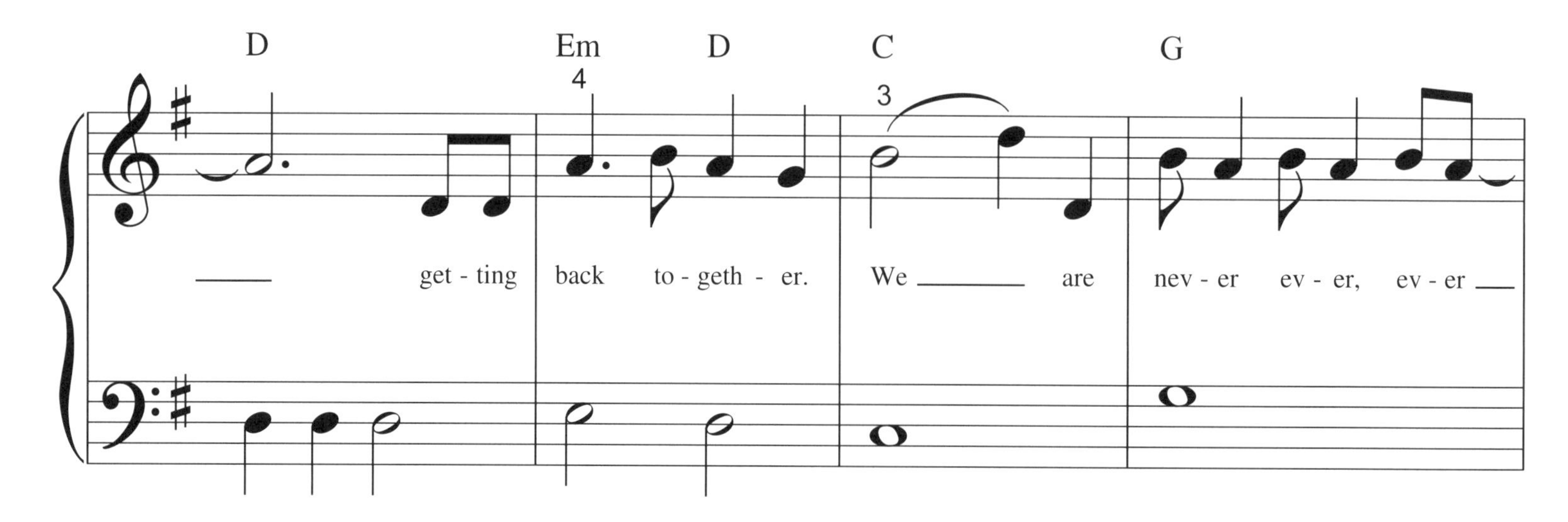
D Em D C G
get - ting back to - geth - er. We are nev - er ev - er, ev - er

D
Em
D
C
get - ting
back
to - geth - er.
You
go
talk
to
your
G
D
Em
D
friends,
talk
to
my
friends,
talk
to
me.
But
C
G
D
To Coda
we
are
nev - er
ev - er,
ev - er,
ev - er
get - ting
back
to-
1.
C
G
D
Em
geth - er.
(Spoken:) Like,
ev - er.
I'm

2.
C
5
G
D
geth - er. Ooh, ooh, ooh. Ooh,
Em
D
C
G
D
ooh, ooh, ooh, ooh, ooh, ooh. Oh, oh, oh.
C
G
3
D
I used to think that we were for -
Em
C
1
G
ev - er, ev - er and I used to say,

D
Csus2
G
"Nev - er say nev - er."
(Spoken:)
So he calls me up and
he's like, "I still love you,"
Dsus
Em
Csus2
and I'm like... I'm just...
I mean, this is exhausting, you know?
G
Dsus
D
D.S. al Coda
Like, we are never getting back
together,
like,
ev - er.
No,
CODA
D
C
G
get - ting back.
We,
ooh,
ooh, ooh,

D
Em
D
C
3
G
ooh, get - ting back to - geth - er. We, ooh, ooh, ooh,
D
1
Em
4
D
C
oh, get - ting back to - geth - er. You go talk to your
G
D
Em
D
C
3
friends, talk to my friends, talk to me. But we are
G
D
N.C.
nev - er ev - er, ev - er, ev - er get - ting back to - geth - er.